STILL COUNTING

STILL COUNTING

Women in Politics Across Canada

LINDA TRIMBLE
JANE ARSCOTT

broadview press

National Library of Canada Cataloguing in Publication

Trimble, Linda, 1959-
    Still counting : women in politics across Canada / Linda Trimble, Jane Arscott.

Includes bibliographical references and index.
ISBN 1-55111-374-0

1. Women in politics—Canada. 2. Sex discrimination against women—Canada. I. Arscott, Jane
II. Title.

HQ1236.5.C2T75 2003   320'.082'0971   C2003-900436-8

Broadview Press Ltd. is an independent, international publishing house, incorporated in 1985. Broadview believes in shared ownership, both with its employees and with the general public; since the year 2000 Broadview shares have traded publicly on the Toronto Venture Exchange under the symbol BDP.

We welcome comments and suggestions regarding any aspect of our publications–please feel free to contact us at the addresses below or at broadview@broadviewpress.com.

North America
PO Box 1243, Peterborough, Ontario, Canada K9J 7H5
3576 California Road, Orchard Park, NY, USA 14127
Tel: (705) 743-8990; Fax: (705) 743-8353
email: customerservice@broadviewpress.com

UK, Ireland, and continental Europe
Thomas Lyster Ltd., Units 3 & 4a, Old Boundary Way
Burscough Road, Ormskirk
Lancashire, L39 2YW
Tel: (01695) 575112; Fax: (01695) 570120
email: books@tlyster.co.uk

Australia and New Zealand
UNIREPS, University of New South Wales
Sydney, NSW, 2052
Tel: 61 2 9664 0999; Fax: 61 2 9664 5420
email: info.press@unsw.edu.au
www.broadviewpress.com

Broadview Press Ltd. gratefully acknowledges the financial support of the Government of Canada through the Book Publishing Industry Development Program for our publishing activities.

This book is printed on acid-free paper containing 30% post-consumer fibre.

Eco-Logo Certified
30 % Post.

PRINTED IN CANADA

This book is dedicated to our fathers,

William R. Trimble
(1926–2000)

and

W. Hugh Arscott
(1924–2002).

Contents

Acknowledgements

We owe a debt of gratitude to the many people who supported us throughout the completion of his book, not least our families. In particular, our children, Rob, Sarah, Sam, and David, tolerated late dinners and tired moms for the duration.

We also wish to extend our appreciation to the team at Broadview Press, with whom it was a great pleasure to work. Michael Harrison (Vice-President and Editor) was keen on the book from the beginning, forgave us numerous delays, and facilitated its speedy production when we finally delivered the manuscript. Production Editor Barbara Conolly made everything run very smoothly. Copy-editor Betsy Struthers whipped our sometimes garrulous prose into shape, greatly improving the flow and tone of the book.

A number of people provided invaluable information. Deputy Clerk of the Yukon Legislature, Floyd McCormick, supplied a wealth of facts and insights; we could not have completed the sections on Yukon without his assistance. Too numerous to list here are all the folks employed at legislative and parliamentary libraries and archives and in the federal and provincial offices of chief electoral officers and political parties, who answered our phone and e-mail queries promptly and thoroughly.

We also want to acknowledge the cartoonists whose work is featured here. Brian Gable drew the 1997 "It's a Guy Thing" cartoon that first inspired our efforts to measure the electoral glass ceiling (permission courtesy of the Cartoonists & Writers Syndicate, www.cartoonweb.com). The barriers to political life faced by women juggling family obligations and public aspirations are summarized in Len Norris's 1970 cartoon (permission courtesy of the Simon Fraser University Electronic Document Centre, Editorial Cartoons Collection). Ben Lafontaine's presentation of Kim Campbell's abrupt removal from the top job punctuates the perils facing women party leaders then and now (permission courtesy of Artizans Syndicate, www.artizans.com). Theo Moudakis's drawing of NDP leader Alexa McDonough as a not-so-successful "spice girl" shows the double bind confronting women in powerful positions (permission courtesy of Artizans Syndicate). And Malcolm Mayes, our "home" cartoonist at the *Edmonton Journal,* penned the Anne McLellan cartoon that so neatly depicts the difference women with power can make (permission courtesy of Artizans Syndicate).

Why Are We Still Counting?

In the beginning, we were both inspired by our fathers, by their love of heated debates about political issues at the dinner table and their real-life examples of active citizenship. Linda's interest in politics was piqued by a pre-election visit to the Alberta legislature in the summer of 1971, punctuated by her father's observation that the power balance was soon to change. Indeed it did, as the Lougheed Conservatives swept to power, ending 36 years of Social Credit rule and prompting Linda's fascination with electoral contests. She was motivated as well by her dad's strong opinions on policy matters such as the death penalty and prison reform and by his penchant for letter writing. Bill Trimble did not hesitate to fire off letters to his Member of Parliament, the local Member of the Legislative Assembly, or any other elected official in need of advice or re-education.

Jane became intrigued with electoral politics after helping her father canvass door to door, handing out campaign literature and talking to people in the lead-up to the provincial election in Saskatchewan in 1962. Years later she edited his political memoir, *Mastering Defeat*, in which he described the Rhinoceros Party as the answer to the unmet demands of Western alienation. Over the years he wrote columns and quips for the *Saskatoon Star Phoenix*. Unlike his waning enthusiasm for political party politics, Hugh's commitment to community service and family values remained strong.

The encouragement of our fathers helped us overcome nay-sayers—such as the teacher who told Linda that "girls" should not worry their little heads about politics—and, alternately, heed the advice of champions like the public school principal—one of the few women administrators at the time—who suggested Jane set her sights on becoming prime minister! Jane dismissed the idea as impossible. More importantly, perhaps, our fathers' support for our career aspirations cultivated in us the fortitude and fiestiness to carry on in a discipline that had little place for women. In the late 1970s and early 1980s the "numbers" were certainly against us becoming political scientists, let alone prime minister or just plain garden variety women legislators. As students of Canadian politics we both chose to count the women in public life rather than count ourselves among their number.

This book was inspired by the observation that, after decades of counting, women continue to be elected to less than half of the seats that would be theirs in a genuinely egalitarian society. Women continue to navigate gender-specific road-blocks and obstacles on their pathways to political power, thereby making the fact that so many have succeeded noteworthy in itself. Like our fathers, female legislators are remarkable for their gumption and perseverance. We would like to see many more of them.

We have been counting women in Canadian politics for nearly 15 years. Linda started working on women's representation in Alberta politics after returning to the province in 1989. She was intrigued by the fact that Alberta had one of the best records for electing women, but one of the worst for responding to the substantive policy demands of the women's movement. She decided to use Alberta as a case study to investigate the link between the election of more women and the effective representation of women's interests. Jane was busy digging through archival material on the Royal Commission on the Status of Women when the Royal Commission on Electoral Reform and Party Financing issued its report in 1994. She noticed certain parallels and concluded that the electoral prospects for women in the 1990s were not much different than they had been 25 years earlier, despite significant gains in some areas of public life.

Our first collaboration began when we realized the time was ripe for a collection of essays about the presence and impact of female politicians in Canada's Parliament and legislatures. Fortunately, it wasn't difficult to find scholars from across the country keen to write about progress made by women in their home (or adopted) provinces. The resulting volume, *In the Presence of Women: Representation in Canadian Governments*, was published in 1997. That collection provided a comprehensive cross-jurisdictional account of the three stages of women's political representation— getting elected, voicing women's interests, and making a difference to public policy. As contributors to the "women in politics" field as well as champions of its continued importance, we were delighted when the work of the pioneers was continued, expanded, and enriched by new scholars.

So why are we still counting women legislators? Why is this book necessary and timely? The answer is easy to understand on the surface yet is complex underneath. Two general reasons and three specific ones remind us why counting matters. The general reasons concern democracy and the values that underlie its institutions, while the specific ones relate to how difficult it has proved to be to achieve balanced, equitable, and fair representation for women over time.

First, in democracies like Canada's, electorates select the decision-makers who make up the nation's legislative assemblies and cabinets. These institutions thus represent the will of the people. When representatives are selected from an excessively narrow pool of aspirants, both the legitimacy of the process and democracy itself is diminished. Democracy and its institutions of representation produce **democratic deficits** when significant portions of the electorate do not take their place as legislators. Secondly, the institutions of a society sustain its health and stability over time. They convey values, meaning, and aspirations to generations of citizens. When social institutions in general and institutions of political representation like legislatures in particular do not make space for significant numbers of the people from whom the representatives are drawn, it becomes necessary to challenge these institutions in order for them to provide better service in the future.

Three specific and relatively simple reasons for continuing to count women in politics remain. We continue to tabulate the number of women elected to public office because by any objective measure women are not even halfway to equal. Women comprise over 50 per cent of the population, but only 20 per cent of elected legislators, 25 per cent of cabinet ministers, and less than 10 per cent of party leaders. A quick glance at the "numbers game" shows that the problem of women's political underrepresentation has not been solved. Secondly, despite this fact, the issue of women's political representation has almost entirely disappeared from the political agenda. Political parties continue to resist the need to address the problem, and media organizations rarely bother to tot up the numbers of women candidates these days, even at election time. We take the view that the number of women in politics ought to be transparent and publicly available over time so that parties and policy-makers can be held accountable for the fact that gender parity has yet to be realized.

Thirdly, the process of counting women in positions of political power is far from easy. Over the past ten years in our collective attempts to offer a comprehensive and rigorous count of women in legislative office, we have discovered that the numbers are by no means readily available to academics, let alone to journalists or interested citizens. Simply gathering the data on women candidates in the most recent federal, provincial, and territorial elections proved tricky and time-consuming. In part these new difficulties have been created thanks (ironically) to gender neutral practices, whereby the sex of candidates in most jurisdictions is not identified. As Sonia Pitre wrote, in an e-mail response to Linda's query about female candidates in New Brunswick, "until I started my research on women in NB politics, I had no idea that men had names like Beverly and Claire!" The fact that the numbers just are not out there in any complete, accurate, or easily accessible form in and of itself is an important justification for this book and its accompanying website [http://stillcounting.athabascau.ca].

We are unwilling to move on to other topics because we believe that not all the relevant questions have been asked or answered. In fact, the

---

BOX 1: Reasons for *Still Counting*

- Women make up over 50 per cent of the Canadian population but only 20 per cent of legislators, 25 per cent of cabinet ministers, and less than 10 per cent of party leaders. Twenty per cent representation by women is wrongly regarded as fair and equitable, thereby contributing to the perpetuation of further inequality.
- In the absence of balance, equity, and fairness for women, objective measures provide strong evidence of the extent of the inequality.
- The credibility and political legitimacy of representative institutions are diminished when gender deficits are not corrected as a matter of public policy.
- Uncorrected gender deficits undermine both democracy and the values that support it.

---

more counting we do, the more questions we reveal. This book began as a paper on women and parties, first presented at the annual meeting of the Canadian Political Science Association in 1997. In it, we summarized the conclusions from *In the Presence of Women* that pointed us in new directions in our research and analysis of the data. We enumerated the percentages of women elected to Canada's legislatures, looked at the proportion of women serving as party candidates, and accounted for the (few) women party leaders. Since the paper raised more questions than were answered by the "big picture" statistics, we began to compare numbers over time and across parties and jurisdictions. We also collected the stories behind the data. When a qualitative analysis was used to colour the statistical outline, a series of interlocking narratives about women and political power emerged. Although these narratives offer some reason for optimism about the prospects for women's political equality, on the whole, however, they show how much gender still matters. As the content of this book demonstrates, gender continues to act as a brake on women's leadership aspirations.

For both of us, the period from 1985 to 2000 involved a struggle to achieve a more or less comfortable place for ourselves in academe and for feminist perspectives in political science. We have seen the number of women political scientists grow in our own institutions and across the country and can now count on a collegial and supportive group of researchers with similar research interests for information, advice, and new ideas. Even so, there is no room for complacency. It is, perhaps, our habit of hyper-vigilance, resulting from many years of work to gain the improvements we see around us today that makes us cautious about assuming that gains by and for women will last. As indicated by the title of *One Step Forward, Two Steps Back*, a book by Gwen Brodsky and Shelagh Day about women's equality claims under the Canadian Charter of Rights and Freedoms, hard-won gains can be lost all too easily.[1] Whether in arguments for women's equality made before the justices of the Supreme Court, numbers of women elected and appointed to Parliament, or feminist comfort levels in academia, the media, or public life, the crucial issue remains the recognition of equality for women. The last 15 years, which have been so formative for us as feminist political scientists, have also been significant in the history of women's progress toward equality in political and electoral representation. Advances for women on all fronts matter, we maintain. How much representation by women is too little, and how much is enough? Our answers to these questions explain why we are still committed to counting women in Canadian politics.

CHAPTER 1

Introduction:
Still Counting

A Gendered Leadership Gap

For several years running, Canada was cited by the United Nations as the best country in which to live, but lost the number one spot in 2001. As well, in all those years, Canada ranked only ninth for females once factors involving social development were calculated. How could Canada have been the best place to live if one was male but not if female? The answer in part is that, despite recent advances, Canada continues to be outpaced by Scandinavian countries in its quality of life for women. This is not the only reason that this country lost its number one position. Our high rates of child poverty, short life expectancy for Aboriginal peoples, and a public health care system that no longer ensures the continued well-being of the population contribute to the slip in the rankings. These factors all differentially affect women because, first, women are the principal caretakers of children living in poverty, and, second, they bear the brunt of the **public policy legacy** that puts members of many Aboriginal communities at risk. Finally, women's generally poorer health, lower social status, financial dependency, and lower lifetime earnings, make it difficult for them to provide for themselves and dependent family members as they age.

If a woman is Aboriginal or less than able-bodied, old, a member of a racialized minority group, poor, or some combination of these, being Canadian falls short of best. While some people—mostly but not exclusively men—have benefited a great deal from being and becoming Canadians, others of us, including many women, are still counting on the hope of a better future. Politics is one of the means available to bring about the social change that would improve prospects for women. However, needed changes are unlikely to be realized as long as parliamentary debate is characterized by punch and counter-punch, body slams, and the displays of daring do, sea-doos, and Howdy Do-style posturing that the media define as political leadership.

In the 1970s, the women's liberation movement criticized Canadian society for its **systemic sexism**, the phenomenon of society-wide sexual discrimination toward women. It also noted a failure to provide equality of opportunity for women to participate fully in all occupations and positions held by men. The media heralded women's demands for equality with such advertising as the famous ad for a women's cigarette in which the manufacturer of Virginia Slims proclaimed, "You've come a long way, Baby." Of course, the commercial referred to women's freedom to be smokers like men, to do it in public, and to believe that smoking would help to keep them svelte and alluring. Thirty years later, female smokers outnumber male nicotine addicts, and women have more respiratory problems and cancers related to smoking than they did before the issue of inequality between the sexes grabbed the headlines. And many women still cringe when they are called "baby." During a 1984 question period exchange in the House of Commons, cabinet minister John Crosbie told Liberal MP Sheila Copps to "Just quieten down, baby."

Copps retorted, "I am 32 years old, I am an elected Member of Parliament from Hamilton East, and I'm nobody's baby."[1] Many women reject being infantalized because such treatment is demeaning and sexist. Instead, they want fairness, equity, and approximately equal shares of key positions in public life, the social realm, and the economy.

What are we to make of the push to advance equality for women over the years? Because progress has been made in some areas but not others, the results are mixed. Women's equality has not come nearly as far or as fast as many of us would like to see. After decades of women's movement activity, policy-making to raise the status of women, and concerted political action, men still hold a disproportionate share of the **top jobs** in public life, thus revealing the persistence of a **gendered leadership gap**, with pernicious effects. Women regularly receive less in wages, status, and high-ranking positions than they have earned. International studies have confirmed the existence of such gendered leadership gaps around the world.[2] This phenomenon produces social, economic, and political shortfalls, with serious implications for the quality of democratic deliberation. As a result, **democratic deficits**—gaps or flaws in the democratic political system that diminish its effectiveness and legitimacy—have emerged.

Two democratic deficits in particular have still to be addressed. One is the underrepresentation of women in public life. Were it not for the legacy of sex bias, women and men would be expected to hold roughly equal numbers and varieties of top jobs in public life as in the rest of society. This is not the case. Many fewer women than men hold high-ranking political positions. As political columnist Hugh Winsor summarizes the point: "Expect lots of gender correctness from this Prime Minister [Chrétien] on the easy files. But when it comes to real muscle, the guys have got it and they are going to keep it."[3] Second, leadership positions continue to go almost exclusively to men, a **gender bias** that occurs despite clear evidence that **sex-based discrimination** is both real and powerful. Further deficits affecting the well-being and political legitimacy of democracy itself will occur if the underrepresentation deficit and the gendered leadership deficit are not corrected. The election of political representatives to institutions of representative government is an integral component of democracy, for elected political institutions foster **popular sovereignty**, **political equality and freedom**, and **popular consultation**.

BOX 1.1: Democratic Deficits in Need of Correction

- *Deficit:* Women are underrepresented in the formal political sphere in Canada.
  Rationale: In a democratic society committed to principles of equity and fairness women and men would hold approximately the same number of top jobs and honours in representing the nation as a matter of simple justice.

- *Deficit:* Women are grossly underrepresented in positions of political leadership.
  Rationale: Leadership positions continue to go almost exclusively to men, which is not only unfair and inequitable but undermines the democratic principles underpinning the electoral and political system.

Many people see nothing wrong with outcomes that disproportionately elect men. They say men are more interested in politics and public life than women. Some go so far as to argue, as does Canadian Alliance strategist Tom Flanagan, that men are better suited to political leadership than are women.[4] From the outset it is important to make clear that such positions do not stand up under careful examination. In a free and democratic society such as Canada aspires to be, principles of fairness and equity demand that women as well as men be leaders in public life. It is a matter of "simple justice."[5] Why, then, does it remain so difficult for women to take their rightful place as leaders in Canadian society? Because systematic sexism, old biases, conventional practices, and current arrangements of political power are difficult to disrupt, never mind topple.

When Liberal MP Carolyn Bennett publicly observed a power imbalance in a January 2002 cabinet shuffle, which promoted only one new woman minister out of ten appointments from the backbenches, the prime minister angrily scolded her during a caucus meeting. As chair of the Liberal women's caucus, Bennett was simply voicing what was obvious— that many Canadians were upset to see the usual line-up of white men waiting to be sworn into cabinet while women and members of minority groups of both sexes remain underrepresented. Her boss, Jean Chrétien, defended the newly constituted cabinet and his government's record of appointing women to powerful posts, including Beverley McLachlin as Chief Justice of the Supreme Court. Indeed, while the number of women in cabinet (including secretary of state positions) dropped from 27 per cent before the January 2002 shuffle to 23 per cent afterwards, the prime minister's appointments have boosted the number of women on the Supreme Court to 33 per cent and female senators to over 30 per cent. But why should women receive any less than half of the top jobs? And why does the prime minister, along with political parties and many media observers, consider this to be good enough representation for women?

By going public with her dissatisfaction about the prime minister's 2002 cabinet shuffle, Carolyn Bennett joined a distinguished group of demanding women. From Sarah Ramsland's "stake out" of a minister's office to gain approval for a $5 expenditure to fix a pothole in her constituency in the early 1920s to Pauline Jewett's challenge to Prime Minister Pearson to grant her a place in his cabinet to Laura Sabia's threat to lead 2,000,000 women in a march on Ottawa in the 1960s, women legislators' presumptuous claims on male authority litter Canadian political history.[6] Like other courageous upstarts, Bennett may know that the most outspoken and audacious among them often break new ground for women. But as the late MP (and trail blazer) Pauline Jewett recognized, "just counting on trail blazers isn't nearly good enough."[7] As she pointed out, "nothing much happens afterward" unless many more women follow in their footsteps, thereby marking, widening, and developing the trail.

It's a Guy Thing

Masculinity and merit continue to be conflated. Male candidates are able to speak as if gender is irrelevant. Not so for female candidates, as their sex continues to be highlighted and stereotyped by the media, other candidates, and political parties. Female party leaders' performances during leadership debates are still described as "shrill."[8] Thus, masculinist norms associated with electoral institutions and processes undermine women's claims as women, as women legislators, and as representatives for women. For example, a 1997 *Globe and Mail* story titled "Political Power continues to elude women reveals study!" summarized the conclusions of a survey conducted by the United Nations to compare electoral outcomes. Worldwide, the study concludes, women remain scarce in high elected office. The political cartoon at the beginning of this chapter depicts the double-edged treatment of women in electoral politics that is the subject of this book.

To think, as the King clearly does, that power and leadership is "a Guy thing" reflects symbols and practices that are patriarchal; for instance, the sceptre held by His Majesty is topped by the international symbol for men ($\male$). In theory, his consort could sit on his throne. A closer look makes it clear to the viewer that the fit is imperfect, impractical, and uncomfortable, because the throne is disproportionate to the size of her body. Moreover, his crown is too big to fit her head. The viewer is affirmed in the understanding that women are not suited to be holders of power. The expression on the face of the "wife of" indicates her dissatisfaction, but she says nothing. Only the male formulates an analysis of the meaning of the gender difference: his perspective dominates. Like the King, men have earned their place, even though they perpetuate exclusionary practices in order to do so. The drawing both challenges the idea that men are better suited to hold power and affirms the point at the same time. Undoing the fact that men are predominantly power-holders, elected or otherwise, will not change as the result of any study. However, the presence of women in all aspects of the life of nations and communities—more women and more diverse women—has great potential to bring about social change.

Overview of Still Counting

The purpose of this short book is to present material on women office seekers and holders in an interesting and provocative manner. We know that this account of women and politics represents only one part of a much larger picture of women's varied and diverse contributions to public life in Canada. Even so, we remain convinced that it is a crucial part. We are still counting women in politics because counting continues to matter. The chapters that follow offer an analysis of the numbers. The book also provides compelling stories, controversial positions, and bold predictions about women's leadership prospects against which to measure developments in the next 15 years.

CHAPTER 2: Counting Matters: The Numbers Game and Women's Political Power

Chapter 2 starts with the story of the first official tally of women legislators in Canada, conducted by the Royal Commission on the Status of Women (RCSW) in the late 1960s. There were so few women in official politics that the commission staff was able to count them by asking around and scribbling (short) lists on pieces of paper. The commission tried to make sense of the fact that, several decades after some Canadian women were accorded the right to vote and run for office, precious few had actually won election. The dilemma of counting something that is so rare fostered a perspective on women's representation that we call a "fetish for firsts." The second section of the chapter points out how this "first woman" narrative, important though it is to an understanding of women's progress, tends to portray women's achievements as merely the result of extraordinary efforts by exceptional individuals. This masks the reality of women's electoral gains, which are in fact the culmination of the efforts of many women working long and hard in the relative obscurity of political party backrooms, riding associations, and women's movement organizations.

The completion of the RCSW's report in 1970 marked the beginning of 30 years of unprecedented change in women's legislative representation. We map this change by comparing the number of women elected, federally and provincially, at 15-year intervals, beginning in 1970. We argue that, while significant, the advances made represent insufficient progress towards fair representation for all women. This point is emphasized in the final section of Chapter 2, which demonstrates the prevailing political convention that women are appointed to top jobs representing Canada directly in proportion to their capacity to get elected. A historical view of the advances made by women in public life identifies the strong and persistent relationship between women's share of legislative seats and the willingness of governments to appoint them to other senior, politically sensitive posts. Chapter 2 uses the three time points—1970, 1985, and 2000—to demonstrate that this convention has been a powerful determinant of women's representation.

Now some would argue that women are winning more and more seats and will sooner or later reach gender parity, thereby eventually erasing the gendered leadership gap. Chapter 3 argues that the assumption underlying this proposition needs to be revisited and revised. As we show in Chapters 3 and 4, the future for women's continued advancement is not bright.

CHAPTER 3: The Electoral Glass Ceiling for Women

There has been an unexamined assumption that women's share of elected positions will continue to increase more or less steadily over time. Chapter 3: *The Electoral Glass Ceiling for Women*, analyzes the number of women elected to Canada's national, provincial, and territorial legislatures in the five most recent elections and argues that the assumption of continued electoral success for women is unfounded. Indeed, a plateau has been reached with the levels of women's representation converging across the country at roughly 20 per cent of seats. This is a political variant of the glass ceiling women have experienced in business and public-sector employment. We discuss the reasons why the numbers of women candidates and office holders increased in the 1980s and 1990s and offer some insights into why these numbers have stalled or are actually dropping. Data on women candidates and their declining numbers in recent elections are offered to support our lack of optimism about further advances in the short-term.

Chapter 3 argues that it is fair, just, and democratic to undertake formal and informal measures to increase the representation of women in Canada's legislatures. However, indifference prevails within political parties about the need for further action. Certainly apathy about the need for change is partly to blame for the lack of government and party initiative to implement proposals for reform to Canada's electoral system, proposals designed to increase the presence of under-represented groups in our Parliament and legislatures. We maintain that **complacency**—that is, self-satisfaction of the sort that tends to support the status quo and does not generally produce self-reflection or reform—actively contributes to diminishing the prospects for women's full participation in public life (and society) in the near future.

CHAPTER 4: It's a Drag: Where Have all the Women Leaders Gone?

When it comes to top jobs in electoral politics—premier, prime minister, and party leader—women remain on the sidelines. To be blunt, women are largely out of the running for these positions. Chapter 4 surveys women's efforts to lead political parties and highlights the revolving door that dispatches most of them in short order. Among the 20 women who have led competitive political parties, three-quarters held the post for less than two years. There are no women on the political scene anywhere in the country who could rival Wilfrid Laurier's longevity in office or Jean Chrétien's assault on the political record books to win a third straight term. These parameters for political leadership elude women entirely.

Most of the 20 women who have served as party chiefs were chosen
to lead moribund, ailing, or soon-to-be decimated political parties.
Often they are chosen in the vain hope that they can perform **partisan
CPR** and revive party fortunes. Those who succeed in making their
parties more competitive are typically nudged aside and replaced by
men, thus reinforcing already well-established practices and assumptions: wielding power is a male prerogative. Those who fail quickly see
their leadership scuttled. Either way, women cannot seem to win.
Chapter 4 shows they cannot win with the press, either, as female party
leaders frequently have their personal lives invaded, their leadership
prospects dismissed based on sexist evaluations, and inappropriate
comments made about them because of their sex. We conclude that the
future for women party leaders looks bleak, as women with sufficient,
or even exceptional, experience are passed over for these important positions. For many, it is now clear that the party leader's post is simply too
much of a drag to be worth the trouble.

CHAPTER 5: Spice Girls and Old Spice Boys: Getting There is
Only Half the Battle

What happens when women enter Canada's Parliament and legislatures
as elected representatives? After all, these institutions were not designed
with women in mind; indeed, women were once expressly excluded from
them, since they were created at a time when women were denied the right
to vote or run for office. Although legal barriers to women's participation
in electoral politics have been removed, female legislators continue to
describe legislatures as "men's clubs." Women involved in Canadian politics say it is still a "man's game," and they recount the perils associated with
treading on masculine turf. The legacy of sex and race discrimination in
Canada's voting laws lingers, while age-old attitudes about a woman's
proper place continue to shape women's experiences in politics.

Chapter 5 begins with a story about a male legislator who called
women on the opposition benches "Spice Girls" and discounted their

interventions as "chirping." We argue that such attitudes and the behaviour that stems from sexist assumptions make legislative politics uncomfortable arenas for women. Many find the overtly combative and argumentative strategies of parliamentary debate incompatible with their own principles and approaches. Even if they learn to live with a conflict-ridden working environment, female politicians often find that their femininity is questioned, and guilt traps are set to make them feel insecure and anxious about their capacity to blend parenting and politics. Some women legislators report having been verbally and sexually harassed simply because they are women. Female legislators who identify themselves as feminists tend to come in for a particularly nasty brand of ridicule and harassment. Chapter 5 ends with the dilemma such an atmosphere fuels—how to change it without more women and how to attract more women without changing it.

CHAPTER 6: Counting for Something: Women in Politics Can Make a Difference

Chapter 6 tackles a question crucial to the issue of women's political representation—what is the purpose of electing more (and more diverse) women? Will they make a difference to political speech and public-policy decisions? The chapter begins with a discussion of what, precisely, "making a difference" for women means. What are "women's issues"? What kinds of changes are women legislators expected to make, and what strategies can they realistically employ to advance women's interests?

Evidence from various countries suggests that women must comprise a **critical mass** of legislators before they can have any significant impact. We look at Canadian studies of women's influence on policy debates and outcomes and argue that the evidence certainly supports the notion that electing more women matters. However, we show that electing a critical mass of women is not necessarily sufficient to make change, as numbers are only half of the story. Party discipline, cabinet solidarity, and the very structure of parliamentary government complicate the representative process, creating both opportunities and challenges for women politicians. For instance, executive dominance of political decision-making gives first ministers and their cabinets control over policy outcomes. We examine the "numbers game" in cabinet as a crucial indicator of women's access to the levers of power.

Generally speaking, "making a difference for women" is assumed to mean promoting the interests of the women's movement. After all, feminist groups are responsible for putting the status of women on the political agenda and demanding the types of policy measures necessary to foster women's full citizenship. Thus, feminist groups, politicians, and academics argue that the central representational issue is that of the representation of feminist ideas and, accordingly, view feminist women legislators as most likely to make change beneficial to women. Evidence supporting this proposition is offered, but Chapter 6 challenges the notion that women politicians only make a difference for women when they represent feminism and the goals of the women's movement. We take the controversial position that all women politicians count for something, regardless of their support for feminism, their desire to advocate on behalf of women's organized interests, or their ideology. In answer to the question, "is it better to elect a feminist man over a non-feminist (or anti-feminist) woman?" we say it is better for women to represent themselves. We discuss Reform/Alliance Member of Parliament (MP) Deborah Grey as an example of what we call the "**Deb Effect**"—the positive impact of electing more, and more diverse, women to serve in Canada's legislatures.

CHAPTER 7: Conclusion: Halfway to Equal

We conclude that the number of women legislators in each jurisdiction and on average across jurisdictions continues to provide a reliable indicator of the pace and level of social change. After sharp gains in the last 30 years, women's progress on the electoral front has stalled, not least of all because it is plain that women do not have good chances of winning the top jobs. Canada is as far from having a handful of women premiers today as it was in 1970. There are more women legislators, but as inter-national bodies such as the United Nations and the Inter-Parliamentary Union have recognized, politics remains very much a man's game, with four out of five positions worldwide being held by men.[9]

This generalization drawn from the international scene holds true for Canada. Given the evidence provided here, there is additional reason to be concerned that women's electoral representation is no longer increasing, having leveled off at about 20 per cent. If what we say here about electoral performance as a predictor of women's representation in public life more generally, the **glass ceiling** discussed in Chapter 3 ought to be a matter for public discussion, unless 20 per cent is good enough representation for women. Our view is that this is neither fair nor equitable. Women's absence from the electoral field has perpetuated women's underrepresentation in other areas related to public life. Our tracking of women's advances in federal, provincial, and territorial politics indicates a microcosm of **systemic sex bias** that limits women's access to top jobs, their career mobil-ity, and their educational and professional opportunities.

Still Counting Website

There are lots of numbers in this book, many of which will quickly become dated as elections are held, cabinets are shuffled, and new party leaders are selected. So, in the interest of helping everyone track the numbers as they evolve, a complete set of tables is available and updated periodically on the *Still Counting* website hosted by Athabasca University at http://stillcounting.athabascau.ca. The website also offers you, the reader, a chance to have your say, and we certainly welcome feedback. We are especially interested to learn about ways readers and surfers use the information provided in the book and on the site to develop their own knowledge. We know there is a lot more fun to be had with this material, and we invite you to offer your opinions, stories, and observations.

CHAPTER 2

Counting Matters:

The Numbers Game and Women's Political Power

"What's the point of them going to all this trouble if you won't put in for Senator, join the RCMP or run a crown corporation?"

Introduction

For a long time, women legislators were too few and far between to be considered worthy of study. In the first 50 years after the official entry of some Canadian women to electoral politics (1916–66), only eight women in all had been elected to the House of Commons, 46 to provincial and territorial legislatures, and nine appointed to the Senate. Thérèse Casgrain was the lone woman to lead a political party; she headed the Cooperative Commonwealth Federation (CCF) in Quebec between 1951 and 1957. Elected and appointed at an average rate of two every three years for the first 50 years, women legislators were assumed not to matter. It was presumed that there was no socially useful purpose to be served by counting them.

Now that more women have won office, the electoral representation of women has been studied more often and in greater depth than ever before. However, the public record still provides no comprehensive description and analysis of women candidates and legislators across Canada. In our effort to compile data for this book, we ran headlong into the same problems faced by the Royal Commission on the Status of Women (RCSW) in the late 1960s. Like the Commission, we soon found ourselves using pencil and paper to list which women won, where, when, and how. While conducting archival research on the RCSW, Jane Arscott came across very short handwritten lists of names of women who served in public life as elected and appointed representatives. Because we had many more women to count, our job has proven more complicated; more than 600 women have now served in legislatures across the country, including the Senate. Arscott's handwritten lists now fill a notebook. But in one respect our experience with counting the women was similar to that of the RCSW: the information we sought was located in no one place. We wrote lists of names, searched old parliamentary guides, and sent email to far-flung legislative libraries in order to complete our count. We also ascertained that we could not trust some of the information on the worldwide web. We were struck by the difficulty in locating the necessary information. Why is counting women in politics so difficult when it matters so much to an evaluation of women's place in public life?

Important though counting women is to us as citizens and academics, it remains relatively unimportant in official government and political party circles, as is evident from the lack of easily accessible information available on the topic. Missing even now is a simple, consistent method of gathering basic information on women's candidacies and legislative positions. The history of women's service to the body politic remains fragmented, divided between historical and current analysis, federal and provincial/territorial jurisdictions, and elected versus appointed positions. When the pieces are put together, a larger story of women's place in Canadian society can be told.

The first section of this chapter outlines the dilemma faced by members of the RCSW: how do you count something when there is so little to count? We discuss the approach and findings of the RCSW regarding the presence of women in politics from 1916 to 1969. While almost all of the progress in getting women elected has occurred since 1970, it is important to remember that the story began unfolding much earlier. As well, we address some omissions in the RCSW's analysis, particularly its lack of attention to the provincial and territorial level of government and to women's ethnic and cultural diversity. We then question the "fetish for firsts" plaguing most of the analysis of the women elected to Canada's legislatures during the lean years when female legislators were few and far between. The focus on the "firsts" ignores the women legislators who were not first but made other important contributions.

The second section of the chapter compares the numbers of women elected, federally and provincially, at 15-year intervals. The comparison of women's status in legislative office in 1970, 1985, and 2000 provides empirical evidence of the significant but still insufficient advances made after the report of the RCSW. This trend makes it all the more important that women's recent electoral progress not falter. However, as this book will demonstrate, continued progress is not assured.

At the end of the chapter, we broaden our focus to consider the relationship between success in electoral office and women's likelihood of being awarded the most prestigious appointed positions. We show that women's overall presence in public life exceeds their electoral achievements only in the case of Senate appointments. The data we present confirms in different ways and over time that success in appointments reflects success in electoral contests. Counting elected women matters in more ways than the arithmetic of power-sharing in electoral politics. The presumption that getting elected equals "deservingness" for appointments to high-level patronage positions is documented over the last three decades. We show that the increased number of women legislators provides women with more and better access to high-ranking appointed positions. Included in these top political posts are federally appointed judges, members of the Privy Council, the lieutenant-governors, and other positions that provide evidence of how well the present government (or any government) does in its recognition of women's contribution to Canadian society.

The evidence we present does not extend to the top ranks of the public service, the courts, or appointments to the foreign service; that is work for another project. Bertha Wilson's study of gender equality in the legal profession published in 1993 and studies of women's status in the public service in 1970 and 1990 provide additional pieces that enrich our account of women's presence in public life.[1] We have provided a comprehensive count of those rankings that involve political representation and that together provide an objective measure of women's presence in public life. These numbers also offer an analysis of women's political status over time, the fairness of the political system, and what the women of this country can expect in the future if the trends continue unchallenged.

The Count Begins

Accounts of women's progress in electoral representation generally began in 1970 when the Royal Commission on the Status of Women (RCSW) systematically raised questions for the consideration of Parliament. This influential body, appointed in 1967, brought the matter to public view and did so in a manner that provided a reference point for subsequent research. The staff of the RCSW set out to measure women's presence in public life. The first problem they encountered was that data on gender in public life were not collected,[2] because gender was not considered to be relevant; woman's sphere was the private or domestic realm, not the public world of the economy and politics. In the political sphere, women did not count, and, in any case, few were present to be counted. Moreover, none of the commissioners or other staff members had any involvement in electoral politics on which to draw for insights into the sort of information that ought to be gathered.[3]

What to do? Women and politics had to be prominent in the Royal Commission's report because political participation had been the first item listed on its mandate. But there was next to nothing to be said about women's electoral success, as there had been precious little of it. In 1967 there were five women senators out of 100, two women MPs out of 264 seats in the Commons, one woman in a cabinet of 25, and an unknown number of female legislators in assemblies in the provinces and territories across the country. There had never been a woman speaker, federal party leader, prime minister, justice of the Supreme Court, governor general, lieutenant-governor, or other highly placed woman parliamentarian. No matter what they counted, it was clear women held fewer than 2 per cent of the top jobs associated with public life. Putting pencil to paper, the RCSW's final tally indicated that women figured as less than 1 per cent of all candidates for election to provincial and federal legislatures.[4]

BOX 2.1: Report of the RCSW[5]

- Between 1920 and 1970 only 18 women were elected to the House of Commons.
- In the 1968 election, only one woman, Grace MacInnis of the NDP, won a seat in the 264-member House.
- No woman sat on the government benches and no woman was a member of the official opposition.
- Between 1920 and 1970, only 49 women were elected to provincial legislatures; in June 1970, 12 women were members in the provincial houses.

In the end, the commissioners developed a view of political life that went beyond electoral representation to emphasize participation in public life in general.[6] They expanded their inquiry to various kinds of appointments controlled by the federal government, including nominations to the Senate, to the bench on federal courts, boards of Crown corporations, and federal agencies.[7] Many of these same positions are listed on the Table of Precedence, which is used to establish the relative importance of offices that serve the government of Canada.

The commission's mandate concerned only the federal jurisdiction, and staff refrained from inquiring if what occurred federally also transpired provincially and territorially. Initially, interest focused exclusively on the national level of government, and the federal data has since been used to represent nation-wide trends. As we found while conducting research for this book, relatively little is known about women legislators at the provincial and territorial level. A systematic analysis of the number of women candidates in each election in every province and territory has not yet been undertaken; the task is, indeed, a daunting one.

Based on a study of the archival materials that document the work of the RCSW, Arscott concluded that the commission's findings raised a conundrum that affected its recommendations.[8] Since women held less than 2 per cent of positions in public life, how could more women receive opportunities to show what they could do without first having women in more positions of political leadership? How could women demonstrate their capacity for leadership without first having many more high-profile opportunities to contribute to public life? Round and round the questions went. Will more female legislators produce more women in public life? Will more women in public life produce more female legislators? These questions remain relevant today.

It was clear in the 1960s that the political parties and the prevailing masculinist political culture contributed to the fact that seats in legislatures continued to go disproportionately to men.[9] As Judy LaMarsh told a Convention of Women, men think that in politics "one woman is a crowd."[10] What she meant was that the men in the top jobs were not used to thinking that women had a role in those areas of public life they regarded as their preserve. Women were not needed to produce a rich and healthy political life; more to the point, they were not wanted. This social norm expressed the conventional political wisdom of the times. Women's efforts to win election to public office also had to overcome a well-established social bias. Electing women proved to be more difficult than involving women in the activities of political parties or reducing the barriers to their participation in elections as candidates. Legislators are elected as individuals who have the support of the highly organized and partisan groups called political parties. Although individual women aspired to prove themselves suitable and meritorious, their success was measured collectively to determine what the country's women deserved altogether. Further opportunities to advance in their political careers was circumscribed by the progress overall in electing women.

In the end, the RCSW recommended the election of more female representatives by appealing to political parties to involve women at all levels of political participation. They recommended, too, that the federal government demonstrate leadership in selecting women for appointments, most certainly to the Senate and also to government-controlled boards and positions—in short, to top jobs. As we will see, no such change occurred. It took another 15 years before women approached the 10 per cent level of representation in federal politics, longer in some provinces and territories. Ten per cent representation by women was by no means certain even 30 years later in several jurisdictions in Canada. Because the increase has been so gradual and over so long a period, it was perhaps unavoidable that the women who did succeed in getting elected and appointed to top jobs would be considered as firsts worth talking about almost exclusively for their novelty value.

A Fetish for Firsts

In a political environment dominated by men, the first male legislator elected in any jurisdiction, the first male speaker, and the first male leader of a political party are not worthy of public comment. Firsts for women, however, have received much more comment, not all of it complimentary by any means. The firsts fast became a topic of comment in the media. We know, for example, that Mary Ellen Smith was the first woman cabinet minister in the British Commonwealth; Agnes Macphail was the first woman elected to the House of Commons; and Cairine Wilson and Iva Fallis were the first women senators appointed by Liberal and Conservative governments respectively. The first woman elected in Quebec was Marie-Claire Kirkland Casgrain; the first woman governor general was Jeanne Sauvé; the first elected woman premier was Catherine

Callbeck; and the first and still only woman prime minister was Kim Campbell. The exceptional nature of their achievements made it difficult for others to see themselves in these positions. Women legislators were exceptions to the rule that the "best" candidates are mostly men; accordingly, few women are selected to govern.

TABLE 2.1: Select Table of Firsts[1] (Chronological)

Year	Name	Achievement, First Woman ...
1917.06.07	Louise McKinney Roberta MacAdams	 AB Leg
1918.01.24	Mary Ellen Smith	BC Leg First woman known to have taken her husband's seat in the British Commonwealth
1919.07.19	Sarah Ramsland	SK Leg
1920.06.29	Edith McTavish Rogers	MB Leg
1921.12.06	Agnes Macphail	ON HoC ON Leg
1930.05.17	Helena Squires	NF Leg Council pre-Confederation
1930.02.15	Cairine Wilson	ON Senate
1935.10.14	Martha Black	YK HoC
1940.03.26	Dorise Nielson	SK HoC
1941.06.02	Corinne Casselman	AB HoC
1943.08.04	Agnes Macphail Margaret Lucock	ON Leg
1953.05.09	Mariana Jodoin Muriel McQueen Fergusson	QU Senate NB Senate
1953.11.05	Nancy Hodges	BC Senate
1955.07.28	Florence Inman	PEI Senate
1960.01.14	Olive Irvine	MB Senate
1960.09.11	Gladys Porter	NS Leg
1961.05.29	Margaret Mary MacDonald	PEI HoC
1961.12.14	Marie-Claire Kirkland Casgrain	QU Leg
1962.06.12	Isabel Hardie	NWT HoC
1963.04.08	Margaret Konantz	MB HoC

[1] The selection is limited to the first women elected to provincial, territorial, and national legislatures and appointed to the Senate and the offices of lieutenant-governor and governor general.

TABLE 2.1: *continued*

Year	Name	Achievement, First Woman ...
1963.04.08	Pauline Jewett	BC HoC
1964.11.09	Margaret Rideout	NB HoC
1967.09.11	G. Jean Gordon	YK Leg
1970.05.11	Jean Canfield	PEI Leg
1970.12.21	Lena Pederson	NWT Leg
1972.04.27	Margaret Norrie	NS Senate
1972.10.30	Monique Bégin	QU HoC
1974.01.17	Pauline McGibbon	ON Lieut.-Gov.
1974.04.02	Coline Campbell	NS HoC
1979.06.18	Hazel Newhook Lynn Verge	NF Leg
1979.09.27	Martha Bielish	AB Senate
1981.10.23	Pearl McGonigal	MB Lieut.-Gov.
1984.05.14	Jeanne Sauvé	Gov Gen (QU)
1985.01.22	Helen Hunley	AB Lieut.-Gov.
1988.09.09	Sylvia Fedoruk	SK Lieut.-Gov.
1990.08.16	Marion Reid	PEI Lieut.-Gov.
1993.03.11	Raynell Andreychuk	SK Senate
1994.06.21	Margaret Norrie McCain	NB Lieut.-Gov.
1996.12.12	Lise Thibault	QU Lieut.-Gov.
1999.10.07	Adrienne Clarkson	Gov Gen (ON)

In general, firsts are selective: the first woman elected to provincial and territorial legislatures, the first woman elected to the House of Commons, the first one appointed to the Senate and to the posts of lieutenant-governor and governor general, and the first woman to be selected to lead a political party. Indeed, there are a large number of firsts for each province and territory. Some jurisdictions met the milestones early; others reached them only after many decades; and still others have yet to appoint their first woman senator or lieutenant-governor. For instance, Newfoundland and Nova Scotia have not yet had a woman in the lieutenant-governor's post. What becomes readily apparent by looking at all of the firsts together is that at the highest levels of government, serving as the Crown's representative in Canada and holding top jobs as political representatives of Canada, women continue to be as seriously underrepresented in 2002 as legislators and as grossly underrepresented as leaders of political parties as they have been all along.

TABLE 2.2: Firsts by Jurisdiction

	Leg	HoC	Senate	Premier	L.-Gov	Gov Gen	PM
Canada		1921	1953			1984	1993
AB	1917	1941	1979	—	1985	—	—
BC	1918	1962	1953	1991	2001	—	—
MB	1920	1963	1960	—	1981	—	—
NB	1967	1964	1953	—	1994	—	—
NF	1975	—	—	—	—	—	—
NS	1960	1974	1972	—	—	—	—
ON	1943	1921	1930	—	1994	2001	—
PEI	1970	1961	1955	1993	1990	—	—
QU	1961	1972	1953	—	1996	1984	—
SK	1919	1945	1993	—	1988	—	—
NWT	1970	1962	—	1991	N/a	—	—
NT	1999	1997	—	—	N/a	—	—
YK	1967	1935	—	2000	N/a	—	—

Much of the history of women's political participation has been treated as an on-going story of exceptional individuals holding positions usually held by men. A fetish for firsts is a natural enough story, one worth telling. However, it also tends further to segregate successes that may be few and far between. Achievements by women are often analyzed in isolation from each other, making it difficult to see larger patterns such as the recent decline in the number of women leaders. Women's achievements in winning election tend to individuate their success, that is, to see its occurrence apart from the success of other women seeking election. Interpreting an individual woman's electoral success as unrelated to its broader social and electoral context makes each woman's election unique. This excessively narrow interpretation routinely draws attention away from the bigger story of women's lack of fair and equitable political representation. The particularities, even the peculiarities, of each woman's achievement continue to divert the public's attention away from questions of fairness in representation. A focus on fairness could be used to "promote the meaningful exercise of the rights and freedoms essential to a healthy electoral democracy."[11]

The strong historical emphasis on firsts honours the elected women at the same time that it sets them apart from the rest of womanhood as odd, peculiar, special, or extraordinary. In addition to seeing their individual achievements as setting a new high watermark for the advancement of women's equality, there was a tendency to emphasize their extraordinary qualities, characters, and opportunities. This approach reinforced how very tenacious and singular of purpose any woman had to be to win election. No one but the truly exceptional girl would aspire to the job, and no one but the most narrowly focused, ambitious, headstrong woman could possibly succeed. Succeed some of them did, after a time. Long before she became mayor of Ottawa Charlotte Whitton published an article in a 1929 issue of *Chatelaine* about the British Empire's first woman privy councillor.[12] Whitton emphasized Margaret Bondfield's special qualities that made it possible for her to lay a claim to many firsts in the labour movement and in national political life in Britain. The first woman delegate to attend a trade union congress, Bondfield was the first woman elected to serve on the trade union executive committee (she later became its chair). She was also the first woman to be a member of a British government, as an under-secretary, and, later still, the first woman member of cabinet. The litany of firsts she achieved makes her appear to have been a most remarkable and exceptional creature.

The support role women play in electoral politics remains as clear today as it was to Canada's first woman MP, Agnes Macphail. Years after her first election, she wrote a much-cited article, "If I Were Prime Minister." Published in 1933, the opinion piece draws attention to the problem of women's place in public life. She did not write "When I am

Prime Minister" or "When I will be Prime Minister." The use of a subjunctive verb emphasizes the reality that neither she nor so many other women legislators had it within their power to turn such an aspiration into actuality. Although it was legally and politically possible for a woman politician to become prime minister, Macphail implied that such an outcome was not at all likely.[13] It remains an unrealizable aspiration for all but one of the women MPs since 1921.

1917–1969: Eligibility for Some = Representation for Few

During the formative years, women legislators were the perpetual bridesmaids of the political system. They supported the legitimacy of democracy with all of its institutions and offices while having extremely limited access to success in the electoral rite themselves. After the first round of elections across the nation in which some women were eligible to vote, that is, in 1917 for some provinces and 1921 for the federal Parliament, very little changed. There was a period of quiescence for the first 50 years in which fewer than 75 women were elected to legislatures and appointed to the Senate. Women candidates did not step boldly to the hustings. Those who did could refer to special circumstances that drew them to politics, namely the death of husbands and fathers serving terms in legislative office. (See Appendix I: Women Legislators and Senators, 1916–1969.)

What generalizations can be drawn from such a listing of who served when and where? The brief summaries in Box 2.2 and Box 2.3 indicate just how few women populated the first 50 years of women's public service as elected legislators. The numbers were so small over such a long period—two additions every three years on average—that the women who did enter the highest level of public office hardly seemed a matter for study. On the federal electoral scene women mounted 380 candidacies, 30 of which were successful. Roughly 8 per cent of those who stood for Parliament won seats.[14] So, it is not so much that women did not offer themselves as candidates, but that few competitive parties nominated women in winnable ridings; as a result, few ran, and fewer still were

---

BOX 2.2: 50 Years of Women MPs—A Summary

- 18 women elected
- six replaced deceased or ill husbands;
- only one was re-elected for a second term;
- seven Liberals, six Progressive Conservatives (PC), two CCF, and three others;
- eight in Ontario, six in the West, two each in the Maritimes and Territories.

BOX 2.3: 50 Years of Women MLAs—A Summary

- 46 women elected
- two-thirds from the West: 17 in BC, 18 in the prairie provinces;
- six in Ontario, two in the Maritimes, one in Newfoundland (pre-Confederation). Most Quebec women were first eligible to vote in 1940.
- The first Quebec woman was elected in 1960, then re-elected.

---

chosen by the electorate.[15] Fifty years following the introduction of some women's eligibility to stand for election, 62 women had succeeded in being elected in federal and provincial jurisdictions.

Until 1929 women were excluded from appointments to the Senate, because they were not considered qualified "persons" as defined by the constitution (the British North America Act). Five women from Alberta challenged this interpretation of Canadian law in a constitutional reference popularly known as the Person's Case. In 1929, the British Judicial Committee of the Privy Council, which was Canada's highest court at the time, decided that women could be considered "persons" qualified to serve in public life.[16] Nine women were appointed to the Senate after the conclusion of the Person's Case and before 1970. These women senators served 130 person-years, an average of 14 years per senator, a feat not continued in recent times when more women have been appointed but some have served for as little as six months before reaching the retirement age of 75.

A poll conducted in 1948 asked readers of *Chatelaine* why there was then only one woman MP. Twenty-two per cent of respondents said women had "other responsibilities" for home and family that preoccupied their attention. Just over one-fifth—21 per cent—said they thought women were afraid to try to win elected office, and 18 per cent opined that women were "indifferent" to the job. A sizeable number of those surveyed suggested sexist attitudes were to blame, as 17 per cent thought the public needed to be educated to consider women as qualified, and 15 per cent responded that prejudice against women hindered their chances of success. Five per cent favoured each of these explanations: that women are "too emotional" to be effective, that men are preferred because they are more suited to the job, and that women rejected the corruption associated with politics.[17] In the 50 years since this poll was taken, women have shown repeatedly that they are capable and willing, but men continue to be overrepresented relative to the distribution of the general population now as in the past. In jurisdiction upon jurisdiction and time after time, women legislators have struggled to take their place on an equal footing and in equal numbers to men.

Including More, and More Diverse, Women: Progress from 1970 to 2000

Journalists writing in the immediate aftermath of the RCSW report pointedly asked, "Where are the women?" and "Why aren't there more of them?"[18] *Chatelaine* magazine noted prior to the federal election of 1971 that female MPs were a rarer breed than whooping cranes (one woman, 56 birds). Like the birds, women politicians did not become extinct; far from it, as so many were qualified for the job. And the diversity of the species increased with the enfranchisement of Aboriginal and ethnic minority women, occurring as it did variously from the late 1940s to the late 1960s.[19] In 1972, *Chatelaine* editor Doris Anderson declared that there were lots of "good women willing and able to run. (In our October issue last fall, without half trying, we turned up 105 of them)."[20] The photograph *Chatelaine* published of the potential candidates had few visible minority women among their number. Over time, the number of women and the diversity of candidates' heritage and life experience has increasingly been a matter for public discussion.

The RCSW, like the political observers of the time, conceptualized group-based **identity politics** as those ideas, values, and behaviours that were shaped by religion, language, and region. The "race question in Canada" was a matter of French versus English.[21] As a result, the commission did not focus attention on the ethnicity of women candidates and office-holders. Nor did it note that some women began to enter legislatures, in very small numbers, well before all women had the right to vote. White, able-bodied women won the franchise provincially and federally between 1916 and 1940, but, like their male counterparts, status Indian women, women of East Indian, Japanese, and Chinese origin, and women with mental or physical disabilities had to wait considerably longer for their political rights. For instance, the federal vote was extended to white female British subjects in 1918, but denied to Canadians of Japanese, Chinese, and East Indian descent until 1948, to the Inuit until 1950, and to status Indians until 1960.[22] Persons with mental disabilities living in institutions were accorded the franchise in 1991, and full access to polling stations for those with mobility and vision impairments was finally conferred as the result of changes to the Elections Act in 1992.[23] Further reforms were made in 2000 to make it possible for adults to vote even if they have no fixed address. It is only very recently, then, that all adult women who are Canadian citizens have had the right to cast a ballot and contest elected office. When the RCSW was conducting its research, many Aboriginal and ethnic minority women were newcomers to the electoral process.

Most of the women elected in the first 65 years of eligibility have been older, white, mainly middle-class, publicly heterosexual women. Few identified themselves as actively broadening the range of opinions offered for

public discussion. Since 1988 many more women and an increasing number
of women from diverse socio-economic and ideological backgrounds have
been elected. While there has as yet been no systematic count of the
Aboriginal and visible minority women elected at either level of government, it is evident that women from these groups remain significantly
underrepresented in Canada's legislatures. Only six minority women
(defined as non-Aboriginal women with ethno-racial backgrounds outside
the two majority origin categories, English and French) served in the House
of Commons between 1965 and 1988, comprising 5 per cent of the total
number of MPs of minority background who served during this time (six
out of 120).[24] It was not until 1993 that the numbers increased significantly,
with 11 minority women elected that year, followed by 17 in 1997 and 19 in
the 2000 federal election (respectively, 3.7, 5.6 and 6.3 per cent of the total
number of MPs).[25] The presence of visible minority women has also
increased, from 1 MP in 1988, to 4 in 2000.[26] Presently there are two
Aboriginal women serving in the House of Commons, Merlene Jennings
and Ethel Blondin-Andrew, both Liberals. As well, four visible minority
women are MPs, namely, Jean Augustine, Hedy Fry, Nancy Karetak-Lindell,
and Sophia Leung. Given that the 1996 census of Canada found over 11 per
cent of Canadians self-identify as a member of a group considered a "visible minority,"[27] these are small numbers indeed. (See Appendix II: Women
Legislators and Senators, 1970–1985.)

It is interesting that the fetish for firsts we discussed in the last section
has focused on the achievements of white women. Nowhere is there a list
of the political achievements for women that mark and celebrate women's
diversity. Table 2.3 offers a different look at the "first woman" phenomenon, with ethno-cultural diversity in mind. It shows just how long
women had to wait to see aspects of their diversity reflected in elected
office and illustrates the continued importance of working to elect more
and more diverse women.

Considering women as a group, we can compare how they were doing
in 1970 to 2000 by updating the measures used by the RCSW. More women
have been legislators in the last 30 years than in the previous half-century.

TABLE 2.3: Table of Firsts Representing Women's Diversity[1]

Year	Name	Achievement
1972	Rosemary Brown	First Black woman elected to any Canadian legislature — BC, NDP
1974	Eleanor Millard	First Aboriginal woman elected to a Canadian legislature —Territorial Councillor/MLA YK, 1974–1978
1976	Jean Alfred	First Black woman to be elected to the Quebec National Assembly, PQ
1979 1991	Nellie Cournoyea	First Aboriginal woman elected to NWT legislature First Aboriginal First Minister, 1991–95 First Aboriginal government leader in Canada
1986	Pearl Calahasen	First Aboriginal woman elected to AB legislature—PC
1988	Ethel Blondin Andrew	First Aboriginal woman elected to the House of Commons—Yukon, Lib
1990	Zanana Akande	First Black woman cabinet minister—ON, NDP
1993 1996	Jenny Kwan	First woman of Asian heritage elected to a Canadian legislature—BC, NDP First woman of Asian heritage in cabinet
1997	Nancy Karelak-Lindell	First Inuit woman elected to the House of Commons—Nunavut, Lib

[1] Additions will be made as we continue to identify "firsts" for women's diversity.

The total number of legislators has grown substantially, and there has been improvement overall. The presence of women across all legislatures in the country improved from under 2 per cent in 1970, then gained and exceeded 10 per cent circa 1985. Now, in the first years of the twenty-first century, the percentage hovers at about 20 per cent. Thus, the percentage of women elected to Canadian legislatures increased tenfold over a 30-year period, with the largest acceleration occurring since the late 1980s.

Women's advances in Canadian electoral politics have occurred in two distinct phases. Some progress began to be made after the RCSW released its report, and between 1970 and 1985 the number of women elected grew

TABLE 2.4: The Three-Quarters Century Mark: Women Elected and Appointed to Federal, Provincial, and Territorial Governments, 1917–2000

Women[1] Period	Half Century Quiescence	Third Quarter Growth Women's Status Emphasized		¾ Century Overview
Position/Years	1917–1969	1970–1984	1985–2000	1917–2000
MPs	18	39	97	154
MLAs	44	66	294	404
Senators	9	14	40	63
Number	*71*	*119*	*431*	*621*
Average of ALL Legislators	Under 2%	Up to 10 %	~ 20%	Less than 10%

[1] Incumbents' terms extend between the groupings listed. We have counted only those women elected or appointed for the first time.

slowly but relatively steadily. However, it was in the last 15 years of the twentieth century that significant increases occurred. Table 2.4 reports the numbers of women who won office or were appointed to the Senate during the three time periods. These women were counted by the date first elected; it is worth noting that many of them won re-election, some several times. As Table 2.4 shows, more than three times as many women won election in the 15 years between 1985 and 2000 than prior to 1985.

Table 2.5 shows progress in percentage terms—women as a percentage of the legislators in each jurisdiction—using 1970, 1988, and 2000 for comparison. We chose 1988 as our end date for the second comparison point both because of election timing at the federal level and to reflect a spate of electoral contests at the provincial level after 1985. Otherwise, the data give the mistaken impression that almost all of the progress occurred from the late 1980s onward. By 1988, the wave of increases that occurred between 1984 and 1986 had been recorded. As the table shows, women's percentage of seats in the House of Commons increased from less than 1 per cent in 1970, to just over 10 per cent in 1988, to slightly over 20 per cent in 2000. Overall the provinces and territories elected more women,

TABLE 2.5: **Percentage of Women Elected or Appointed, 15 Year Intervals, 1970–2000**

Jurisdiction	1970		1988		2000	
	% Women	# women/ total	% Women	# women/ total	% Women	# women/ total
House of Commons	0.4	1/264	9.6	27/282	20.6	62/301
Senate	4.5	4/88	11.9	12/101	36.6	34/93
Prov/Terr.	2.3	15/639	12.2	92/752	22.3	165/738
ALL WOMEN	2.0	20/991	11.5	131/1135	23.1	261/1132

Sources: Arscott and Trimble, *In the Presence of Women*, federal, provincial and territorial websites; Parliamentary Guides.

with 2 per cent women elected as members of legislative assemblies (MLA) in 1970, 12 per cent in 1988, and 22 per cent in 2000.

An interesting observation can be drawn from Table 2.5—women have, at all three points, been somewhat better represented in the appointed Senate than in elected legislatures. Women comprised about 5 per cent of senators in 1970, 12 per cent in 1988, and about 37 per cent in 2000. Although appointments of women to the Senate have outstripped elected women MPs by an increasingly wide margin over time, men and women are not appointed at equal rates. Since 1985 a new pattern is emerging in Senate appointments. In the second term of the Chrétien government, women have been appointed almost in equal numbers to men. As a result the representation of women in the Senate is now substantially higher than women's record of election to the House of Commons.[28] However, women have tended to be appointed later in life than men and to serve relatively short terms by longevity standards for that chamber. The gender balance in the Senate over time is as important as the number of women appointed. Achieving gender equity in the Senate is a simple matter compared to electoral contests, the results of which are influenced by so many factors other than the candidate herself.

Only time will tell if gender parity will be achieved sooner in the Senate than in the House of Commons and what that might mean for women's substantive representation.

Counting Matters:
The More Elected, the More Selected

It appears that remarkable progress had been made in a relatively short period in the mid-1980s. Following the election of the Mulroney government in 1984, many more Conservative women were elected than ever before, and, for the first time, women comprised almost 10 per cent of the membership of the House of Commons. Numbers were slightly lower at the subnational level, as there were only 50 women legislators out of 647 in provincial and territorial legislatures across the country (7.7 per cent). However, women politicians had been elected in more than token numbers, and women's political representation thus could finally be considered a serious subject for academic inquiry. In 1985, the first two books analyzing women in federal politics were published.[29]

But what happens when we broaden the analysis of women's presence in public life, as did the RCSW, to include appointed positions? In the year following the 1984 federal general election, there were 12 women senators out of 101 (12 per cent) and 6 women in a cabinet of 39 (15.4 per cent). In 1985, no women represented the Crown or sat in the speaker's chair. (In the preceding 15 years there had been three women lieutenant-governors, one woman governor general, and one woman speaker, Jeanne Sauvé, who occupied the post from 1980 to 1984.) In 1985, there were no female federal party leaders and no women prime ministers, justices of the Supreme Court, or premiers. Women had broken the 10 per cent level federally, but most of the top jobs associated with public life continued to elude them entirely.

Women count in electoral politics, as in life in general, when their presence creates general public expectations about what they merit. To count is to matter. It means being important, worthy of being taken into account. When something comes to matter that did not matter before, it may be necessary to go back and search out that which previously was overlooked as being of no significance. When new matters emerge, gathering evidence is part of the effort required to dignify the phenomenon with appropriate understanding. When women were absent from elected political office, there was no expectation that they would head up government departments, hold ambassadorships, represent Canada on international bodies, sit on the bench, or become premier or prime minister. As long as women were absent from legislatures, they were invisible to those who make such appointments. They were seen to have no claim to the honours and public profile that grateful nations can bestow on their worthy citizens.

In Canada, women have been regarded as meritorious in society in proportion to their presence in public life. Moreover, the primary indicator of merit used in this country has long been women's capacity to get themselves elected. This social fact is a political convention that appears in no policy document but which plays out as the recurrent theme explaining why women continue to be excluded from equal shares of high-profile public positions. There appears to be an unwritten rule that women earn prominence in public life in direct proportion to their capacity to win election, expand their presence in the government party caucus, and "earn" cabinet posts. For more than 30 years, this attitude has been used to support the political convention we describe as "the more elected, the more selected": the more women legislators are elected, the more they are likely to be selected for political appointments.

Collecting the numbers of women elected and appointed to top jobs shows a strong correlation between women's level of representation in the House of Commons, seats in cabinet, and their profile in the public service and on the federal bench. The trend that becomes immediately apparent is that as the federal general elections go for women, so goes the nation. In Chapter 6 we show an even more specific correlation between women's presence in the government caucus and the number of cabinet positions awarded.

The significance of tracking women's electoral performance (which is one of the most important career paths to leadership positions in politics) can be established in two ways. First, anecdotal evidence supports the existence of a political convention of earned electoral entitlement that can be backed up with empirical evidence. The memoirs and personal papers of women aspirants to political jobs express their frustration that they could not make the power-holders of the day understand that they had earned the position they sought. Their demands for consideration were routinely deflected, with remarks, like the one received by Pauline Jewett when she asked Lester B. Pearson for a post in his government's cabinet. They already had one woman (Judy LaMarsh), she was told.

In February 2002, a quarrel broke out between Prime Minister Jean Chrétien and Carolyn Bennett, Chair of the Status of Women Caucus for the Liberals. Although we discussed the dispute in Chapter 1, the story is worth mentioning again here because it so clearly illustrates the "more elected, the more selected" phenomenon. Bennett publicly criticized the underrepresentation of women after a major shuffle resulted in one fewer position for women at the cabinet table. The prime minister chastised her for pointing out the inequity in public. He defended the government's record of appointing women to top jobs, pointing to a governor general, a Supreme Court justice, and eight lieutenant-governors (six of whom served at the same time).[30] An article published in the *National Post* indirectly defended the prime minister by observing that the percentage of women in the new cabinet (23 per cent) actually exceeded the percentage of women in the House of Commons (20.6 per cent).[31] In other words, in the newly constituted Chrétien cabinet, women got slightly more than they deserved. Election to Parliament has been taken as a measure of women's "deservingness" for key appointments.

The second technique for measuring this phenomenon is provided by the Table of Precedence of Canada, an official ranking of positions of importance in the government of Canada overseen by the Department of Heritage. Our analysis of the Tables, at 15-year intervals, examines the increased representation of women in key public positions. Does the growth in women's electoral presence occur at the same time as advances in other measures of women's representation such as membership in the Senate, cabinet appointments, and high-profile appointments representing the Crown?

Table 2.6 makes it clear that women's position in cabinet, in government, in most federally controlled, high-level appointments is strongly influenced by the number of women elected. No women, no status. Twenty per cent elected equals about 20 per cent of prestigious positions, nothing more, sometimes less. Not only is the correlation strong, it has operated for decades.

At one level it has been generally known that this is the case. Demonstrating that the more women elected federally results in more top jobs in public life shows government policy being directed by the heavy hand of political convention and past practice. The empirical data—the hard, consistent evidence—reveals that this phenomenon indeed has existed for more than 30 years. The convention of the more elected, the more selected shows no signs of changing in the near future. Is this the best way of deciding what Canadian women merit? Probably not. So long as women's electoral representation has been steadily increasing, so has women's share of the most powerful political posts. However, what happens if the electoral project stalls, as we argue it has in Chapter 3? The marked progress that occurred between 1970 and 1985 and the steady but gradual increases that characterized 1985-2000 have indeed slowed to a near standstill. What, then, can women expect? Will there be fewer top jobs for women and a corresponding lack of further improvement in increasing women's presence in public life?

We maintain that a plateau in political representation by women has already been reached. There has been a leveling off in women's electoral representation, a trend discussed more thoroughly in Chapter 3. Based on past experience this halt in further progress bodes ill for women's aspirations for equality and fairness in Canada, at least in the short term. What do these trends forecast for women's status in society more generally? What place will women have in political representation and public life 15 years hence?

TABLE 2.6: Tables of Precedence for Canada, 1970, 1985, 2000[1]

Rank	Position	1970	1985	2000
1–5	1–Gov Gen., 2–PM, 3–Chief Justice, 4–Speaker Senate, 5–Speaker HoC.	0/5	1/5	3/5
6	Ambassadors, High Commissioners, Ministers, Plenipotentiary[2]	—	—	—
7	Members of the Cabinet[3]	0/30 —	6/39 [15%]	10/36 [27.8%]
8	Leader of the Opposition	0/1	0/1	0/1
9	Lieutenant-Governors	0/10	2/10	6/10
10	Members of the Queen's Privy Council, not of the Cabinet	3/101 [3.0%]	10/175 [5.7%]	30/224 [13.4%]
11	Representatives of Major Religious Denominations	—	—	—
12	Premiers of the Provinces	0/10	0/10	0/10
13–16	Justices of the Supreme Court, Justices of highest courts of each Prov. and Terr., Judges of other superior courts in the provs. and terrs.	N/A	N/A	N/A
17	Members of the Senate	4/88 [4.5%]	12/101 [11.8%]	33/93 [35.5%]
18	Members of the House of Commons	1/264 [0.4%]	27/282 [9.5%]	62/301 [20.6%]
19	Consuls-General of countries without diplomatic representation	N/A	N/A	N/A
20	Chief of the Defence Staff	0/1	0/1	0/1
21	Members of the Executive Councils, Provincial, within their Provinces	[~2.5%]	[~8.3%]	[~25%]
22–24	Speaker of the Legis. Council in Provs., Members, Speaker of Leg. Assemblies	—	—	—
	Members of Legislative Assemblies within their Provinces	15/639 [2.3%]	67/647 [10.3%]	165/738 [22.3%]
Total	**Elected and Appointed Representatives of Canada**	**27/1313 [2.1%]**	**102/1365 [7.5%]**	**359/1720 [20.9%]**

[1] Effective dates 19 December 1969, 1 March 1985, and 1 April 1999.

[2] Our count is a best case: two women ambassadors in 1970 (B.M. Meagher, High Commissioner to Kenya and Uganda, and Pamela Ann McDougall, Ambassador to Poland) out of 121, 0/85 in 1985, and unknown for 2000. Women's representation in the foreign service needs further study.

[3] Not counted in the tabulation because listed again under Members of Parliament.

Why Counting Women Will Still Matter in 15 Years

In 1970, the RCSW asked why women were not more active in public life and why they were so poorly represented in political office. In 2002, we are still asking variations of the "where are the women" question. Why do women hold only 20 per cent of the seats in Canada's legislatures when they comprise over 50 per cent of the population? Why have there not been more women MPs, MLAs, and leaders of political parties? Why are women's prospects for future leadership roles so dim? Why do women continue to earn so relatively few of the highest political appointments compared to men?

A key concern of this book is the complacency surrounding women's underrepresentation in political life. As a matter of public policy do Canadians need any longer to be concerned about counting the number of women who get elected to high public office? The answer offered here is a resolute "Yes." But in 1991 another Royal Commission, this one on Electoral Reform and Party Financing (RCERPF), concluded the answer to this question was "No," that policy interventions were no longer necessary to secure women's place in electoral politics. The RCERPF argued that, once 20 per cent representation had been achieved federally, this level of participation would be sufficient to keep the upward momentum going to sustain further improvements to electoral representation by women. This minimum was achieved in the federal general election of 1997 as well as in many provincial and territorial jurisdictions. It would seem that women's numbers among the country's legislators is no longer a problem. The once hot topic concerning how to get more women elected to top jobs no longer has any place on the public agenda even at election time. So, does this mean the problem of women's underrepresentation in political life has been solved?

Our answer is, "Hold on. Not so fast." Important issues that affect women's full participation in the life of the nation remain much as before, and these still need to be given their due. Our data provide a base of information from which to predict what the political status of women is likely to be by the time we approach the centenary of (some) women's electoral participation in 2015. Unless unforeseen events intervene to shake the roots of Canadian society, the patterns from the past remain the best predictor of what is to come.

Consider the following: in the 1970s the conclusion drawn by the RCSW was that women had to be encouraged to participate more directly and effectively in political life to demonstrate their worthiness for government appointments. By 1985 what progress had been made still barely reached the 10 per cent level, and then only on the prime indicator of electing women to the House of Commons. At the millennium 15 years later, 20 per cent representation by women had been reached, again not uniformly in legislatures across the country but only in the House of Commons. Given the evidence, much of which is presented in the next chapter, there is no strong reason to believe that significant progress will be made in the next 15 years. We expect 2015 to bring the level of representation in elected positions to about 26 per cent. If Senate appointments for women continue in the current vein, it is possible that women will comprise 40 per cent of the Upper House by 2015. Symbolic representation for women will thereby far outstrip women's access to positions of political power and policy spaces where key decisions are made.

Women in Canada hold less than half of the top jobs that would be theirs were it not for the political convention that women will only merit more of these positions when they earn them through the ballot box. Although the data come almost entirely from the federal scene, our work comparing provincial and territorial jurisdictions to the situation federally leads us to hypothesize that the trend probably holds more universally than the evidence provided here. As this and the remaining chapters show, the pattern that emerges is crystal clear: prevailing attitudes, political conventions, and practices have established 20 per cent, and little more, as women's share. When it comes to matters of leadership of governing political parties, competitive political parties, senior cabinet posts, and national honours, men continue to be selected for four out of every five posts. Historically, the numbers have circumscribed what women actually got as their share in public life.

TABLE 2.7: Summary of the Advancement of Women in the Canadian Political System, 1970–2000

	1970		1988		2000		2015 (estimated)	
Women	%	#	%	#	%	#	%	#
MPs	0.4	1/264	9.6	27/282	20.6	62/301	~25	77/310
Senators	4.5	4/88	11.9	12/101	36.6	34/93	~40	41/101
MLAs	2.3	15/639	12.2	92/752	22.3	165/738	~26	188/750
TOTAL	2.0	20/991	11.5	131/1135	23.1	261/1132	~26	306/1161

Note: Some Senate seats were vacant in 2000; also, between 1988 and 2000, the overall number of legislative seats declined at the provincial level.

Source: Canadian Parliamentary Guides, various years.

Conclusion

Counting elected women involves the production and reproduction of social meanings about women's place in Canadian society. These meanings are used to justify limiting women's entitlement to scarce resources such as seats in cabinet, federal and provincial judgeships, senior positions in government and the public service, appointment to the Senate, and opportunities to represent the crown and Canada in capacities selected by the government. It is not merely that society has more or less women sworn in to each new sitting of our country's legislatures. More importantly, there exist long-standing conventions that are part and parcel of the patterns of governance. The norms and values that underpin these patterns lend their support to the well-established practice that women will be appointed roughly in proportion to their capacity to fill the seats in legislatures.

Counting women in politics continues to matter because women legislators continue to be seen as being collectively responsible for the status of women in Canadian society. Feminist or not, female legislators continue to be looked to for strong support in matters affecting equality for women, regardless of their partisanship or their commitment to the humanity of all people. This social obligation to other women past, present, and future provides them with both a legacy and a challenge. Our legacy is the path beaten through the electoral wilderness over many years and under difficult conditions by not just the "firsts" but the many other women who followed them. Our challenge is to blaze additional pathways to leadership so that the Canadian political system demonstrates fairness and equity toward all women.

CHAPTER 3

The Electoral Glass Ceiling[1]

Introduction

Until the mid-1980s, women were novelties in Canada's legislatures, comprising less than 10 per cent of elected representatives in most jurisdictions. Female representatives were so rare that in some legislatures it was thought unnecessary to have women's washrooms close to the chamber. Women elected to the House of Commons in the 1970s used the washroom in the "Parliamentary Wives' Retiring Lounge." Not much had changed in this regard by the 1990s. Shortly after the late Liberal MP Shaughnessy Cohen was elected in 1993 she missed a vote in the House while she searched for the women's washroom. Cohen protested, and a few weeks later a large men's washroom off the lobby of the chamber was divided into two smaller facilities, one for women.[2] On the provincial scene, Manitoba MLA June Westbury lobbied for the renovations necessary to afford bathroom access to the two women legislators.[3] Alexa McDonough, the lone woman in the Nova Scotia legislature in the 1980s, had to "stand in line with the tour groups to use the public washroom because only the men had a toilet."[4] And as Rosemary Brown recalls:

> In 1972 when I entered the BC legislature, I discovered that all the washrooms in the building meant for the use of elected members had been built with urinals in them. In the particular washroom being used by female politicians and staff, the urinal had been concealed behind a temporary box-like wood structure—a clear indication that our legislative forefathers had not conceived the possibility of women one day serving as elected members in that building, and that our presence there is still accompanied by the hope that our sojourn will be temporary.[5]

Now, in the early years of the new millennium, about one-fifth of officeholders in provincial, territorial, and federal legislatures are women. As of November 5, 2002, including recent by-elections, just over 20 per cent of the representatives at the provincial and territorial level and 21 per cent at the federal level are female, with an overall average of about 21 per cent. Women's electoral representation now approximates the level considered by the Royal Commission on Electoral Reform and Party Financing to require no further action on the part of governments to boost the number of women in Canada's legislatures.[6] Gender is no longer regarded in most quarters as an issue affecting **balanced, equitable, and fair representation**. This chapter argues that a false sense of continuing achievement prevails, further stalling progress for women, and **complacency** itself now contributes to the continued underrepresentation of women in electoral politics in Canada. The number of elected women has stopped far short of a fair outcome. Instead, electoral representation lacks gender balance and so tends to be inequitable and unfair.

Current numbers have led some observers to conclude that the problem of women's underrepresentation in electoral spaces is well on its way to being solved. We disagree, for four reasons. First, while Canada's record with respect to electing women stacks up well against several other countries, including the United States, the United Kingdom, and France, we continue to lag behind the Nordic countries, Australia, New Zealand, and Germany.[7] Indeed, Canada ranks only thirty-fourth in the world when it comes to electing women to its national Parliament (lower house), below many similarly industrialized nations.[8] Secondly, the percentage of elected women in Canada continues to fall far short of 50 per cent. In contrast, some countries are approaching gender parity. Denmark, Iceland, Finland, Netherlands, and Norway feature more than 35 per cent women in their national assemblies, and 43 per cent of Sweden's parliamentarians are women. Yet over 80 per cent—four out of five—of the elected representatives in Canada's legislatures are men. Nowhere in Canada do women comprise more than one-quarter of the legislators.

Thirdly, electoral progress for women in Canada appears to have stalled. A relatively steady increase in the numbers of elected women since the 1980s obscures the fact that most recently, in several jurisdictions, the percentage of female legislators has either stayed the same or actually dropped slightly. For instance, Alberta and British Columbia briefly elected more than 25 per cent women MLAs until spring 2001 elections pushed the number of women down. The Yukon Territory featured over 29 per cent women in its small legislature until the November 2002 election reduced this number considerably, to just under 17 per cent. Women's representation in Canada's federal Parliament has reached a plateau at about 21 per cent.

Finally, not all women are equally well-represented as women. Who, exactly, is making progress? Female politicians are certainly no more representative of the general public than are male politicians; in general, they are overwhelmingly white, middle to upper class, able-bodied, relatively privileged in their amount of formal education, and publicly heterosexual.[9] So, when we take account of the fact that, on average, close to one-fifth of our elected representatives are women, we must remember that many Canadian women and some men do not see themselves (or people like them in important respects) in public office. At present, only the already relatively privileged women are likely to be selected. Women's diversity in its entirety is not currently represented in our legislative institutions, and, as we explore more fully in Chapter Six, this lack of diversity has clear implications for effective public policy-making.[10]

Despite a recent modest increase in the overall percentage of elected women, the political environment is still a difficult one for female political aspirants, activists, legislators, and party leaders. Significant barriers remain to women's substantive representation in formal arenas of political deliberation and decision-making. This chapter examines one of these constraints. We maintain that, as in the business world and other areas traditionally dominated by men, electoral politics features its own version of the **glass ceiling**:[11] the invisible barriers that effectively keep women from rising beyond a certain level in hierarchical organizations. Moreover, it is this electoral glass ceiling on which female political aspirants are now bumping their heads.[12]

We believe the political variant of the glass ceiling has stalled women's electoral progress and will prevent women's legislative representation from exceeding 25 per cent in the near future. Why? There are a variety of reasons, but the most important is the behaviour of the gatekeepers[13] to legislative office, that is, political parties. The increased number of women in Canada's legislatures in the 1980s and 1990s reflected the fact that all political parties, particularly the NDP, nominated women in greater numbers than ever before. In the late 1990s, most Canadian political parties reached, or came close, to the 25 per cent mark for women candidates and went no further. Fortunately, as women began to contest nominations in **winnable ridings**—that is, electoral contests a particular party is expected to win, or "safe seats," those the party has won for more than three consecutive elections— they were no longer the **sacrificial lambs** served up as mere standard-bearers in ridings the party does not expect to win. When members of underrepresented groups are put forward in these ridings, the parties downplay their certain defeat and instead emphasize their inclusiveness in the selection of diverse candidates.

BOX 3.1: Reasons for Concern Despite 20 Per Cent Representation by Women

---

- Other countries consistently elect more women than Canada.
  Challenge: Why doesn't Canada do better?
- Several countries are approaching gender parity (50 per cent women).
  Challenge: Why is the goal of gender parity only half realized in Canada?
- Electoral progress for women in Canada has recently stalled.
  Challenge: Why has concern about women's underrepresentation fallen off the political agenda?
- All women are *not* equally well-represented.
  Challenge: How can representation become increasingly balanced, equitable, and fair?

This chapter begins with an overview of women's electoral progress across Canada. We then offer evidence to substantiate the electoral glass ceiling argument, illustrating the recent slow-down in the number of elected women. The third section shows that political parties must take a large part of the responsibility for the electoral glass ceiling, as they consistently fail to advance women candidates in numbers approaching gender parity. In conclusion, we describe some measures designed to increase women's representation in electoral spaces. However, we remain pessimistic about prospects for change, hypothesizing that the electoral glass ceiling for women will remain around 25 per cent for the foreseeable future.

Women's Electoral Progress: Reaching the 20 Per Cent Mark

Most of the progress towards improved representation of women in Canada's legislatures has been made in the last decade. Women did not cross the 10 per cent mark at the federal level until 1988, and provincially the average percentage of female legislators was below 10 per cent until 1989.[14] In the mid-1980s, the percentage of women legislators ranged from 2 per cent in Newfoundland to 19 per cent in the Yukon. Now the span is broader, from under 10 per cent in Nova Scotia to just under 25 percent in Manitoba, with an average across the country of about 20 per cent. Most provinces and territories crossed the 10 per cent mark by the mid-to-late 1980s; the exceptions include the Yukon, which jumped this hurdle much earlier, in 1967, and Saskatchewan, Newfoundland, and Nova Scotia, where the numbers were below 10 per cent until the 1990s. Nova Scotia was last, electing women to about 12 per cent of its seats in 1998, but the progress was short-lived, and this is now the only province with female representation below 10 per cent. On the other hand, the western Canadian provinces, the Yukon, and Quebec have established a benchmark of 20 per cent. And four jurisdictions have elected women to one-quarter of the seats in their assemblies: Yukon in 1989 and 2000, BC in 1991 and 1996, PEI in 1993, and Alberta in 1997.

Why did women make such dramatic electoral progress in the late 1980s and 1990s? Lisa Young and Elaine Campbell suggest several reasons for this.[15] First, the improving economic and social status of women in Canadian society puts more women in professional categories considered good recruiting ground by political parties when they go looking for prospective candidates. In other words, women are now more likely to have the types of educational and social backgrounds displayed by male candidates and office-holders and, therefore, are more likely than before to be considered to have the "right stuff" for political candidacy. Secondly, the hard work of feminist activists both within and outside political parties in demanding better representation of women and their interests has pressured parties to nominate more women and even to offer modest amounts of financial assistance to women candidates.[16] Thirdly, reformed election finance rules at the federal level and in some provinces have helped level the playing field, making electoral competition more affordable to some women. Fourth, there are more seats up for grabs in any given election, as **incumbency** is less of a barrier in

Canada than is the case in many other countries. Canada has a relatively high rate of electoral turnover, as many incumbents decide not to seek re-election, thereby creating opportunities for parties to nominate women in winnable ridings. Increased party competition and electoral volatility can also dampen the incumbency effect. According to Lynda Erickson, the emergence of new political parties, as well as renewed support for moribund parties can open **windows of opportunity** for women to enter Canada's legislatures.[17]

Finally, and most importantly, many political parties have followed social cues and responded to demands from feminist party activists by nominating more women. In particular, the NDP has led the way at the federal and provincial level, selecting significantly more women candidates than other parties.[18] As a social democratic party committed to equality goals in public policy, the NDP has adopted various affirmative action tactics designed to improve the number of female party officials and candidates. Similarly, the Parti Québécois (PQ) has supported initiatives to enhance women's participation in the party, promote feminist policy demands, and increase women's representation as candidates.[19] Social democratic parties have acted as trend-setters, in many jurisdictions having a **contagion effect** on other parties, inspiring competitors to offer similar numbers of female candidates.[20] Also, with the growth of the women's movement in the 1980s, and the emergence of a small but noticeable gender gap in party support and public opinion, "parties saw that nominating women candidates and having women MPs [and MLAs] in their caucuses could become part of a strategy for attracting women voters."[21] As a result, women candidates began to win nominations for competitive parties in winnable ridings. Because they were no longer being served up mostly as sacrificial lambs for fringe parties or standard bearers in unwinnable ridings for competitive parties, women began to win office in greater numbers. While at the federal level female candidates are still slightly less likely to be successful in their bids than their male counterparts, in some cases at the provincial level they have a marginally better chance of winning than do men.[22]

> **BOX 3.2: Summary of Reasons for Progress in Absolute Numbers**
>
> - More women with professional qualifications are available to seek elected office.
> - Strong, effective support within parties and by the women's movement has increased representation by women.
> - Financing prospects have improved for women candidates.
> - Turnover rates provide opportunities for women and other newcomers.
> - Measures taken by some parties to boost the number of women candidates may influence other parties to do the same (see contagion effect).

Progress in the absolute number of women elected has certainly been made over the last 15 years, but recent evidence indicates that the **electoral project** for women (the goal of electing more and more women until gender parity is reached) has stalled at about the 20 per cent mark. Table 3.1 shows the number of women elected to Canada's legislatures as of elections held by November 4, 2002 and ranks them in order, names the governing party, and indicates the degree of change in each jurisdiction since the previous election. The western Canadian provinces and territories continue to lead the way, with Manitoba, BC, Saskatchewan, and Alberta electing women in at least one-fifth of the seats in their legislatures. Quebec has also consistently elected women at or over the 20 per cent level since 1989. PEI is the anomaly in the Atlantic region, with more than 20 per cent women in its legislature. Along with the Northwest Territories (NWT) and the new territory of Nunavut, the Atlantic provinces are home to the lowest numbers of elected women in the country.

The change column on the right hand side of Table 3.1 suggests a slowdown in the electoral project; in two jurisdictions there was no increase from the previous election, and in four provinces and territories the percentage of women elected actually dropped. In jurisdictions where progress was made, it was very slight indeed. Figure 3.1 paints a broader

TABLE 3.1: Women in Canadian Legislatures: Most Recent Elections as of November 2002

Province/ Territory	Party Elected	Date of Most Recent Election	Number of Members	Number of Women Elected	% of Women Members	% Change Since Last Election
Manitoba	NDP	1999	57	14	24.6%	+ 5.3%
Quebec	PQ	1998	125	29	23.2%	+ 4.8%
BC	Liberal	2001	79	18	22.8%	- 3.9%
Sask.	NDP	1999	58	13	22.4%	0%
PEI	PC	2000	27	6	22.2%	+ 7.4%
CANADA	Liberal	2000	301	62	20.6%	0%
Alberta	PC	2001	83	17	20.5%	- 6.0%
NB	PC	1999	55	10	18.2%	+ 1.8%
Ontario	PC	1999	103	18	17.5%	+ 2.9%
Nfld.	Liberal	1999	48	8	16.7%	+ 2.1%
Yukon	Yukon	2002	18	3	16.7%	-12.7%
NWT	N/A	1999	19	2	10.5%	+ 2.2%
NS	PC	1999	52	5	9.6%	-1.9%
Nunavut	N/A	1999	19	1	5.3%	N/A
TOTAL			1044	206	19.7%	

NOTES

1. In Nunavut, another woman, Rebekah Uqi Williams, was elected in a December 2000 by-election, bringing the total to 2 (10.5%).

2. In Nova Scotia, 5 women were elected in 1999, but Eileen O'Connell died in 2000 and was replaced by a male legislator in a by-election.

3. In Quebec, as of July 2002, by-elections have brought the number of women MNAs to 35 out of 125, or 28%.

4. Regarding the Canadian Parliament, federal by-elections on 13 May 2002 increased the number of women in the House of Commons to 63.

Sources: Federal, provincial, and territorial websites (downloaded June and August 2001, November 2002), Elections BC, via email, 6 June 2001.

picture of change over time. It indicates that, while over the five most recent elections in each jurisdiction the percentage of women in federal, provincial, and territorial legislatures has climbed, recent progress is minimal. From the mid-1980s to the early 1990s, the number of elected women more than doubled, from 9 per cent to 18 per cent. Since then, progress has stalled; over the last decade the overall percentage of female legislators has crept from over 18 to just under 20, a very small increase. This pattern, which we first noticed in 1997,[23] supports the hypothesis that there exists an electoral glass ceiling for office-seeking women.

Figure 3.1: Percentage of Women Elected in Five Most Recent Elections

(Average across federal, provincial, and territorial legislatures)

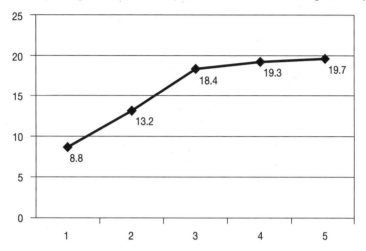

The Electoral Glass Ceiling

In 1990, Chantal Maillé calculated that, "if women continue to increase their number of seats [in Parliament] at the same rate as between 1984 and 1988, and the number of MPs remains constant at 295, it will take nine elections, or as long as 45 years, until an equal number of women and men are elected to the House of Commons."[24] Maillé's scenario is based on a continuous increase in the number of female MPs, but recent elections show this trend to be waning. Since 1988, progress has slowed considerably. For instance, the same number of women (62, or about 21 per cent) was elected to Parliament in the 2000 election as in 1997, and this represented only a marginal increase from the 18 per cent elected in 1993. As Figure 3.1 clearly indicates, we can no longer expect that the number of women elected to political office will continue to climb.

The overall trend of gradual increases in women's electoral representation masks both plateaus and dips. When the five most recent elections are analyzed for each jurisdiction, four patterns emerge. Each trend will be discussed in its turn.

The first trend is a steady increase in women's representation. This pattern is evident in only three places—Manitoba, Quebec, and

---

BOX 3.3: Summary of Trends Resulting in No Further Significant Advances

---

- Continued steady increase (Manitoba, Quebec, Newfoundland).
- Holding pattern (Canada, Saskatchewan, New Brunswick).
- Partial recovery (NWT, PEI, Ontario).
- Decreases (BC, Alberta, Nova Scotia, Yukon).

Newfoundland—and is shown in Figure 3.2. While these provinces have each experienced one plateau, the numbers continue to edge upwards. Electoral change in Manitoba's 1999 election, which brought an NDP government into office, increased the percentage of female legislators from 20 to 25 per cent. The number of women in the Quebec National Assembly climbed to 23 per cent in the 1998 election, which gave the PQ a third mandate. An election must be held in Quebec by 2003, and it seems reasonable to expect another increase in the number of women office-holders if the competitive parties continue to nominate women candidates in 20 to 25 per cent of the ridings. In fact, Quebec by-elections held in 2002 boosted the number of women in the National Assembly to 35, a total of 28 per cent of the seats in that province. Newfoundland has also shown strong growth since 1993, when only 6 per cent of the legislators were women. This number climbed with the election of Liberal governments to almost 15 per cent in 1996 and 17 per cent in 1999; that being said, the percentage of women in the Newfoundland Assembly remains below the 20 per cent average.

Figure 3.2: Pattern Number One: Continued Steady Increase

(Percentage of women elected in the five most recent elections in Manitoba, Quebec and Newfoundland)

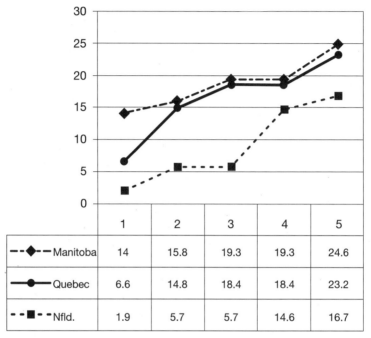

	1	2	3	4	5
— ◆ — Manitoba	14	15.8	19.3	19.3	24.6
——●—— Quebec	6.6	14.8	18.4	18.4	23.2
- - ■ - - Nfld.	1.9	5.7	5.7	14.6	16.7

Sources: Arscott and Trimble, *In the Presence of Women,* federal, provincial, and territorial websites (downloaded June and August 2002).

The second trend is the holding pattern evidenced by the federal, provincial, and territorial averages that we saw in Figure 3.1. Figure 3.3 indicates that, in three jurisdictions—Canada, Saskatchewan, and New Brunswick—electoral progress has slowed to a standstill. As mentioned above, no growth was achieved in the recent federal election, which re-elected the Chrétien Liberals. Similarly, in Saskatchewan, the re-election of the NDP, albeit to a minority government coalition with the Liberals, did not budge the percentage of female legislators from the 22 per cent achieved in 1995. And, as Figure 3.3 shows, while the number of women increased marginally in the most recent New Brunswick election, the number has hovered around 18 per cent for the last three elections despite a change in government. The Conservatives led by Bernard Lord defeated the Liberals in the 1999 provincial election without opening electoral windows of opportunity for women.

Figure 3.3: Pattern Number Two: Holding Pattern
(Percentage of Women Elected in the Five Most Recent Elections in Canada [House of Commons], Saskatchewan, and New Brunswick)

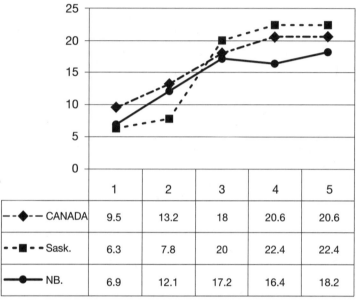

	1	2	3	4	5
— ◆ — CANADA	9.5	13.2	18	20.6	20.6
■ — Sask.	6.3	7.8	20	22.4	22.4
● NB.	6.9	12.1	17.2	16.4	18.2

Sources: Arscott and Trimble, *In the Presence of Women*, federal, provincial, and territorial websites (downloaded June and August 2002).

A third pattern warns that recent increases provide no reason for optimism as they merely represent partial recoveries from earlier drops. As Figure 3.4 illustrates, the percentage of women legislators increased in the most recent NWT, PEI, and Ontario elections. It is important to note that, with only 19 MLAs in its legislature, the election or defeat of only one woman can make a dramatic difference to the overall percentage of women representatives in the NWT. NWT elected the same number of women in 1995—two—but with the smaller number of legislators, the percentage rose accordingly. NWT elected three women (13 per cent) in

1983 and again in 1991, but has not yet reached this record again. Likewise, in PEI and Ontario, recent increases have not brought the number of women back to record levels previously achieved. Female representation in PEI went from 15 per cent in 1996 to 22 per cent in 2000, an increase of 7 per cent. However, as Figure 3.4 shows, this is down from an all-time high of 25 per cent in 1993 and only slightly better than PEI's level of 22 per cent in 1989. Similarly, Ontario has not yet climbed back to its record of 22 per cent women elected when Bob Rae's NDP won office in 1990. When the Harris Conservatives won a surprise victory in 1995, overcoming the Liberals, the percentage of female Members of the Provincial Parliament (MPP) dropped dramatically to under 15 per cent. The re-election of the Conservatives in 1999 brought a few more women into a smaller legislative assembly, but the overall percentage (18 per cent) is still below the countrywide average of 20 per cent.

Figure 3.4: Pattern Number Three: Partial Recovery

(Percentage of Women Elected in the Five Most Recent Elections in NWT, PEI, and Ontario)

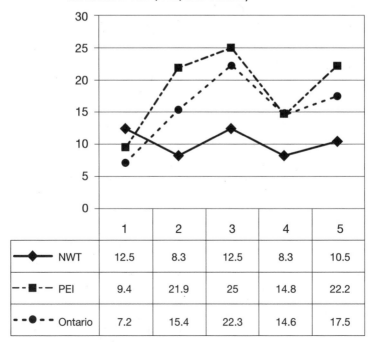

	1	2	3	4	5
NWT	12.5	8.3	12.5	8.3	10.5
PEI	9.4	21.9	25	14.8	22.2
Ontario	7.2	15.4	22.3	14.6	17.5

Sources: Arscott and Trimble, *In the Presence of Women*; federal, provincial, and territorial websites (downloaded June and August 2002).

The fourth pattern is the clearest indication that electoral progress for women is by no means certain. This trend turns downward and is shown by recent elections in BC, Alberta, Nova Scotia, and Yukon. Prior to elections held in BC and Alberta in the spring of 2001, the percentage of women legislators was above the 25 per cent level, but now they have fallen below it. The slip in BC, where the Liberal party led by Gordon Campbell swept the province, winning all but two of the province's 79 seats and defeating former NDP Premier Ujjal Dosanjh, bumped the number of women from 27 per cent down to 23 per cent. A larger drop occurred in Alberta, where Ralph Klein's Conservatives decisively won a third mandate, succeeding in all but nine of the ridings, and the percentage of women fell from 27 per cent to 21 per cent. Nova Scotia continues to struggle to elect women. Figure 3.5 indicates a subtle decrease, from 12 per cent female legislators

Figure 3.5: Pattern Number Four: Decreases

(Percentage of Women Elected in the Five Most Recent Elections in Yukon, British Columbia, Alberta, and Nova Scotia)

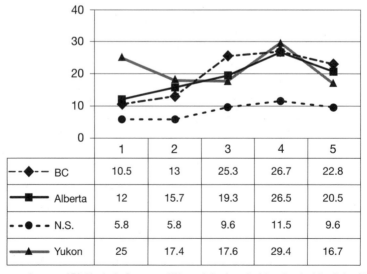

	1	2	3	4	5
– ◆ – BC	10.5	13	25.3	26.7	22.8
■ Alberta	12	15.7	19.3	26.5	20.5
– ● – N.S.	5.8	5.8	9.6	11.5	9.6
▲ Yukon	25	17.4	17.6	29.4	16.7

Sources: Arscott and Trimble, *In the Presence of Women;* federal, provincial, and territorial websites (downloaded June and August 2002, and for Yukon, November 2002).

elected in 1998 to only 10 per cent in 1999, but the picture is even bleaker since the death in 2000 of a woman legislator. A subsequent by-election was won by a male NDP candidate, and as a result only four women now serve in the Nova Scotia legislature; at 8 per cent, this is the lowest level of representation for women in all of Canada. Finally, a precipitous decline occurred in the most recent Yukon election, held November 4, 2002. While the number of women only dropped by two (from 5 to 3), given the small number of seats overall this translated into a big percentage loss. As a result the Yukon has slid from the top of the "electing women" chart to near the bottom.

What do these four trends tell us about women's efforts to occupy more electoral space? Overall, recent progress is very slight indeed. While three provinces (Manitoba, Quebec, Newfoundland) display steady growth in the number of female legislators, and three jurisdictions are in a holding pattern (Canada, Saskatchewan, New Brunswick), the rest paint a bleaker picture. Recent increases in PEI, Ontario, and the NWT followed drops, and overall women have lost ground in these jurisdictions. Alberta, BC, Nova Scotia, and Yukon also show that progress can be short-lived. Alberta and BC crossed the 25 per cent mark in the late 1990s but slipped well below it in the 2001 elections. On the whole, the pattern of the electoral glass ceiling is clear; the 25 per cent limit seems unlikely to be cracked in the near future.

The 25 Per Cent "Solution": Political Parties and the Glass Ceiling

While parties can take some of the credit for women's electoral progress overall, they also bear a large part of the responsibility for the presence and persistence of the electoral glass ceiling for women. Table 3.2 tabulates the number of women candidates chosen by competitive parties in the most recent elections, and it supports our hypothesis that the electoral glass ceiling is set at about 25 per cent of the elected representatives. With the exception of social democratic parties such as the NDP, the PQ, and BQ (Bloc Québécois), none of the parties consistently nominates women in more than one-fifth of the electoral contests.

The NDP averages 31 per cent female candidates, ranging from a high of about 50 per cent in New Brunswick and Yukon to a low of 20 per cent in Newfoundland. But declining support for the NDP, both federally and in some provinces, has acted as a brake on women's electoral progress. The party may nominate more women than its competitors, but without electoral success, NDP women will not find themselves in the legislative arena. The Liberal Party has won office at the federal level and in three provinces and territories, but with an average of 21 per cent women candidates, it reproduces the status quo without effectively challenging the glass ceiling. The Liberal party recently surpassed the 25 per cent mark in only two jurisdictions, BC and Yukon.

The Progressive Conservative party continues to lag behind its main competitors, with an average of 17 per cent women candidates. Given the fact that the Conservatives hold office in five provinces, its relatively low proportion of female candidates has played a role in stalling the electoral project. For instance, in Nova Scotia, where the Conservatives were elected in 1999, female representatives were nominated in only 14 per cent of the ridings. Following the election women comprised only 10 per cent of the governing party caucus. In the most recent elections, the Conservatives have nominated women to more than 20 per cent of the ridings in only two provinces, PEI and Alberta. Similarly, in Yukon, where a 2002 election brought the ideologically conservative Yukon Party back into office, the victor's low number of female candidates (11 per cent) played a key role in reducing the number of elected women to three, down from five in 2000.

In general, then, the political parties, each for its own reasons, have done little in recent years to increase electoral representation by women. Very simply, women cannot win office if they do not run. Candidate numbers indicate why the electoral glass ceiling remains, on average, at slightly less than half of what would be expected in a society that had no sex bias in the electoral system. For the glass ceiling to be raised, more

TABLE 3.2: Women Candidates in Most Recent Elections, by Party (December 2001)

Jurisdiction/ date of election	Political Party			
	NDP	Liberal	PC	Other
CANADA (2000)	88/298 (29.5%)	**65/301** **(21.6%)**	39/291 (13.4%)	CA 32/298 (10.7%) BQ 18/75 (24.0%)
British Columbia (2001)	19/79 (24.0%)	**20/79** **(25.3%)**	—	—
Alberta (2001)	26/82 (31.7%)	18/83 (21.7%)	**17/83** **(20.5%)**	—
Saskatchewan (1999)	**14/58** **(24.1%)**	7/58 (12.1%)	—	SP 12/58 (20.7%)
Manitoba (1999)	**17/57** **(29.8%)**	11/50 (22.0%)	15/57 (26.3%)	—
Ontario (1999)	32/103 (31.1%)	19/103 (18.4%)	**17/103** **(16.5%)**	—
Quebec (1998)	—	30/124 (24.2%)	—	PQ 31/123 **(25.2%)** AD 21/124 (16.9%)
New Brunswick (1999)	28/55 (50.9%)	8/55 (14.5%)	**10/55** **(18.2%)**	—
Nova Scotia (1999)	20/52 (38.5%)	13/52 (25.0%)	**7/52** **(13.5%)**	—
Newfoundland (1999)	7/35 (20.0%)	**9/48** **(18.8%)**	7/48 (14.6%)	—
Prince Edward Island (2000)	10/27 (37.0%)	3/27 (11.1%)	**7/27** **(25.9%)**	—
Yukon (2002)	9/18 (50%)	5/18 (27.8%)	—	**YP 2/18** **(11.1%)**
TOTALS	270/864 (31.3%)	208/998 (20.8%)	119/716 (16.6)	—

Note: bold type indicates the governing party; also, the "other" category only includes competitive parties, defined as parties that have elected at least one representative.

NDP = New Democratic Party
Liberal = Liberal Party
PC = Progressive Conservative Party
CA = Canadian Alliance [formerly Reform]
BQ = Bloc Québécois

PQ = Parti Québécois
AD = Action Démocratique du Québec
YP = Yukon Party
SP = Saskatchewan Party

women candidates need to be selected, or women candidates have to win in unprecedented proportions. Nominating more women candidates is the more certain route to increased representation for women.

The numbers suggest that political parties in general now seem to regard one in four women representatives as satisfying the goal of equality. This view was clearly articulated by the federal Liberal party in the October 1993 election, when it openly declared its goal of recruiting women to 25 per cent of the candidacies.[25] They only managed to nominate women in 22 per cent of the ridings, despite the prime minister's controversial decision to circumvent the regular nomination process by directly appointing a number of candidates, including nine women. In the run-up to the 1997 election, the party announced that the target (25 per cent women) and the method for reaching it (leader-appointed candidates) would remain the same as in 1993.[26] In fact, the 25 per cent mark was surpassed, and 28 per cent of the party's candidates were women. However, in the most recent federal election, the Liberals were silent on the issue of women's representation and fell short of the 25 per cent goal, with women representing the party in only 22 per cent of the constituencies. The Liberal party apparently did not think it necessary to continue advancing women's equality by supporting their electoral success in federal politics.

This example raises three points worth considering further. First, 25 per cent was considered "good enough" representation for women by the federal Liberal party in 1993 and 1997. Or to put it differently, the 25 per cent level "merely establishes the status quo as a benchmark."[27] Secondly, having surpassed this target in 1997, the Liberals decided to rest on their laurels in 2000, and women lost ground as a result. Fewer women were selected as candidates for the party virtually guaranteed to win a third majority, and this fact certainly played a role in the unchanged percentage of women MPs. Thirdly, rather than addressing the rather obvious problems with the nomination process, especially the exorbitantly high cost of contesting nominations in some Ontario ridings, the Liberals instead appointed women as candidates in a few cases (nine in 1993, six in 1997). Furthermore, the decision selectively to by-pass the "normal" nomination process generated a huge fuss inside and outside the party, with critics labeling the appointment of women candidates undemocratic and arbitrary.[28] Men were appointed too, but for different reasons, and with significantly less adverse publicity. The negative response to the appointment of women candidates reveals a presumption that the over-representation of men, assisted by a nomination process that favours them, is democratic and fair while any effort to increase the representation of women constitutes "special treatment."

BOX 3.4: Summary: Sources of Women's Continued Inequality in Electoral Office

- The view is that 25 per cent women legislators equals "good enough" representation for women; nothing more needs to be done to improve electoral success for women aspirants.
  Implication: No challenge to the status quo.
- There is complacency among parties that reach the 25 per cent level of female candidacies.
  Implication: Inaction makes the situation worse by producing a decline in numbers of women nominated and elected.
- Policy measures designed to improve women's representation are deemed to be undemocratic and unfair.
  Implication: Policy inaction maintains and extends women's underrepresentation in political life.

The glass ceiling is built and supported by the assumption that party measures designed to promote gender parity in candidate selection are undemocratic or otherwise unfair. According to this line of thinking, women should win nominations on the basis of "merit," an assumption that historically has favoured men. Resistance to affirmative action does not apply to all Canadian parties; social democratic parties and even parties of the centre and centre-right have expressed a desire to nominate more women.[29] But what makes the glass ceiling especially impenetrable is the practice known as **local riding association autonomy**, which simply means the right of local party riding associations to choose "their own" candidates at meetings of constituency members. This right is fiercely guarded, making it difficult for party officials to impose and then achieve targets in the proportion of females and males who stand for election to the country's legislatures. Even the federal NDP has been unsuccessful at reaching gender targets despite specific constitutional provisions allowing the federal council to intervene in the selection process and mandatory selection procedures designed to facilitate affirmative action goals.[30] Despite stating an objective of 50 per cent women candidates, the NDP only succeeded in nominating 84 women in 1993, or 39 per cent of the total. Since then the gender parity policy has proven difficult to implement, as the percentage of women candidates dropped to 36 per cent in 1997 and fell again to just under 30 per cent in 2000.

Have parties given up trying put forward larger numbers of women candidates? At the federal level it appears so. Figure 3.6 shows that only the BQ succeeded in nominating more women candidates in the 2000 federal election (24 per cent) than in 1997 (21 per cent) and 1993 (13 per cent). As detailed above, the Liberals and NDP nominated fewer women in 2000 than in 1997, failing to reach previous targets. The Conservatives have selected fewer and fewer women to run for federal office and in 2000 barely managed to offer the electorate more female candidates (13 per cent) than the Canadian Alliance (11 per cent). In particular, the emergence and recent electoral successes of first the Reform Party and now the Canadian Alliance Party have stalled the upward progress of women's representation in the House of Commons. The presence of small "c" conservative parties in the House is a contributing factor to continued underrepresentation of women, because few women have recently contested office under the Conservative, Reform, or Alliance party banner. Indeed, the Alliance rejects the notion of encouraging women candidates through formal or informal means. As a result, with women comprising just 5 per cent of the Reform Party's caucus in 1997, and 10.6 per cent of the Alliance caucus in 2000, the party "has achieved the lowest rate of representation of women of any major Canadian party at the federal level in fifteen years."[31]

Figure 3.6: Percentage of Women Candidates in Recent Federal Elections, by Party

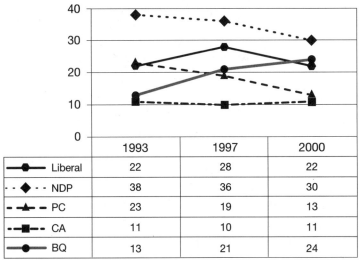

	1993	1997	2000
———♦——— Liberal	22	28	22
· · ♦ · · NDP	38	36	30
– –▲– – PC	23	19	13
·—■—·· CA	11	10	11
———●——— BQ	13	21	24

Liberal = Liberal Party of Canada
NDP = New Democratic Party of Canada
PC = Progressive Conservative Party of Canada

CA = Canadian Alliance [formerly Reform Party]
BQ = Bloc Québécois

We believe the electoral project for women has lost ground, as gains made between the 1980s and 1990s are now being eroded. Some political parties, notably the Alliance, reject out of hand the idea of recruiting women candidates and setting gender goals at election time. As well, the political parties that made efforts to boost the number of women candidates and run women in winnable ridings in the 1990s now seem to be resting on their laurels. Most Canadian political parties assume that more representation for women—up to 25 per cent of candidates and seats—is good enough. Parties that have tried to challenge this assumption, notably the federal and some provincial wings of the NDP as well as the BQ and PQ, have failed to achieve gender parity. As a result, the electoral representation for women will continue to languish at or below 25 per cent for the foreseeable future. The number of female representatives certainly cannot break the 25 per cent barrier if parties do not assist the process themselves by selecting women to run in more than one-quarter of the ridings.

Can (and Should) the Glass Ceiling be Raised?

Why should parties try to break the electoral glass ceiling? The first and most important reason is simple fairness. As Janine Brodie argues, "a fundamental premise of our democratic value system is that no one social group is or should be systematically excluded from the exercise of political power."[32] To achieve full citizenship and wield the decision-making authority that is their due, women must be elected in roughly equal numbers to men. Secondly, in our edited volume *In the Presence of Women*, we argued that representation by women (which can be done only by women) must be distinguished from representation for women (which can be undertaken by either men or women).[33] Male legislators may be able to articulate women's political perspectives and policy needs, but evidence suggests that women's diverse experiences, interests, and goals are more likely to be voiced by female representatives.[34] And, while men can represent many of women's interests, they "cannot claim power for women and they cannot hold power in women's stead."[35]

Thirdly, creating spaces for feminist voices in political parties and legislatures is essential in the wake of **neo-liberal** restructuring and **neo-conservative** discourses.[36] It is important that women's opinions be heard in the decision-making process because neo-liberal deficit-reduction efforts, cuts to programs and services, privatization, and deregulation have significant consequences for women's social status, economic independence, and political citizenship. Moreover, women should have a strong voice in cabinets and legislatures when neo-conservative policies designed to champion the traditional sexual division of labour in the family and to invoke greater state regulation of women's private lives are being discussed. If women do not hold positions of power during this era of state restructuring, "they risk being marginalized, since crucial discussions will take place and irrevocable decisions will be made without their input."[37] Arguably this has already happened. Since 1993, the Chrétien, Klein, and Harris (now Eves) governments have led the way in introducing neo-liberal values and policy changes, including dramatic de-funding of the **welfare state**. While some women support such measures, those who have been harmed by them now find themselves with fewer sites of resistance within the state.

What can be done to break the electoral glass ceiling, or at least to raise it? In its 1991 assessment of electoral democracy in Canada, the Report of the Lortie Commission (the Royal Commission on Electoral Reform and Party Financing) made several recommendations for government action at the national level. The proposed measures were also applicable to the provinces and territories. The report suggested offering parties financial incentives for nominating women, in the form of extra reimbursement of election expenses for registered parties that succeed in electing women to 20 per cent of the seats held by the party. It also recommended that Elections Canada regulate the nomination process by imposing spending limits on nomination campaigns and extending tax credits to contributions to support prospective candidates seeking nomination. Since the nomination process can be very expensive, especially in competitive ridings, the financial burden of winning the nomination can be a formidable barrier for women candidates.[38]

Political parties have strongly and repeatedly resisted any attempt by government to regulate their internal procedures, including candidate nomination processes. They appear unlikely to change their attitudes, not least of all because no immediate electoral benefit appears to accompany such a change. In any case, Canadian governments seem quite comfortable with the underrepresentation of women, having neither implemented the Lortie Commission's suggestions nor any other significant measure designed to encourage women candidates. In federal elections, child care costs are now recognized as legitimate campaign expenses, a positive step according to Manon Tremblay, but "plainly insufficient to increase the number of female MPs in the Commons."[39] Perhaps federal, provincial, and territorial governments remain unwilling to legislate gender equity in representation because of the public's intensely negative reaction to proposals for gender parity in the Senate, proposals that were discussed along with a variety of constitutional changes in the Charlottetown Accord. At that time, the premiers of three provinces agreed to equal representation of women in a reformed Senate. However, many politicians, media commentators, and members of the general public labeled this proposal "unfair, insulting, undemocratic, repugnant and absurd."[40]

Arguably the electoral glass ceiling can best be addressed by internal party efforts, whether constitutional (candidate selection processes designed to increase numbers of women and other underrepresented groups) or informal (leader and/or women's commission efforts to recruit women candidates to winnable ridings). But, as we have shown, even parties that enthusiastically support such measures have not succeeded in achieving gender parity in nominations. This failure has been due in large part to local party control over candidate selection. For this reason, some observers argue that nominating women to half of the constituencies remains unlikely and is perhaps even impossible, unless the electoral system is changed. Local riding association autonomy is difficult to challenge in **single-member plurality systems (SMP)** like Canada's. In contrast, **proportional representation (PR)** or **mixed-member plurality (MMP) electoral systems** could give more control over candidacy to the central party hierarchy.[41] However, changing the electoral system may or may not increase women's representation; its success would depend heavily on the will of political parties to ensure that women's names appear on the nomination lists. Countries with PR systems that have successfully elected women in 30 to 45 per cent of the seats in national parliaments have the advantage of a proportional electoral system coupled with political parties willing to guarantee women a large number of the places on the candidate list. Given current evidence of their lack of political will, Canadian political parties have no reason to do what they have not done for the last ten years when there was considerable pressure—within parties and from the feminist movement—to change. Now, any change for the better in women's representation seems unlikely.

Also, while there is increased interest in PR in Canada among the general public and some activists,[42] there is little incentive for governing parties, which benefit from the "winner take all" effects of our single-member plurality system, to advocate a switch to proportional representation or a mixed system. In the absence of changes to the electoral system in its entirety, the political will of the parties (or their lack of it) remains a crucial factor in the electoral underrepresentation of women.

Another option, one that would require less drastic change to the present electoral system, is the dual-member constituency idea proposed for the new territory of Nunavut and subsequently defeated in a referendum.[43] This electoral system would have ensured gender parity by electing one man and one woman in each constituency. However, it is likely that if such a proposal were suggested now for the Canadian electoral system, it would be resisted across the country as it was in Nunavut and for the same reasons. The idea of quotas or guaranteed seats for women is very controversial, even among women themselves. Many women and men argue that women must "make it" according to the time-honoured rules of the game because this test alone determines genuine merit. During the Nunavut referendum, opponents of dual member constituencies said implementing "special measures" for women imply that women fail to compete effectively. Critics of the proposal also argued that women elected under such a system would not be taken as seriously as their male counterparts. The Nunavut debate also revealed that a dual-member constituency system has practical implications, requiring either fewer constituencies or much larger (and more expensive) legislative assemblies. Finally, the form of the dual-member representation proposal made it appear as if gender is the only representational issue that needs to be addressed by electoral reform. Aboriginal Canadians, persons with disabilities, ethnic minorities, and gay, lesbian, bisexual, and transgendered Canadians remain profoundly underrepresented in our legislatures. There is no guarantee that a dual-member constituency system will fully diversify electoral representation.

Conclusion

At present in the political environment, the electoral glass ceiling is not considered an important matter. Deficit reduction, bureaucratic downsizing, and cuts to programs and services dominate the policy agendas of Canadian governments, and women's concerns are considered peripheral, even hostile, to the neo-liberal consensus. Voices on the left, including the NDP, have been weakened, leaving few champions for gender equality in sites of formal political power. In this context, and in the absence of substantial gender gaps in party support, political parties remain unconvinced that there is any electoral payoff in nominating women candidates or supporting policy initiatives designed to raise the status of women. Moreover, the mass media now rarely address the issue of women's representation in political life. Tallies of women candidates and office-holders were regularly offered by newspapers and news programs in the late 1980s and 1990s as women's electoral representation grew, but are now rarely seen. An elite consensus—that 20 to 25 per cent representation for women is "good enough"—provides the solid underpinnings of the electoral glass ceiling for women. Sustaining the existing electoral space for women will be difficult given the predominance of masculinist assumptions about power and leadership, assumptions which seem immune to demands by women and other marginalized groups for equal representation.

CHAPTER 4

It's a Drag:
Where Have All the Women Leaders Gone?

Introduction

When Toronto transvestite Enza "Supermodel" Anderson announced her bid for the leadership of the Canadian Alliance in December 2001, she said Stockwell Day's short-lived and troubled experience in the post suggested the job is "a real drag." As a self-declared "drag queen-super-model extraordinaire," Enza concluded she was perfect for the post.[1] The experience of female party leaders in Canada certainly supports Anderson's contention that the job is not easy. Women are typically pulled into the role to prop up ailing parties, often in the (vain) hope that they can miraculously resurrect political organizations destined for electoral destruction. They face infighting, backstabbing, and challenges from those backroom boys who cannot accept a woman as party leader. They endure media treatment which, if not overtly sexist, is certainly shaped by gender-based assumptions and value judgements. Indeed, women party leaders are so far off the media map that Pat Duncan, who led her Liberal party to a surprise win in Yukon on April 17, 2000, was bemused by news reports of "*Mr.* Duncan's" victory.[2] Leadership is still assumed to be masculine territory. When women leaders are successful at rebuilding moribund parties through sheer determination, often following years of hard work, they are likely to be patted on the head and sent on their way so the party can then restore its essentially masculine identity as personified by male leadership.

In all of Canada's history only 20 women have headed mainstream Canadian parties—that is, parties that have succeeded in electing representatives to the legislature either before or during the woman leader's term as party leader. One woman, Alexa McDonough, led two parties, the Nova Scotia and federal wings of the NDP. The first woman party chief certainly had little hope of gaining power or even winning a provincial seat. Suffragist, peace activist, and human rights proponent, Thérèse Casgrain, was selected leader of the Quebec wing of the CCF in 1951 and led the party until 1957. The CCF never established a strong electoral presence in Quebec, and Casgrain failed to win a seat in the National Assembly, though she persisted in trying.[3] However, her prominence within Quebec society and her various forms of political involvement made her a key figure in her day. The first woman head of a competitive party was Yukon Conservative Hilda Watson, who held the post for a few short months in fall 1978, but resigned after her defeat in the territorial election that November.[4]

Most female leaders ascended to the top party job in the late 1980s and early 1990s, with 1993 as the high-water mark for women party leaders. In that year, ten women led mainstream political parties at the federal and provincial level. Now, with Alexa McDonough's resignation from the leadership of the federal NDP, there are only three women leaders across the country: Elizabeth Weir (New Brunswick NDP), Joy MacPhail (BC NDP), and Pat Duncan (Yukon Liberals). Duncan alone among them briefly held power, as Yukon premier from April 2000 to

November 2002, and the other two have little hope of bringing their parties into office.

This chapter addresses the transitory and troubled nature of women's party leadership, answering a question posed by an *Ottawa Citizen* headline: "Why Don't Female Leaders Last in Canadian Politics?"[5] Our answer is that the revolving door for female leaders reflects a societal sexual division of labour and reinforces the patriarchal assumption that wielding political power is a male prerogative. Despite Enza "Supermodel" Anderson's quip that the Alliance can be refashioned by a leader with flawless makeup and great outfits,[6] female leaders find that what they wear provides no great advantage to them or their parties. Their gender, not their fashion sense, acts as a drag on their leadership aspirations.

The Revolving Door: Women's Party Leadership in Canada

With few exceptions, leadership for women has been transitory. For many the post is best characterized as a **revolving door**. Women who have ascended to party leadership positions tend to get spun about and then expelled in short order, sometimes in less than a year, and almost none give the door a second try. The NDP has chosen female leaders who have served the longest. The record holder is Alexa McDonough, who led the NDP in Nova Scotia from 1980 to 1994 and served as leader of the federal NDP from 1995 to 2002, thus holding a leader's post for more than 21 years. In addition she is the only woman to have led both a provincial and a federal party. Elizabeth Weir is in second place, having headed the New Brunswick NDP for 14 years, beginning in 1988. None of the other women leaders comes close to these veterans. Manitoba Liberal Sharon Carstairs led her party for over ten years, and Lynda Haverstock (Saskatchewan Liberals) and Audrey McLaughlin (federal NDP) are tied at six years apiece. Their longevity of service is all the more remarkable because three-quarters of the women leaders served less than five years, or an average of two years each. Of the five leaders who held the leader's post for more than five years, their average term as leader is just over 11 years. These statistics indicate that women's leadership of political parties is typically precarious and short-lived. Rising female stars like Kim Campbell fall to earth only to be buried six feet under, politically speaking. These experiences do not mirror the meteoric rise of Pierre Trudeau, Jean Chrétien's ability to outlast all competitors, the phoenix-like return of Joe Clark, or the ease with which Jean Charest was able to jump ship, from the federal Conservatives to the Quebec Liberal party. Women politicians lead much less charmed careers.

TABLE 4.1: Women Party Leaders[1] in Canada, Most to Least Recently Elected

Leader (in alphabetical order)	Jurisdiction	Party	Elected Representative While Leader?	Dates Served as Party Leader	Years/ Months Served as Leader[2]
MacPhail, Joy	**BC**	**NDP**	**yes**	**06/01–present**	**1 year, 6 months**
MacDonald, Helen	NS	NDP	no[3]	07/00–04/01	10 months
Duncan, Pat	**Yukon**	**Liberal**	**yes**	**02/98–present[4]**	**4 years, 11 months**
MacBeth, Nancy	Alberta	Liberal	yes	05/98–03/01	2 years, 10 months
Barrett, Pam	Alberta	NDP	yes	09/96—02/00	3 years, 6 months
Hasselfield, Ginny	Manitoba	Liberal	no	10/96–12/97	1 year, 2 months
Verge, Lynn	Nfld.	PC	yes	04/95–03/96	10 months
McDonough, Alexa	Canada	NDP	yes	10/95–01/03	7 years, 3 months
Callbeck, Catherine	PEI	Liberal	yes[5]	01/93–08/96	3 years, 5 months
Campbell, Kim	Canada	PC	yes	06/93–12/93	6 months
McCarthy, Grace	BC	Social Credit	no[6]	11/93–05/94	6 months

Note: Women presently in leadership positions are in bold type.

TABLE 4.1: *continued*

Leader (in alphabetical order)	Jurisdiction	Party	Elected Representative While Leader?	Dates Served as Party Leader	Years/ Months Served as Leader[2]
McLeod, Lyn	Ontario	Liberal	yes	02/92–11/96	4 years, 9 months
Johnston, Rita	BC	Social Credit	yes	07/91–01/92	6 months
Mella, Pat	PEI	PC	yes	11/90–05/96[7]	5 years, 6 months
Haverstock, Lynda	Sask.	Liberal	yes	04/89–11/95	6 years, 6 months
Baird-Filliter, Barbara	NB	PC	no	11/89–04/91	1 year, 6 months
McLaughlin, Audrey	Canada	NDP	yes	12/89–10/95	4 years, 10 months
Weir, Elizabeth	**NB**	**NDP**	**yes**	**06/88–present**	**14 years, 6 months**
Carstairs, Sharon	Manitoba	Liberal	yes	03/84–06/93	10 years, 3 months
McDonough, Alexa	NS	NDP	yes	11/80–11/94	14 years
Watson, Hilda	Yukon	PC	yes	09/78–11/78	2 months

[1] This table includes leaders of competitive parties only, that is, parties with elected representatives in the legislature during the woman's term as leader. Thus Thérèse Casgrain is not listed here (though she is discussed in this chapter). Also, we have not included women who have served as interim party leader, heading parties in between leadership contests. For instance, Shirley Dysart, Liberal MLA from New Brunswick, served briefly as interim leader in the 1980s, as did Bettie Hewes (Liberal, Alberta, 1993).

[2] For contemporary women leaders, we counted time served until the end of December 2002.

[3] Helen MacDonald was elected to the NS legislature in a by-election in November 1997 and was re-elected in the 1998 general election. However, she was defeated by a narrow margin in 1999, thus was not an elected MLA when she won the leadership of the party.

[4] Duncan was unofficially acclaimed leader of the Yukon Liberals in February 1997, and officially elected to the post 7 February 1998.

[5] Callbeck was an MLA in PEI from 1974 to 1978. She then served as an MP in Ottawa from 1988–93, a position she resigned to become leader of the Liberal Party and premier of PEI in 1993.

[6] McCarthy had been a member of several Social Credit governments as an MLA from 1966 to 1991 and served as a cabinet minister in the Bennett and Vander Zalm governments. She resigned in 1991; thus, when she won the leadership of the Social Credit Party in 1993, she did not have a seat in the legislature.

[7] Mrs. Mella announced she was stepping down as leader in December 1995, but stayed in the post until the new leader was selected, May 1996.

TABLE 4.2: Women First Ministers, 1867–2001

(in order of election, least to most recent)

Name, Jurisdiction and Party	Dates Served* (yy-mm-dd)	Length of Tenure	Notes
Johnston, Rita BC, Social Credit	02/04/91 to 17/10/91	6 months	Johnston was named deputy premier on 9 August 1990, amid speculation that a general election would soon be called. Following a criminal charge that stemmed from conflict of interest in his personal business, Premier Vander Zalm resigned effective 2 April 1991, making the deputy premier the interim leader and acting premier. Johnston's leadership was then confirmed at a party convention in July.
Cournoyea, Nellie NWT, none	12/11/91 to 16/10/95	3 years, 11 months	NWT features a no-party system, with MLAs elected as independents. Fellow legislators elect the premier and cabinet. Cournoyea was elected by MLAs to lead the government; thus, properly speaking, she is the first woman elected to lead a sub-national government in Canada. As well, Cournoyea is the first Aboriginal government leader in Canada.
Callbeck, Catherine PEI, Liberal	25/01/93 to 10/10/96	3 years, 9 months	The first woman elected to lead a government via general election, Callbeck was selected party leader, then led her party to victory in the subsequent election. She replaced popular Premier Joe Ghiz as party leader.
Campbell, Kim Canada, Progressive Conservative	25/06/93 to 25/10/93	4 months	Campbell served briefly as prime minister, having won the leadership of a governing party (the Mulroney Conservatives). The Conservative government was soundly defeated on 25 October 1993. All but two PC candidates, Campbell among them, lost their seats. She was replaced as leader by Jean Charest on 14 December 1993.

TABLE 4.2: continued

Name, Jurisdiction and Party	Dates Served* (yy-mm-dd)	Length of Tenure	Notes
Duncan, Pat Yukon, Liberal	17/04/00 to 04/11/02	2 years, 5 months	Duncan was acclaimed as leader of the Yukon Liberals, a party that held 3 of 17 seats in the legislature, in February 1997, and was elected leader a year later, in February 1998. With the Liberal victory in April 2000, Duncan became the second woman to bring her party to office in a general election. However, her government was defeated by the Yukon Party in the November 2002 election, just 2 and a half years into its first term.

* Dates served as first minister.

For one thing, women party leaders are not very successful at leading their parties to victory in general elections. As Table 4.2 indicates, we can still count the number of women first ministers on one hand. Two of them, Kim Campbell and Rita Johnston, became heads of government by assuming the leadership of governing parties. In both cases their tenure as first minister was remarkably brief, because their unpopular parties lost power in general elections. Only in two cases have women led their political parties to victory. PEI Liberal leader Catherine Callbeck has the distinction of being the first woman leader elected to lead a government in a general election, achieving this victory in 1993. Pat Duncan is notable for bringing the Yukon Liberals to office for the first time in 2000 and also for being the first woman to win an election in which competing parties were led by men. Not all leaders have had to win the approval of political parties. In 1991, Nellie Cournoyea was elected Territorial Leader by her peers in the NWT legislature, where all members are independents and MLAs vote to elect the political executive. Cournoyea is, therefore, the first woman elected (albeit by MLAs, not voters) to lead a sub-national government in Canada. She also has the distinction of being the first Aboriginal first minister in Canada. Of the three contemporary women party leaders, Duncan was the only head of government, and her hold on power was short-lived. As Table 4.1 shows, the other women currently at the helm of Canadian parties are Joy MacPhail, who assumed leadership of the BC NDP after it was unceremoniously removed from office and reduced to two seats in the 79-member legislature in the 2001 election, and perennial New Brunswick NDP leader Elizabeth Weir, who holds the sole NDP seat in that province's legislature.

In an op-ed piece written for the *National Post*, Tom Flanagan noted that women party leaders are significantly less successful than their male counterparts, as they fail to win office and typically see their party's fortunes flag under their watch.[7] Flanagan explains this outcome by suggesting that men are genetically programmed to be more competitive and power-seeking than are women. This "biology is destiny" account falls flat, not least because there is a much more obvious explanation. One simply needs to look at the political fortunes of the parties women are elected to lead. Typically, women take over parties that potential male aspirants regard as being too uncompetitive to be worthy of their political ambition. Once selected, the women are expected to assume the role of healer or caretaker.

The female leadership model then typically follows one of three trajectories. In the first case, women are expected to nurture electorally decimated and demoralized parties until they have been revitalized and once again appear to be viable, at which point they are often unceremoniously dethroned, and then replaced, by men. Secondly, governing parties whose popularity is plummeting sometimes see a woman leader as their last hope. But when the unfortunate female party chief fails to stage a miraculous electoral recovery, her leadership is scuttled. In the third trajectory, women win the leadership of competitive parties, parties with at least a reasonable chance of winning, or retaining, office; however, if they do not manage to stage an electoral victory, these women quickly fall from grace. And, as we shall see, even winning a general election is no guarantee of security in the leader's post. In short, Canadian political parties have briefly turned to women leaders for their novelty value, but their inability to parlay the much overplayed "gender factor" into electoral miracles has led the media and party strategists to conclude, as an Alberta news magazine editor put it, "we don't do really well with lady political leaders."[8]

BOX 4.1: Three Paths for Women Party Leaders[9]

- Women take over electorally decimated and moribund parties (the most common trajectory).
- Women assume the leadership of governing parties careening toward defeat.
- Women win leadership of competitive parties (parties recognized as having a chance of winning or keeping office).

When No One Else Wants the Job

BOX 4.2 Women Leaders of Moribund or Electorally Decimated Parties

- Pam Barrett, Alberta NDP, 1996–2000
- Barbara Baird-Filliter, NB PC, 1989–91
- Sharon Carstairs, Manitoba Liberals, 1984–93
- Ginny Hasselfield, Manitoba Liberals, 1996–97
- Lynda Haverstock, Sask. Liberals, 1989–95
- Joy MacPhail, BC NDP, 2001–present
- Grace McCarthy, BC Social Credit, 1993–94
- Alexa McDonough, Nova Scotia NDP, 1980–94
- Pat Mella, PEI PC, 1990–96
- Elizabeth Weir, NB NDP, 1988–present

There are numerous examples of women assuming the leadership of defunct, electorally decimated, or **uncompetitive political parties**. Most of the pioneer female party leaders, those elected to head parties in the 1980s and early 1990s, including Lynda Haverstock, Sharon Carstairs, Pat Mella, Elizabeth Weir, and Barbara Baird-Filliter, took over party organizations that had fallen gradually into a moribund state or that had suffered massive electoral defeats. The experience of Lynda Haverstock fits into the first category and reveals much about the gendered nature of the leadership game. Haverstock became leader of the Saskatchewan Liberal party in 1989, when the organization had no elected representatives, and secured a formal role for the party in the legislature when she won her own seat in 1991. She then orchestrated a couple of by-election wins, increased the party's percentage of the popular vote by 10 per cent, and succeeded in having the party promoted to the status of official opposition in 1995, after it won 11 seats in the 58-member legislature. However, this recovery was not sufficient for some party members, as party in-fighting led to a caucus revolt and a nasty post-election leadership review, which prompted Haverstock to resign. A year later she was replaced by Jim Melenchuk. She publicly expressed frustration and dissatisfaction concerning the lack of support she received from the party establishment, decrying the sexism underlying leader evaluations: "When women are called strident, men are called tough. When women are called abrasive, men are called straight talkers." Gender-differentiated expectations for politicians, she implied, had a good deal to do with her decision to resign. Haverstock refused to lead a party that pursued "back-room, patronage-driven, elitist regimes" like those she associated with her political opponents.[10] The party subsequently imploded, with three members transferring their allegiance to the fledgling Saskatchewan Party, and Haverstock and another woman MLA leaving the party to sit as independents. However, in 2000, Haverstock was rewarded for her years in the political trenches when she was appointed lieutenant-governor of Saskatchewan.

Another case of a woman chosen to rebuild a party is that of Sharon Carstairs, who was elected leader of the nearly defunct Manitoba Liberal party in 1984. When she took over as party leader, says Carstairs, Manitoba Liberals were an endangered species.[11] There were no Liberals elected in the provincial election of 1981, and the party was leaderless in 1982 and 1983. Carstairs rebuilt the party, bringing Liberals back into the legislature by winning her own riding in 1986, and establishing the party as the official opposition with 20 seats won in 1988. As the second largest party in a minority government, Carstairs's Liberals played a significant role in Manitoba's handling of the controversial Meech Lake Accord.[12] But the proposed constitutional amendments, as well as her stance on the Accord, proved divisive within her caucus, and an exhausted and disillusioned Carstairs resigned the leadership after the Liberals lost 13 seats in the 1990 Manitoba election, held a few short months after the Meech Lake Accord was defeated. Even now Carstairs's haircuts and the timbre of her voice are more likely to be remembered than the seedbed of new MLAs she nurtured, her prominent role in Manitoba politics, and her current position as government leader in the Senate.

Pat Mella of PEI won the leadership of the Conservatives in 1990, at a time when the party seemed perpetually destined for the opposition ranks thanks to the popularity of the Liberals and their leader, energetic Premier Joe Ghiz. The Ghiz-led Liberals won 30 out of 32 seats in the 1989 election, and the party cruised to victory once again in 1993, with Catherine Callbeck at the helm, obliterating all but one Conservative representative from the legislature. But when Liberal fortunes began to flag in 1995, and the Conservatives looked electorally viable, the local press reported rumours of a move to replace Mella. This backroom backstabbing suggested that "the powerful men within the party had supported Ms. Mella only while there was little chance that the party would form the government."[13] Haverstock's experience was repeated. Mella stepped down from the leader's post shortly thereafter, and the Conservatives went on to win office in 1996, with a male leader, Pat Binns, at the helm. Mella now serves as treasurer in the Binns administration.

Haverstock, Carstairs, and Mella led their parties for significant periods of time, rebuilding party fortunes over more than five years. Other female leaders have been ushered out of the revolving door much more quickly, especially those who failed to revive party fortunes after sizeable electoral defeats. Since Sharon Carstairs's departure, the Manitoba Liberal party has been marked by declining electoral support and a succession of leaders, including Ginny Hasselfield, who won the post in 1996 but failed to survive a leadership review just over a year later. A newspaper article described Hasselfield's reign as "tumultuous," noting that in October 1997 "she threatened to sue a former colleague for defamation after he publicly questioned her leadership abilities."[14]

In New Brunswick, Barbara Baird-Filliter bravely assumed the leadership of the "demoralized and decimated" Progressive Conservative Party in 1989, two years after Richard Hatfield's ignominious defeat to the Liberal party led by Frank McKenna.[15] The party had no seats in the legislature, and Baird-Filliter was condemned for refusing an invitation extended to opposition leaders by the Liberal government to participate in question period. After enduring two years of often-unjustified criticism and unsubstantiated innuendos, Baird-Filliter resigned unexpectedly during a television interview.

Yet another woman to take over the difficult task of rebuilding a party nearly wiped out in the polls is BC NDP leader Joy MacPhail. MacPhail was a cabinet minister in the NDP government that lost power, and all but two of its seats, in 2001. Leader Ujjal Dosanjh failed to regain his seat, leaving MacPhail and relative newcomer Jenny Kwan as the lone NDP members. MacPhail was appointed party leader shortly after the election. The two-member NDP caucus has been denied the title and trappings of official opposition status, despite being the only opposition party in the legislature.[16] MacPhail has her work cut out for her if she wishes to rebuild the party.

Grace McCarthy's story certainly follows the "woman nurturer of ailing party" narrative so common to women's leadership experiences. McCarthy was elected as a Social Credit MLA in BC in 1966 and steadily climbed the ranks within the Bennett and Vander Zalm regimes, serving variously as minister of the departments of Economic Development, Human Resources, and BC Transit, as well as being deputy premier in the 1970s and 1980s. After a lengthy and distinguished political career, she left political life in 1991, having lost the Social Credit party leadership race to Rita Johnston. The Socreds were beaten badly by the NDP in the 1991 election, and Johnston stepped down as leader. The party seemed headed for political extinction when a new leadership contest was called in 1993. Party members pleaded with McCarthy to enter the race and save the ailing party. Indeed, a *Vancouver Province* cartoonist depicted her as a ballerina falling into the arms of the dead Social Credit party, and a *Victoria Times-Colonist* editorial, written after her May victory, described her as a "faith healer for still-sick Socreds."[17] With the leadership in hand, McCarthy sought a legislative seat in a February 1994 by-election, enduring threats of defections from Social Credit MLAs if she failed to win. Lose she did to a Liberal candidate. The Vancouver *Sun* then pronounced, "The Song's Over for Socreds."[18] A few weeks later, three of the Social Credit caucus members defected to the fledgling BC Reform party. In April, an all-out leadership rebellion was staged, with **party elites** telling the press they were "tired" of McCarthy. Two party directors publicly urged her to resign,[19] which she did on May 4, 1994, just six months after winning the post.

Albertan Pam Barrett's experience with party leadership is a bit of an anomaly within this trajectory. Although she took over a party that had been virtually erased from the electoral map, the end to Barrett's leadership came at a time of her own choosing. Like Alexa McDonough who elected to exit the position of leader of the Nova Scotia NDP to contest the leadership of the federal party, Barrett chose to leave rather than being made to leave by disgruntled party insiders. She had served as a vocal and popular NDP MLA from 1986 to 1993 and was touted in 1989 as a woman with leadership prospects. However, she left political life before the 1993 election, which re-elected the Conservatives under the leadership of Ralph Klein and left the NDP with no seats in the legislature. Barrett was lured back into the fray in 1996. Her "mighty mouse" persona and high public profile helped the party win a legislative toehold of two seats in 1997, when she reclaimed her old riding of Edmonton Highlands. The media favoured her because she was colourful and outspoken. Barrett even had the approval of the government because she drew attention away from the official opposition, the Liberals. So she secured plenty of headlines, many news-bites, and a reputation as a zany, slightly off-base, but dedicated leader. Barrett's leadership faltered in January 1999, when she asked the party for a six-week leave of absence to deal with "stress and problems in her personal life."[20] Just over a year later, she resigned and declared her intention to leave politics for good, following what she described as a "near death experience" in the dentist's chair and a subsequent spiritual awakening.[21] Critics of the Klein government's Bill 11, which allows private medical facilities to set up shop and perform surgical procedures requiring overnight stays, were dismayed. They had been counting on Barrett to help rally forces against the legislation.

None of the women party leaders who inherited unpopular parties were able to achieve an electoral miracle, though during their watch, Haverstock and Carstairs rebuilt their parties to the status of official opposition, and Barrett reclaimed a few seats for her party. Most women leaders have tried without much more success than their male counterparts to revive parties beset by **opposition party syndrome**—the nagging doubts about electoral prospects, back-room squabbles, and perpetual infighting that characterize party organizations with slim electoral prospects. But, as Sharon Carstairs observed about women leaders, "once we fall from grace, we do it with a thud that the male candidates don't seem to do. There seems to be very little tolerance for women's failure."[22]

Partisan CPR: Women Leaders as the Party's Last Gasp

BOX 4.3   Women Leaders of Governing Parties Headed for Defeat

---

- Kim Campbell, Federal Progressive Conservatives, 1993
- Rita Johnston, BC Social Credit, 1991–92

A variant of the "woman as the last hope of parties in decline" trend is that of women who win the position while their party is in office but is headed for certain defeat. We call this **partisan CPR** because the women are expected to resuscitate the party's electoral prospects after the last breath has gone from a once vital partisan body. This has occurred twice, and the best-known example is the political career of Kim Campbell. She took the helm of the federal Conservatives from Brian Mulroney at a time when the party's popularity was barely in double digits. Campbell herself recognized that the party was "looking for a miracle worker to stop the Tories' slide into oblivion."[23] The party's standing in the polls in late 1992 reflected a mere 18 per cent approval rating, and the prime minister's popularity was at 13 per cent. The other traditional parties were far ahead of the Conservatives, with the Liberal party boasting the support of 44 per cent of decided voters and Liberal leader Jean Chrétien at 28 per cent.[24]

As is typical for a new party leader, Campbell enjoyed a honeymoon at the polls during the summer after her victory. However, voters were inclined to punish the government that had introduced the unpopular Goods and Services Tax (GST) and presided over a painful recession. The criticism soon began. Most commentators agree that Campbell made significant mistakes in 1993, and that the Conservatives ran a poor campaign. Some, but not many, analysts refused to blame her for the party's near-obliteration. No one envied her for having "to drag the corpse of Brian Mulroney around with her," as one party activist put it. Moreover, the media and the Conservative Party alike exhibited blatant sexism in their treatment of Canada's first woman prime minister, by focusing on her looks, her clothing, her marital status, and her sexuality. A mere six weeks after the election Campbell was, to use journalist Sydney Sharpe's words, "brutally terminated" by the party she had led for less than seven months.[25]

The second case of a woman heading a government only to be unceremoniously dumped after an election defeat is that of Rita Johnston, who became Social Credit (Socred) leader and, briefly, premier in British Columbia. Like Campbell, Johnston inherited a scandal-ridden and extremely unpopular governing party, and, like Campbell, her term as party leader lasted less than seven months, from April to October 1991. Johnston was named deputy premier on August 9, 1990, amid speculation that a general election would soon be called. Following a criminal charge that stemmed from conflict of interest in his personal business, Premier Vander Zalm resigned on April 2, 1991, making Johnston the interim leader and acting premier. Her leadership was then confirmed at a party convention in July. However, the Socreds lost badly to the NDP in a general election held a few months later. Retaining only seven seats, the Socreds were bested as official opposition by the revitalized BC Liberal party. Defeat at the polls is the proverbial kiss of death for the female leader who acquires a government without winning a general election, especially one who loses her own seat. Johnston resigned the post in January 1992. As mentioned above, her opponent in the 1991 leadership race, Grace McCarthy, was next in line for the job, but her tenure was short-lived, and the party has since disappeared into the political ether, having failed to elect an MLA in subsequent elections.

But Can She Win? Women Leaders of Electorally Viable Parties

BOX 4.4: Women Leaders of Electorally Viable Parties

A) Parties with reduced numbers, but not out of the running
- Nancy MacBeth, Alberta Liberals, 1998–2001
- Helen MacDonald, NS NDP, 2000–01
- Audrey McLaughlin, Federal NDP, 1989–91
- Alexa McDonough, Federal NDP, 1995–2003

B) Parties with hopes of forming government
- Lyn McLeod, Ontario Liberals, 1992–96
- Lynn Verge, Nfld. PC, 1995–96
- Pat Duncan, Yukon Liberals, 1998–present

C) Popular governing parties
- Catherine Callbeck, PEI Liberals, 1993–96

A few female leaders have won the top job in parties with at least modest electoral prospects. This category includes political parties in decline but not yet out of the running, parties on the upswing, and governing parties. Four women have won the leadership of parties that had lost support at the polls yet were expected to rebound (or at least not lose any more ground). Nancy MacBeth was elected to head a party that had suffered surmountable losses, and she was initially considered capable of rebuilding the party. After a close loss to Ralph Klein's Conservatives in 1993, the Alberta Liberal party, led by Grant Mitchell, lost seats in the March 1997 election, declining from 32 MLAs to 18. Mitchell resigned soon thereafter, and a competitive four-way leadership race ensued. Three members of the Liberal caucus threw their hats into the ring, along with Nancy MacBeth. MacBeth had been a cabinet minister in the Conservative government of Don Getty (1985–92) and had sought the leadership of that party when he resigned. In that contest she lost to Ralph Klein. Although she handily won the May 1998 Liberal leadership race, as well as a summer by-election to gain a seat in the legislature, MacBeth's leadership of the official opposition mostly went unnoticed, though the defection of one MLA to the Conservatives received considerable press coverage.[26] In the lead-up to the 2001 election, some commentators argued that a MacBeth-led Liberal party would attract disaffected Tories. Others maintained that Klein's popularity was unassailable.[27] An intensive and costly TV advertising campaign did not improve the party's fortunes, and the Liberals lost badly in the March 2001 electoral contest, retaining only seven seats. MacBeth, who lost in her own riding, resigned at a snap news conference four days after the election.[28]

Nova Scotia NDP leader Helen MacDonald experienced an even briefer tenure as head of her party, which saw its fortunes quickly rise and fall in the late 1990s. In March 1998 the NDP, led by Robert Chisholm, elected 18 members and formed the official opposition with the largest NDP caucus in the province's history. MacDonald, who had entered the legislature in a 1997 by-election, was returned to office in

1998. But the minority Liberal government quickly fell, and Nova Scotians went back to the polls in 1999. The NDP, considered by some commentators to be "on the brink of power," actually lost seven seats, including MacDonald's. Robert Chisholm resigned, and, in July 2000, a four-way race for the NDP leadership, featuring three members of the NDP caucus, resulted in MacDonald's victory on the third ballot.[29] She then led a party with sizeable, albeit declining, legislative presence (11 members). But without a seat in the legislature herself, MacDonald had to direct the party from the outside. A poor showing in a March 2001 by-election—MacDonald placed third in a race on her home turf, a riding where she had taught school for 30 years—led caucus members to plot a leadership coup.[30] Warned of the plan, MacDonald resigned immediately, having held the leader's post for less than a year.

The federal NDP has the distinction of being the first national party to choose a female leader, Audrey McLaughlin, and is notable for electing another woman, Alexa McDonough, to replace her. No other party has elected two women leaders in a row. Both women leaders have played a significant role in breaking a path for other female leadership aspirants, McLaughlin because she defied criticism that she was elected leader because of her sex. She then went on to champion a non-traditional leadership style. McDonough is remarkable because of her ability to beat the odds and hang on to the leader's job despite losses at the polls in the 2000 election, heavy criticism, and rumours of her imminent defeat.

The federal NDP's best showing was in the 1988 election, when, led by Ed Broadbent, the party won 43 seats. When Broadbent retired, the leader's post was hotly contested, and the 1989 contest featured seven contenders, including high-profile former BC premier Dave Barrett. As a Yukon MP and relative newcomer to federal politics, Audrey McLaughlin's leadership aspirations were initially not taken seriously by pundits. McLaughlin wrote in her autobiography that the press persisted in evaluating her as a "lightweight." Her speeches, they said, lacked "substance."[31] Despite a highly organized campaign boasting considerable support from caucus members, labour leaders, and party insiders,

McLaughlin was accused of winning the leadership merely because of the novelty value of her sex. As she recalled: "I knew that many in the media and in the party were saying that I had won the leadership primarily because I was a woman, that I was an 'interim' leader, a caretaker who would see the party through the next election before handing things over to another, better leader, presumably a man."[32] McLaughlin's statement illustrates that, in matters of political leadership, male gender continues to be presumed to be preferable, even required. It is not that the electorate will not vote for women; they will, but the leadership of political parties remains—as it has always been—almost exclusively a male prerogative.

Audrey McLaughlin was determined to be true to her convictions and model a new, consensus-based, non-hierarchical style of leadership. This approach, however, was criticized as ineffective, especially by a press corps conditioned to expect personality conflicts, rhetorical fireworks, and classic macho posturing.[33] And when the party experienced a serious setback in the 1993 election, electing only nine members, and winning under 7 per cent of the popular vote, her tenure was questioned. Although she led the party for a few more years, the dramatic loss of seats in 1993 prompted McLaughlin to leave the post in 1995.

In the party leadership game, Alexa McDonough has been the ultimate survivor, able to outwit critics, outplay party competitors, and outlast female and male leaders alike. In many respects, her story reflects the first trajectory, that representing women heads of electorally decimated parties. But McDonough's leadership, first of the Nova Scotia NDP, then of the national party, defies this classification because of her longevity and particularly because of her refusal to do what many female (and male) leaders do—that is, immediately step aside in the wake of an electoral setback.

In 1995, McDonough took over the leadership of a party in decline, inheriting a tiny parliamentary caucus, one without official party status in the House of Commons. She increased the NDP's fortunes in the 1997 federal election, improving the party's vote share to 11 per cent, more than doubling the party's seats (from nine to 21), securing official party status, and sneaking past the Conservatives to become the fourth largest party. Her years of experience as leader of the Nova Scotia wing of the party served her well, as did her strong support base in her home province, where the party won six of 11 seats in 1997. The NDP slipped in 2000, managing to hold only 13 ridings and losing five of the Nova Scotia seats due to Liberal enticements. Almost immediately the media began to criticize McDonough's leadership and predict her departure.[34] But McDonough prevailed, winning an 80 per cent vote of confidence from delegates to the party's November 2001 convention and defying both a leadership challenge and a proposal to scrap the NDP and build a new, more radically left-wing party.[35] Like Broadbent, who gradually increased the party's electoral support over the 14 years of his leadership, McDonough gained in political stature the longer she held the post. When she announced her resignation from the leader's job on June 5, 2002, columnists applauded her dedication to the party and to public life, noting that she plans to say on as MP for Halifax. "In Ottawa, she became the voice of conscience in question period, the one who asked constantly after social housing and pharmacare, even when the rest of the opposition was taking more political tacks," wrote the *Globe and Mail*.[36] Her willingness to step aside in a timely fashion, thus allowing the new leader an opportunity to rebuild the party before the next election, was noted with approval by all but McDonough's most persistent critic, Canadian Autoworkers Union president Buzz Hargrove. "Too bad she had to quit to get our attention," said political columnist Susan Riley.[37] The revolving door has now expelled Canada's most experienced female party leader.

Two women leaders have won the leadership of opposition parties with a realistic chance of winning office. Lynn Verge became leader of the Newfoundland Conservatives in 1995, at a time when party fortunes were on the upswing. Indeed, the party was expected to displace the governing Liberals. But Brian Tobin, fresh from "Captain Canada" fame as Minister of Fisheries during the highly publicized dispute with the Spanish government over off-shore fishing rights, replaced Clyde Wells as Liberal leader and claimed victory in the 1996 election. The Conservatives lost seats, and Verge resigned soon after the election. Verge, who had led the Conservatives for slightly less than a year, exemplifies the long-serving, highly respected woman politician who expends all of her political capital in one election and is disposed of shortly thereafter. Of course, the same fate befalls many long-serving male legislators who eventually become party leaders, except that there is an endless supply of them. When well-established women leave the political scene this way, there is a chilling effect on women's place in the political arena. As journalist Susan Riley pointed out, women who challenge the hold of patriarchs over political affairs are punished when they get "uppity."[38] Similarly when women aspire to lead political parties in Canada, and fail, their deaths—politically speaking—are certain. Women political leaders are an endangered species, in part because they fail to reproduce their kind in captivity.

Similar to Verge's experience is that of Liberal leader Lyn McLeod in Ontario. David Peterson brought his Liberal government to a hasty election in 1990, and, although he lost to the NDP, the party remained electorally competitive. The Liberal party was actually poised to win the 1995 election with McLeod at the helm. She won a competitive leadership race in 1992 and by February 1993 had overseen an increase in the party's approval rating to 45 per cent support of decided voters, far surpassing that of the Conservatives and NDP, both of which had the declared support of only 26 per cent of Ontarians.[39] McLeod remarked on the gender factor, saying she would have to overcome gender-based stereotypes to become the province's next premier. Her efforts in the 1995 election fell short of the target. The Liberals only managed official opposition status, with the Harris Conservatives staging a surprise victory. A male colleague, Dalton McGuinty, replaced McLeod as leader on December 1, 1996. Like McLeod, McGuinty failed to bring the Liberals to office in the next provincial election (1999), but his leadership remains secure.

An *Ottawa Citizen* columnist described McLeod's demise in this way: "In the testosterone temple that is Toronto's Maple Leaf Gardens, Lyn

McLeod, t*o be known forever as a mother of four,* surrenders the leadership of the Ontario Liberal Party on Saturday ... McLeod steps aside after
4 1/2 years as leader and one disastrous election, having never quite
escaped *the nurturing role*" (emphasis ours).[40] While there is considerable evidence to suggest that the men in the party backrooms are largely
responsible for this gendered typecasting, the quotation indicates the
media are at least partly to blame.

Only one woman has staged a come-from-behind victory, though her
success was fleeting. The Yukon's Pat Duncan led the Liberals to power
for the first time in April 2000. Earlier, the party had established a
competitive presence in the territory, securing three seats in the 17-
member legislature in the 1996 election, including the seat won by
Duncan. But Liberal leader and MLA Ken Taylor lost in his riding and
stepped down. In February 1997 Duncan was acclaimed as leader of the
Yukon Liberals, a post to which she was officially elected in February 1998.
Although the party had not won office since the territory adopted a party
system and had endured serious leadership troubles before Taylor's stint
in the job, its prospects were quite good when Duncan assumed the leadership. The Liberal share of the popular vote was up, and the Yukon Party
had lost support over its more than ten years as the government. As well,
under Duncan's leadership, the Liberals won a 1999 by-election that
vaulted them into the role of official opposition, thus laying the ground-
work for the April 2000 victory. Still, the Liberal win, a majority of 11 seats,
surprised some media observers and political pundits.[41]

The defection of three Liberal backbenchers in spring 2002 left
Duncan with a minority government. According to one newspaper
report, Duncan's leadership created "what some felt was a centralized,
controlling regime, in which her caucus mates and opponents had little
say," prompting the three disgruntled caucus members to sit as independents.[42] Party-infighting and desertions of this sort are unusual in
majority government situations, leading us to wonder whether female
leaders face higher levels of dissent and even public challenges to their
authority because of their gender. While the support of one independ-

ent member allowed the government to make it through the spring session, its prospects of surviving key votes scheduled for the fall sitting were slim.[43] A possible defeat at the polls was judged to be less risky than a certain defeat via non-confidence motion in the legislature, and Duncan called an election just two-and-a-half years into her government's term in office. The move backfired, as the Yukon Party won a decisive victory (12 of 18 seats), and the Liberals were reduced to just one seat, Duncan's. In the days immediately following the election, Duncan was noncommittal about her future as leader of the Yukon Liberals. Normally a loss of this magnitude would lead to immediate calls for the leader's resignation; as we have seen, female leaders do not typically survive electoral disasters. However, as Duncan is the lone representative of the party in the legislature it is possible that she will be encouraged to retain the leadership, at least in the short term.

One woman has taken the reins of a still-popular governing party; ironically, this example bodes ill for female leadership hopefuls. PEI's Catherine Callbeck, who inherited a strong governing party from popular Liberal Premier Joe Ghiz, engineered yet another stunning electoral victory for the Liberals in 1993, shortly after assuming the leadership. But she resigned in August 1996 at the tail end of her first successful term in office, "with not much of a reason for quitting."[44] One newspaper columnist suggested that the PEI Liberals failed to rally around her when the party's popularity fell below that of the Conservatives in the polls and even fuelled rumours of "a leadership *putsch* just days before her surprise resignation."[45] With her withdrawal, the "Backroom Boys" once again asserted control over the party and do not seem disposed to loosen their control again any time soon.[46] Callbeck was replaced by Keith Milligan, who called, and then lost, an election to the Conservatives in 1996. Again, Sharon Carstairs's reflections seem apt; "in their heart of hearts," said Carstairs, "these men politicians think that they can do a better job."[47]

Just Like a Girl: Media Portrayals of Women
Party Leaders

The metaphoric language of election coverage is often aggressive and glad-
iatorial, replete with images of the boxing ring, competitive sports, and
the battlefield. Describing election events with masculinist imagery disadvantages female political actors, as women do not generally come to mind
when we conjure up images of pugilists, soldiers, or sports stars. Therefore,
applying macho metaphors to women creates cognitive dissonance; "nice
women" don't punch out their opponents or annihilate the enemy.[48]

As this suggests, if "nice" women do not have what it takes to thrive in
politics, women who aspire to top jobs in political parties confront a classic catch-22. Gender stereotyping casts women as nurturers, kind and
gentle enablers. But the portrayal of political news is dominated by
metaphors of warfare, sports, and other types of violent confrontation.
If women choose to "join the fray," they are criticized for being too aggressive (thus unwomanly), and their actions are even exaggerated and
misrepresented. Elizabeth Gidengil and Joanna Everitt compared the
actual behaviour of women party leaders in the 1993, 1997, and 2000
federal party leaders' debates with TV and newspaper coverage of these
events. They found that the female leaders were characterized as more
aggressive than their male counterparts, even though their words and
actions were demonstrably less confrontational.[49] On the other hand,
women leaders are often portrayed as inherently unable, because of their
sex, to play the game according to rules set by their male predecessors.
They are cast as electoral weaklings by journalists and pundits; indeed,
they are often written out of the game simply because they are women.
Shannon Sampert and Linda Trimble's study of national newspaper
headlines covering the 2000 federal election documented the presence of
military imagery involving fights and force. Aggressive figures of speech
and sports and battle metaphors were applied significantly more often to
coverage of male party leaders than to stories about the lone woman party
chief, Alexa McDonough.[50] The crucial first-actor position in headlines

(the first name mentioned), accompanied by the language of aggression (fight, punch, attack, strike, and bomb), was rarely associated with McDonough, but frequently with the male party leaders. The overall effect was to relegate her to the margins of the electoral game.

Prevalent gender codes—that is, assumptions about sex-appropriate characteristics, aptitudes, and roles—continue to frame politics as a man's game. Women politicians, especially party leaders, are anomalies, and the media are hard-pressed to fit them into the usual masculine stereotypes of hard-hitting, ruthless, warrior kings. As Gertrude Robinson and Armande Saint-Jean have observed, one strategy employed by the news media to resolve the seeming contradiction of a female political leader is to draw attention to the feminine attributes of the woman occupying a man's role.[51] In this way, the media frequently remind readers that while these women wield power, they remain essentially women, concerned with beauty, femininity, and traditional domestic roles. A variety of discursive techniques are used to "domesticate" and feminize women leaders, including paying undue attention to their household tasks, emphasizing their personal relationships, and making pointed observations about their wardrobe, hair, make-up, and weight. Consider this description of BC NDP leader Joy MacPhail: "But the 5-foot-2-inch Ms. MacPhail is a formidable foe. Even her critics say the sharp-tongued politico, *known for her trademark cropped red hair and stylish wardrobe*, will keep them on their toes" (italics ours).[52] Even more blatant is a 1997 news story about Alberta NDP leader Pam Barrett and her party's mid-election standing in the public opinion polls. The article's version of the NDP leader's election strategy was entirely personal and domestic, as it focused on Barrett's bathing rituals and her preparation of gravy for a Sunday dinner with family and friends.[53] More recently, portrayals of women ministers in Jean Chrétien's cabinet exaggerate them as squat and physically unfit compared with relatively trimmer and more athletic male politicians.

Another feminizing ritual is to associate female leaders with sex. Questions, especially about a woman leader's inferred sexuality, crop up repeatedly as a way of making unattached women appear to be less knowledgeable about the needs of the people than male politicians with so-called "traditional" families. For example, supporters of Jean Charest's 1993 bid for the leadership of the federal Conservatives constructed his marital status and parenthood as a virtue that was contrasted with Kim Campbell's well-publicized marital history. After Campbell's defeat in the 1993 federal election, in addition to the typical questions posed in post-election interviews, *Maclean's* magazine asked the former prime minister, "Have you found love?"[54] Indeed, her sexual exploits remain the subject of much media scrutiny. Her "new man" was the focus of a lengthy story about her post-political life in the *National Post* in 1999. Her partner was featured prominently in a 2000 *Globe and Mail* profile of older women and their "hard-bodied toy boys."[55] The *Post* article, which referred to Campbell as "twice married and seldom without a man in her life," is typical of this strategy.

Then there is the persistent observation that women leaders just do not fit in. Their voices are shrill, their brightly coloured dresses provide a stark contrast to the sombre grey or navy of men's suits, and their rhetorical punches are just plain wimpy. A 2000 pre-election score-card/profile of the federal party leaders, printed in the *Globe and Mail* and called "Ready to Rumble," evaluated the "most effective punch" of the five contenders. Alexa McDonough was presented as an electoral lightweight with this evaluation: "Float like a butterfly, sting like a, er, mosquito."[56] Similarly, the March 1997 Alberta leaders' debate inspired headlines like "Leaders take their corners" and "Lots of sparring, but no knockout punches." These newspaper reports were liberally sprinkled with terms like poke, jab, hammer, attack, swipe, ruckus, hound, and punch. Evaluations of the leaders (three men and one woman) were laden with gendered assumptions; the men were described as strong, relaxed, sincere, cool, and in command, while the lone female leader was characterized as shrill, aggressive, and out of control.[57] Her choice of attire for the event was also a focus of media attention. In the manner of the lifestyle or entertainment pages, an *Edmonton Journal* article (titled "Dressed to Kill") began: "Pam Barrett will be dressing for success tonight, dahling. The New Democrat will debut her new tailor-made, kelly-green, wool gabardine creation ..."[58] Tongue-in-cheek though this was, it diminished her politically. These few examples, among many, illustrate the tendency of journalists and editorial writers to judge women unfit for the electoral game because of their gender. Clearly, a critical examination of media coverage of women in politics is essential to an understanding of the revolving door for female party leaders.[59]

Where Have All the Women Gone? Leadership Prospects

The future for female political leaders looks bleak for two reasons. First of all, the trend of women taking over non-competitive parties in a cheer-leader mode continues, except that there are fewer of them. At present there are only three women leaders: all lead opposition parties with only one or two seats and slim chances of forming a government. Secondly, there are fewer women who seem willing to take the gamble. When we first presented a version of this chapter in 1997, we expected at least three or four new women leaders of competitive parties to emerge by 2000, speculating that Janice MacKinnon and Frances Lankin of the Saskatchewan and Ontario NDP, respectively, might be among them. Male leaders now head these parties. We also saw possibilities for women in Newfoundland and Quebec. But when Lucien Bouchard stepped down as PQ leader in January 2001, Deputy Leader Bernard Landry claimed such extensive support within the party and caucus that the sole female contender, Pauline Marois, decided to bow out of the contest and support him.[60] In Newfoundland, Brian Tobin's cabinet featured four women who gained the experience often required of politicians with aspirations to lead their party. However, none of them competed for the job when Tobin elbowed his way past all other possible contenders. Later, when he resigned from provincial politics to return to the House of Commons, yet another male leader, Roger Grimes, replaced him as premier.

At the federal level, Sheila Copps is an unlikely successor to Jean Chrétien.[61] She is rarely mentioned in the press as a serious contender but is likely to be encouraged to run so that the electoral platform is not exclusively male. A few female cabinet ministers were noted as Liberal leadership aspirants in 1998, including Copps and two other high-profile cabinet ministers, Jane Stewart and Anne McLellan. More recent newspaper columns flag Paul Martin Jr. as the frontrunner, with Allan Rock and John Manley as potential rivals.[62] Besides Copps, the Liberal women seem to have faded from columnists' memories. As an *Elm Street* article observed, it is interesting that "over the past year or so, Stewart's and McLellan's names have mysteriously dropped from the media's lists of potential Liberal leadership contenders."[63] And Copps herself is ridiculed in the press for making a third run at the leadership.

In 1998 the federal Conservatives turned to a former leader and prime minister, Joe Clark, to revitalize the troops. This leadership contest revealed much about gender, party politics, and leadership in the late 1990s, as neither the party nor the news media cited any women's names in the aftermath of Jean Charest's decision to leave federal politics and seek the leadership of the Quebec Liberal party. While former Mulroney cabinet ministers like John Crosbie were singled out, no one mentioned Barbara McDougall or Kim Campbell. Indeed, the *Globe and Mail* conducted a public opinion poll regarding public reaction to several possible Conservative contenders, all of them men.[64] In the wake of Clark's summer 2002 decision to step aside, the media reported that the candidates for his job include MP Peter MacKay, party strategist Hugh Segal, and Toronto businessman John Tory.[65] No woman is expected to compete for the position despite the fact that the Conservatives need to do better with women voters to improve their position in the House of Commons.

Ironically, one (admittedly remote and fleeting) possibility of a new woman party leader on the federal scene resulted from the leadership travails of the Canadian Alliance, a party distinguished by its paucity of women candidates and unabashed lack of concern for gender equity in political representation. The entry of Alliance MP Diane Ablonczy into the party's second leadership race in as many years illustrates the pattern of women seeking leadership of troubled parties. But it is important to note that, despite party-infighting and the departure of 13 MPs from the party caucus in protest of Stockwell Day's mismanagement, six of whom later returned to the fold, the Alliance leadership is still a job many men want. Former Reform MP Stephen Harper and Alliance MP Grant Hill contested the post, as did the beleaguered Day. Ablonczy was recognized as a serious contender, having gained a high profile during the Human Resources Development Canada (HRDC) scandal with her dogged and pointed questioning of Minister Jane Stewart. Early speculation in the *Globe and Mail* anticipated a two-way race between Ablonczy and Harper, but Ablonczy lacked crucial support from current caucus members. As well, her stance on a merger with the Conservatives was unpopular in some circles of the party.[66] As the leadership race unfolded, she fell far behind the male frontrunners. As the first round of voting began, she told a reporter that, for the first time in her nine-year political career, she confronted the limitations posed by her gender. "Some people in the Alliance are asking if a female leader could have the strength and vision and determination ... to lead the party," Albonczy said, "I do think people still tend to think of leaders more in the male context."[67] On March 20, 2002, Stephen Harper decisively won the contest on the first ballot, with 55 per cent of the vote. Ablonczy came in third, with 4 per cent of the vote, keeping her just ahead of Grant Hill.

The departure of Alexa McDonough from the leadership of the federal NDP has inspired a leadership race in which all the confirmed and rumoured contestants have been male. The one woman mentioned in the immediate aftermath of McDonough's resignation was Elizabeth Weir, presently leader of the New Brunswick party. Weir unequivocally ruled herself out of the running, saying "No. Never in a trillion years."[68] Political columnist Susan Riley summed up the state of affairs with this comment on McDonough's resignation: "until the larger culture changes, the best jobs in federal politics will remain the preserve of mostly male workaholics."[69]

Conclusion

A high-water mark in terms of women's leadership of political parties was achieved between 1992 and 1995. Since then, the number of women leaders has dropped significantly, and further advances are unlikely in the near future. The leadership experiences of, among others, Baird-Filliter, MacBeth, Haverstock, and Verge certainly do not recommend the job to female aspirants. The electoral glass ceiling makes it difficult to maintain a strong, steady supply of women politicians who might entertain hopes of eventually being selected leader. And the few women who seek leadership positions face a revolving door that shunts out most women aspirants in a matter of a few years or less. Women are chosen to nurture demoralized party stalwarts and to revitalize failing political parties, but this caregiving role creates a classic catch-22 situation for them. If they are successful, and the party becomes electorally competitive, then the leader's post is once again attractive to male political aspirants and, often, they are pushed aside. On the other hand, if the female leader is unsuccessful at winning power within a relatively short period of time, she may well be sidelined in favour of a male candidate.

The mass media persist in judging women leaders according to a gendered yardstick and, not surprisingly, tend to suggest that women just do not measure up. Journalists domesticate female party leaders by highlighting their femininity, looks, clothing, relationships, and the tone of their voices—anything but their political skills and policy acumen. Women at the head of parties routinely endure inappropriate scrutiny of their personal lives and are constantly reminded by the press that they are different. When describing politics, especially elections, the news media employ masculinist discourses, evoking images of warring parties fighting it out on the battlefield, and party leaders as pugilists, punching, kicking, and attacking their way to victory. In this context, women are anomalies; they are not men; they do not fit in.

Worse still, these two patterns have coalesced. The revolving door for female leaders in Canada has recently expelled a number of experienced women from political life, reinforcing the view that women cannot succeed in the top jobs. And media treatment of them accentuates patriarchal assumptions about leadership styles and women's "proper" roles. As a result, party leadership has become even more of a drag for the women currently holding the post than was the case in the early 1990s. The top jobs are unappealing to those women politicians who might otherwise consider seeking them.

CHAPTER 5

Spice Girls and Old Spice Boys:
Getting There is Only Half the Battle

Introduction

Frustrated with heckling directed at him during a spring 1998 session of question period in the Alberta legislature, Acting Premier (and then Treasurer) Stockwell Day complained, "It's sometimes difficult to maintain a focus with all the *chirping from the Spice Girls* over there" (emphasis ours).[1] Day's likening of female members of the Liberal opposition to the "girls" in the then popular British band was not well received by the women he targeted. Liberal MLA Colleen Soetaert felt the comment showed "a lack of respect for women in the legislature." Her colleague Sue Olsen summarized her reaction this way, "I'm getting tired of the sexist comments that are being made." Day's remarks came close on the heels of heated personal invective directed at newly elected Liberal leader Nancy MacBeth, including pointed observations about repeated changes

100

to her hairstyle.[2] The media loved the hairdo comments and ran with the Spice Girls story by linking female opposition MLAs with the appropriate band members. Laurie Blakeman, with her red hair, had a clear resemblance to Ginger Spice, but was Colleen Soetaert Baby or Scary? Soetaert, master of the quick quip, responded later in question period by calling a government member "Old Spice," referring to a cologne marketed to the over-50 crowd as an aftershave for the "man's" man.

This incident, and the media response to it, reveals a great deal about the circles of constraint that continue to restrict the advancement of women legislators. The Spice Girls, female newcomers to political office, women with ideas, energy, and confidence, represent a new generation of women politicians who, like the flamboyant pop group, are not afraid to claim "girl power." On the other hand, the Old Spice Boys—men with legislative experience and an expansive sense of entitlement "earned" by dint of hard work and decades of male dominance of political office— have various ways of expressing their discomfort with these female upstarts and their "chirping." Female legislators are quite routinely shouted down, verbally and sexually harassed, heckled, and ridiculed because they are women. The proverbial battle of the sexes continues to be fought between the new Spice Girls and the Old Spice Boys, with the media eager to report every verbal jab, personal insult, and personality clash.

Legislatures remain, much as they have long been, men's clubs. Women intrude at their peril. Their presence is annoying but tolerable so long as they keep to their place on the sidelines. After all, women are not typically contenders for positions of leadership. Women who do contest the top jobs quickly discover that they are intruding on masculine turf. Sheila Copps learned this lesson in her bid for the leadership of the Ontario Liberals. She lost, but surprised many observers by posing a solid challenge to the victor, David Peterson. After the convention, Copps was treated differently by the male powerbrokers in the party.

Funny—when I had been the "sweet young thing" from Hamilton Centre, the only woman in caucus, I'd been no great threat. But the leadership convention changed that. For the first time, the men in my caucus realized that women could be more than tokens in our party, that we could wield influence—even power. That notion frightened a number of my colleagues.... While I had failed in my bid to lead our party, I had shown that it might be possible for another woman at another time. That realization threatened men who might themselves seek greater political roles.[3]

No longer formally excluded from legislatures, women are still seen as outsiders, strangers in a foreign culture, aliens in the "testosterone tabernacles"[4] that make political judgements and direct policy decisions. This chapter begins by exploring the assumptions and attitudes that underlie the construction of politics as a man's game. We then look at the consequences for female political aspirants, including barriers to engaging fully in political debate, the role conflict faced by female legislators with children, and sexist behaviour in legislatures. While some women legislators manage to take up the Spice Girl challenge and rise above the petty politics of the Old Spice Boys, gender-based circles of constraint tend to make legislatures difficult and even unsafe work environments for female legislators. As a result, those women who stay in the game a long time demonstrate considerable courage, persistence, and fortitude.

A Man's Game

One of the very few women who sought a party nomination to run for a seat in the PEI legislature in the 1950s said the male activists in her party "didn't want women mixed up in it. It was a man's legislature."[5] This is a consistent refrain, even by women who have broken into these formerly men-only environments.[6] Canada's legislatures were indeed originally constituted as men's legislatures. They were developed at a time when women were expressly denied not only the right to membership in them, but even to vote for the men seeking political office.

In the beginning, the seats of power were fashioned for a very select group of men. The first federal electoral law denied all but white male property owners the right to vote and singled out women and "mental incompetents" as particularly undeserving of this privilege. A varied and formidable list of reasons was offered to support the exclusion of women from the vote: women were too weak to participate in the excitement of elections; they lacked the mental acuity necessary to comprehend political issues; woman suffrage defied Biblical teachings; the vote would "unsex and degrade women, destroy domestic harmony and lead to a decline in the birth rate"; women could better achieve their goals by means other than the vote, especially by their use of "loving persuasion"; women were said not to want the vote; and, finally, even if granted the right to vote, women would not bother to cast ballots.[7] The very idea of granting women political rights was considered so radical that the first group devoted to winning the female franchise, formed in 1876, felt compelled to disguise its intentions with the moniker "Toronto Women's Literary Club." After seven years of subterfuge, emboldened by an Ontario law that gave property-owning spinsters and widows the right to vote on municipal by-laws, the club unveiled its true intentions by renaming itself the Canadian Woman Suffrage Association.[8]

Many Canadians, including women, were denied political rights on the grounds that they did not possess the necessary qualities to exercise the duties and enjoy the privileges of citizens.[9] The "ideal of citizenship" resulted from a process that systematically excluded all but "an elite class of male landowners [who] ... first laid claim to the reasoning faculties that alone, in their view, made them competent to influence policy."[10] For much of our post-Confederation history, Canadians were legally or logistically excluded from voting and running for political office simply because they were women, Aboriginal, poor, members of ethnic minority groups, or disabled. Women were neither regarded as a category of person worthy of positive recognition in the eye of the law and in policy, nor were they treated as a unified category. As we saw in Chapter 2, some women won the vote federally in 1918, but other women (and men) waited considerably longer for their franchise to be granted. For some—

Canadians of Asian or East Indian origins—the vote was not achieved until the late 1940s; for most Aboriginal Canadians the franchise was won in the 1960s; and for persons with disabilities it did not come until the early 1990s.

Politics was designed as a (white, able-bodied) man's game. As its masculinist ethos was consolidated, women were excluded from political activity, including entry to legislatures, on the basis of their sex, ethnicity, class, and mental/physical ability. Notions about a woman's "proper place" included assumptions that lingered long after most women were accorded the right to vote and run for office. After all, women were seen as biologically destined for the domestic household, not the houses of Parliament. In the first few decades after Confederation, political, scientific, and clerical elites clearly delineated a woman's place with statements like "woman's first and only place is in the home" and "woman exists for the sake of the womb."[11] A woman's true calling was to be a good wife and mother. Given attitudes like these, it is not surprising that when Canada's first female MP, Agnes Macphail, tried to enter the House of Commons in 1921, an employee blocked her way. "You can't go in there, Miss!" she was told.[12] In she went. Since Macphail's entry, 154 more women have won admission to the national legislature where formerly they could not go.

**BOX 5.1: Politics As a Man's Game—
            Features and Assumptions**

- Formal exclusion of women from the exercise of political power (voting; contesting elected office; seeking appointments).
- Informal exclusion of women from elected and appointed office is based on a series of assumptions:
  - the idea that political participation is "unwomanly" or "unfeminine";
  - the belief that women are properly suited for the domestic household, not the houses of Parliament;
  - the assumption that racial minority women are risky choices as candidates; and
  - the notion that women don't "merit" more power.

Since the social context was pervasively sexist, it is not surprising that several of the first women legislators were elected as replacements for male parliamentarians. In her memoirs, the late Judy LaMarsh, Liberal MP from 1960 to 1968, recalled: "throughout my years in the Liberal party, I never saw evidence that any real attention was paid to seeking out and grooming women as ... parliamentary material, except in one area and that was the importuning of fresh widows of Members of Parliament to seek their husbands' unexpired terms."[13] The first woman elected in BC, Mary Ellen Smith, replaced her late husband in a by-election held in 1918.[14] Nine women have been elected to the House of Commons as political substitutes for male relatives, one as recently as 1982. Between 1921 and 1970, only 17 women were elected to the House of Commons, taking 74 out of 3,821 seats (2 per cent); seven of them took over the role from recently deceased husbands. At the provincial and territorial level, at least six, and likely many more, women were chosen by party gatekeepers to substitute for their departed spouses or fathers. Why? Party officials figured the pity factor could easily be parlayed into a by-election win, and the grieving but grateful widows or daughters would faithfully carry on in the tradition of their departed relatives. Electing women family members also "solved" in the short term the problem of providing for the family of a loyal party man. Ordinarily a suitable male candidate could then be vetted and nominated in the lead-up to a general election. However, not all surrogates stepped aside graciously.

New Brunswick's Margaret Rideout, the first woman from the province to win election federally or provincially, typifies this path for early women politicians. Rideout's husband, Sherwood, had been the Liberal MP for Westmorland when he died of a heart attack. His death left the Liberal minority government in a precarious position; thus, the 1964 by-election was both very important and hotly contested by opposition parties with "no intention of allowing this election to be given away to a grieving widow."[15] But Margaret Rideout's campaign posters and pamphlets suggested that this was precisely why voters should support her, and she won quite handily. As "Mrs. S.H. Rideout," the traditional homemaker, she posed no threat to the male powerbrokers of the day. Electing her provided needed support to the status quo. The women who entered legislatures on their own terms were not welcomed, for they threatened entrenched attitudes and structures of privilege.

In an exchange that took place in 1985 between then President of the National Action Committee on the Status of Women, Judy Rebick, and Newfoundland Conservative John Crosbie, he irreverently needled, "We can't have women representing themselves or the next thing you know we'll have to have the crippleds and coloureds."[16] Crosbie later said he thought his comment was funny. Occasionally persons with disabilities and non-white individuals have been elected, but not consistently or in large numbers.[17] Members of newly enfranchised or politically active groups disrupt established patterns when they speak out about their collective underrepresentation or other matters affecting the fairness and equity of the political system. Not only women but members of racial minority groups, persons with disabilities, and members of Aboriginal communities have great potential to expose and challenge taken-for-granted notions about who should hold power. A few legislators have commented openly about the potential and actual power of elected members of underrepresented groups to bring attention to injustices.

For example, in the early 1970s BC NDP Rosemary Brown had reservations about seeking elected office. Encouraged by NDP leader Dave Barrett to contest a nomination, Brown said she and her husband laughed at the idea. "We both knew that no Vancouver riding would choose a person who was Black, female and an immigrant to be its elected representative." The couple had experience that supported their prediction. Brown recalled, "It made very little sense to me that people who had for years refused to rent me accommodation or hire me for employment would entrust me with the responsibility of representing them in the place of power, where laws governing their lives were drafted and enforced."[18] However, events took a different turn. A majority of voters was persuaded that she was the right candidate for Vancouver-Burrard, where she won a provincial seat in 1972. Nevertheless, in anticipating negative reactions to her candidacy due to her race and heritage, Brown had not miscalculated the negative reception typically given those who challenge the status quo.

In another tightly fought contest, this one for the Liberal nomination in Rosedale prior to the general election of 1979, social worker and community activist Anne Cools, herself an immigrant, saw her campaign for the nomination marred by racial slurs. The National Film Board documentary, *The Right Candidate for Rosedale*, collected images that used negative racial stereotypes to depict the candidate. Cools lost the nomination to an eminent male candidate, John Evans, President of the University of Toronto; he subsequently was defeated in the election by Conservative incumbent David Crombie.

The reaction to women who entered legislatures at a time when female representatives were few in number clearly illustrates the patriarchal presumptions of the Old Spice Boys. Sheila Copps, freshly elected to the Ontario legislature in 1981 as one of only six women in the House and the only female member of the Liberal caucus, found that her colleagues "clearly saw me as an ornament to the party—nice to have around as long as I knew my place." At least one cabinet minister saw her proper place as the domestic sphere. Irritated by her persistent questioning, he suggested she go "back to the kitchen."[19] When Alexa McDonough was the lone female MLA in the Nova Scotia legislature in the early 1980s, her son received telephone calls from drunks demanding to know why Alexa "wouldn't just do the proper thing and keep to the kitchen."[20] Below the surface but still readily apparent runs the message: "You do not belong here; in this arena you have no merit."

Have attitudes and behaviours changed since women began winning election to legislatures in more than token numbers? Much of the evidence, empirical and anecdotal, suggests that female politicians continue to experience resistance to their inclusion, not just as tokens, but as leaders and decision-makers. Claims for substantive power for women invariably smash up against two sides of the merit argument. First, there is the idea that women have not earned, and thus do not merit, more power. Secondly, merit in electoral politics operates in a gender-specific manner. While women's merit is questioned, most men have their merit taken for granted. Merit has long been used in political circles as a code word for those who have power. And because traditional gender roles have been challenged but not fully uprooted by the women's movement, the assumption persists that women belong in the household, performing duties as wives and mothers. Women are mired in the muck of the traditional dichotomy of gender *versus* politics.

"Are You a Politician or a Woman?"

In the 1970s, the notion that political careers and traditional feminine roles were mutually exclusive options was epitomized by a question frequently posed by reporters to MPs Flora MacDonald and Judy LaMarsh: "Are you a politician or a woman?"[21] It is still often presumed that parenting and governing are incompatible roles, at least for women. Mothering, as it is socially constituted, does impose internal and external constraints on women's political participation. Because child bearing and rearing are seen as the responsibility of women, it is

> assumed that family constraints are irrelevant for male candidates but relevant for females. Males are expected to act in the worlds of business or politics, and the factors that would constrain them become someone else's responsibility, usually the candidate's spouse's. It is often assumed that men have a stable support system within the home; the wife's contribution to the man's candidacy is taken for granted. Obviously, family constraints cannot be so easily minimized for most female candidates because the sexual division of labour denies them the same support system.[22]

A double standard emerges, one that was pointedly summed up by Sheila Copps in her book *Nobody's Baby*: "If a young man ascends the political ladder and successfully combines that effort with a happy family life, he becomes complete. If you are a woman, there is always the question, 'How can you look after your children?'"[23] BC MLA Judy Tyabji found this out the hard way when she was denied custody of her three children because the judge felt her political ambition was incompatible with parenting.[24] In reaction to the decision, outraged women politicians asked why the same reasoning was not applied to former Prime Minister Pierre Trudeau, who, as a single father of three young boys, governed the entire country.[25]

The role conflict experienced by women politicians is not simply a reflection of the actual demands of the job. After all, lots of women combine paid work with child-rearing, and most male politicians have children. But social expectations of fathers remain modest, while mothers are still expected to put their children, husbands, and domestic duties first. As Janine Brodie suggests, "the supposed incongruence between the role of homemaker or mother and the role of politician is imposed as much by the idealization of motherhood as by the actual demands of motherhood." After all, "'good wives' or 'good mothers' do not abandon their husbands, homes or children to pursue political careers."[26] Again, Sheila Copps provides a pithy take on this presumption:

> When I married in the summer of 1985, I had already been working full-time in politics for eight years, yet an amazing number of people asked me whether I planned to quit my job. The unstated reason was that I had now snagged a man and should get down to the real business of womanhood, having babies. And everyone knows that babies and politics don't mix.[27]

Despite the fact that some or even a great deal of this role conflict is socially constructed, women politicians are greatly affected by it. Iris Evans, now a cabinet minister in Alberta, says women with political ambitions used to be relegated to the local school board. "The attitude was, 'Dearie, we'll take care of the important stuff [namely provincial and national politics] and you look after the kids,'" Evans recalls.[28] Some women politicians have described the guilt and anxiety they endure as

a legacy of the traditional sexual division of labour in Canadian society.[29] In her memoirs, Rosemary Brown related this story about how the
"are-you-a-politician-or-a-mother?" conflict affected her first campaign
for a BC legislative seat in 1972:

> The only hostile questions directed at me concerned the hypocritical
> fear that my children would suffer as a result of my political activities,
> and accusations of their impending neglect. At first the question made
> me defensive because I shared these concerns myself. I felt guilty about
> spending a lot of time away from the children, aged fourteen, twelve
> and five, so I handled the question badly. In time it became clear that
> the Socreds realized they had found my Achilles' heel. I was not fooled.
> I knew that the questioners cared not one whit about my children, but
> they saw that their questions wounded me and so, smelling blood, they
> kept tearing away, heckling, questioning and accusing me every chance
> they got.[30]

Brown struggled with her guilt, recognized that similar attacks would
not be directed to a male candidate, and in the end used humour to
deflect the criticisms. She also pointed to her child-rearing work as
invaluable experience for a legislator.

Female politicians without husbands or children are not exempt from
traditional assumptions. Those who eschew marriage and motherhood
are questioned about their femininity. Kim Campbell was criticized by
members of her own party because, when she sought the Conservative
leadership, she was single and had no children. Indeed, unmarried
women politicians are often assumed to be lesbians.[31] The subtext
conveyed by these examples is clear; a "womanly" woman doesn't enter
the aggressive and competitive political arena. Pauline Jewett's biogra-
pher says this trail-blazing MP, who served for the Liberals in the 1950s
and the NDP in the 1980s, was questioned about her femininity and
single status: "Her independent spirit and firm opinions were perceived
as unwomanly and masculine; she was not seen as a 'real' woman."[32]

Power-seeking women are, therefore, considered unfeminine, perhaps abnormal, and certainly a threat to the status quo.

Role conflict for women politicians is about much more than sexual innuendo and feelings of guilt. There are tangible barriers to blending parenting and politicking for male and female politicians alike, but women in the political realm are more likely to point them out. According to a BC study, many female MLAs say long hours, the lack of a fixed schedule during legislative sessions, and night sittings make the Legislative Assembly less than woman-friendly.[33] The sheer unpredictability of the legislative schedule makes it difficult to integrate work and family life, arrange child care, and find time for friends and family.[34] Travel is also a burden, especially for female legislators whose homes are geographically distant from the capital. For example, Conservative MP Pat Carney, then a single parent, was told in 1984 that the MP's family travel benefit was only for spouses. Consequently, she could not use the fund to fly her 15-year old son to Ottawa. Carney protested by refusing to perform her duties until the rule was changed. When that tactic failed, she appealed to the first woman Speaker of the House, Jeanne Sauvé, who agreed to extend travel allowances to "designated next of kin."[35]

BOX 5.2: An Inhospitable Working Environment?

The legislator's job features:
- night sessions of legislatures;
- long, unpredictable hours; and
- lack of a set schedule.

(these three features have been changed at the federal level for MPs— why have they not been changed at the provincial and territorial level?)
- travel to and from the constituency, often on a weekly basis;
- lack of time for friends and family.

Now, many Canadian parents cope with long hours spent on the job, but in the public and private sectors, employees can predict their working hours and plan ahead for their time off. Provincial and territorial politicians often do not have this luxury. A sudden election call or a prolonged legislative session plays havoc with the lives of elected representatives, their friends, and their families. These problems are easily addressed, as changes to House of Commons rules made in the mid-1980s show. MPs now have a fixed schedule, no night sittings, an on-site day care centre, and the predictability that results from a parliamentary calendar set months in advance. Kim Campbell wrote that the regular hours in particular "were a boon to the family life of all MPs."[36] But it seems that, although these simple provisions make life so much easier for both male and female representatives, women politicians at the provincial and territorial level have not been able to find support for the necessary changes that improve the work environment all around. The underlying assumptions about the incompatibility of parenting and politics remain uncontested.

Sexist Circles of Constraint

In 1997, the Angus Reid polling firm, in collaboration with the CBC, conducted telephone interviews with 102 female politicians across Canada.[37] Most of the women legislators agreed patriarchal attitudes constrained their political careers. Eighty-one per cent said it is accurate to describe politics as an "old boys" club. Many reported personal experiences with sexist behaviour: 60 per cent had fielded inappropriate or demeaning gender-based remarks, and 31 per cent dealt with unwanted sexual advances or propositions. Almost one-third, 30 per cent, said they were held back in their political careers because of their sex. They agreed *en masse* that women politicians face gender-related personal pressures resulting from scrutiny by colleagues, the press, and voters of their private lives, their appearance, wardrobe, family responsibilities, weight, and age. These women also expressed the opinion that the style of politics would change with more women in the legislature: 63 per cent believed that with more women elected, legislatures would become more civilized and respectful environments for discussion and debate.

The survey confirmed what many women politicians had been thinking. It certainly codified the sexist circles of constraint women politicians confront regardless of their stance on feminism. In autobiographies and interviews, women legislators have related their first-hand experiences involving sexist attitudes, assumptions, and behaviours. The similarities in their narratives about the job and its perils are striking. Two key themes emerge. First, women politicians say it is unpleasant to work within such a masculine and adversarial environment as legislatures, especially because they find it difficult to reject traditional aggressive and conflict-ridden approaches and participate on their own terms. Secondly, they describe a working environment at times so hostile to their participation that it is experienced as emotionally abusive. In particular, women legislators who advocate for women's rights, especially those who identify themselves and their policy goals as feminist, have been ridiculed, heckled, mocked, and harassed.

Entering the "Testosterone Tabernacle"

Many women have commented on the masculine and war-like trappings of Parliament. A central symbol is the mace, a ceremonial staff originally designed as a medieval war club. Seating in legislative chambers was designed to keep opposing sides two sword-lengths apart. The Speaker of the House is still afforded ceremonial protection against the once very real danger of having his head lopped off. And titles like the "Gentleman Usher of the Black Rod"[38] and "Sergeant-at Arms" continue to evoke a "men's club" atmosphere. Even the artwork speaks to the glory days of gory battle. Trudeau-era Liberal cabinet minister Iona Campagnolo had this to say about the paintings decorating the House of Commons: "they're all men and war and swords and blood."[39] Male heroes abound in portraits and statues, while the only women to adorn the halls and grounds of Parliament are a few female monarchs and, as of October 2000, the "famous five" women from Alberta who secured legal person status for women.[40] The memoirs of female politicians express their dismay at this old-fashioned and (to them) arcane institutional culture. Former NDP leader Audrey McLaughlin devoted an entire chapter of her autobiography to her experiences in "the men's club"; likewise Sheila Copps called one chapter "When a House is Not a Home." Former Manitoba Liberal leader Sharon Carstairs titled her book *Not One of the Boys*. Spoken as well as unspoken rules of the parliamentary "men's club" result in the exclusion of women.

Women politicians who are new to the legislative arena arrive full of optimism and enthusiasm. They are keen to voice their own ideas and their constituents' needs, but often have a rude awakening when they begin their jobs as political representatives. They soon discover that the true role of the legislator is not all they hoped it would be. Parliamentary representatives act neither as idealized political representatives, wisely discerning the best ideas and the common interest, nor as the community's liaisons for constituent ideas and opinions. Rather, the legislator's principal job is to champion his or her party and critique the opposing group, regardless of the issue, its nuances, and complexity. The rules of political discourse are, therefore, simple—us versus them, no holds barred. The parliamentary system of government is an intrinsically adversarial contest, with opposing "teams" (parliamentary parties) engaging each other in rhetorical battles. Sometimes, the conflicts verge on the physical, as when Reform MP Darrel Stinson stepped away from his desk, rolled up his sleeves, and invited a Liberal member to duke it out. In the end, fisticuffs were not the order of the day, but at least one of the combatants declared himself ready, willing, and able.

Journalist Sydney Sharpe maintains the institution itself is designed to facilitate verbal battles. "In the Commons, enemy MPs are staked in rows on either side of a wide, carpeted isle, a psychological moat across which they fire their modern versions of the flaming arrow—epithets like 'liar,' 'jerk,' 'scumbag,' and 'asshole.'"[41] Liberal cabinet minister Sheila

Copps agrees that the "traditions of the House create an atmosphere which is combative, not conciliatory; aggressive not consultative—a forum in which many women feel there is no place for them."[42] Pat Duncan, former premier of the Yukon, said "the high testosterone level in our Legislative Assembly gets to me at times."[43] It is no wonder many women describe the atmosphere as alienating and off-putting. Indeed, "Put Off by Parliament" is the title of an article in *Elm Street* that described federal politics as "Ottawa's macho game." In the piece, journalist Susan Delacourt wrote, "politics functions along the same lines as a sports team or a military unit, emphasizing discipline, tradition, loyalty and bravura performance. The cliché 'Politics is a blood sport' is simply accepted as a fact of life."[44] But for women in the House of Commons this so-called "fact of life" often prevents them from doing the job in their own way, with a lower profile and less confrontational strategies.

BOX 5.3: Politics as a "Blood Sport"

- Symbols and trappings of power are masculine, evocative of bloody warfare.
- Traditions and procedures organize parliamentary debates as a "team sport," with party teams facing off against each other in rhetorical battles.
- Style of debate is adversarial, combative, and aggressive.

The highest profile parliamentary battleground is the daily question period, where ministers are grilled by opposition members with the intent of catching them off guard or exposing government errors. Some women have gone on record as disliking question period because of the hyper-confrontational style and vitriolic tone adopted by many legislators in an effort to score points with their parties and secure ten-second sound bites on TV and radio. Seasoned Liberal cabinet minister Anne McLellan refers to it as a brand of torture equivalent to dental work without Novocaine: "It's about 'gotcha' and 'ha ha.' And I hate that. I hate that."[45] In her autobiography, written while she was leader of the federal NDP, Audrey McLaughlin said: "I remember how amazed Marion [Dewar, also an NDP MP] and I were when we sat through our first Question Period. The posturing, the banging on desks, and the shouting made us think of school kids. And like children in the school yard, the men seemed to be constantly jockeying for territory and dominance."[46]

For women politicians whose job experience is in the professions, particularly health care, teaching, and social service, and who are trained to take a more collegial, holistic approach to decision-making, the political landscape seems alien, riddled with landmines, and difficult to navigate. Many women do not want to play the game by the age-old masculinist rules; it is just not their style. A female legislator in BC explained the atmosphere this way: "it functions on anger, pure and simple, and the ability to control, manipulate, use, display anger, and of course, along with anger goes a big, loud, voice, being tall, being imposing, all of those things which obviously play to male experience, male strengths, male conditioning."[47]

In this sense, then, women politicians are damned if they do, damned if they don't. If they avoid the fray, they may be squeezed out of important discussions, overlooked, or not taken seriously. They may not be able to get the job done. On the other hand, if they embrace the aggressive and adversarial techniques typical of parliamentary exchanges, they run the risk of being labelled unwomanly. The classic example is the much-broadcast and pilloried image of Liberal "rat packer" Sheila Copps leaping over chairs to confront Sinclair Stevens, a Conservative cabinet minister caught out in a conflict-of-interest scandal and bent on avoiding questions from a parliamentary committee. This "chair hopping" incident happened almost 20 years ago but is still used to brand Copps's behaviour as hyper-aggressive and unseemly. And it has served to caution other female aspirants, as political scientist Don Desserud's interviews with women politicians in New Brunswick found. Two female politicians told him that it was important "for women not to be too aggressive."[48]

Babes in Boyland:[49] A Hostile Working Environment

The CBC-Angus Reid survey discussed earlier in this chapter provided statistical verification of women politicians' experiences with sexism and sexual harassment in Canada's legislatures. The majority of female legislators, 60 per cent, said they had endured inappropriate or demeaning gender-based remarks, and 31 per cent reported fending off unwanted sexual advances or propositions. First in the capacity of an MPP and, later, as an MP, Sheila Copps experienced it all, wrote journalist Sydney Sharpe: "Copps came in for a special brand of sexist insult. Over the years, she was called 'baby,' 'slut,' 'witch' and 'a goddamn ignorant bitch.'"[50] Copps reported in her autobiography that government members of the Ontario legislature regularly commented on her looks, weight, bra size, and voice.[51] The 1980s were a particularly difficult time for women politicians; although they were relatively few in number, they seemed poised to challenge the complacency of the old boy's clubs. Alexa McDonough still has the nasty notes male MLAs passed to her when she was the lone woman in the Nova Scotia legislature in the early 1980s.[52]

Some of the maltreatment women experience includes sexual harassment and sexual assault. A fellow MPP attempted to sexually attack Sheila Copps, then a member of the Ontario legislature, a move Copps referred to as a "pass."[53] In the late 1980s, Alberta NDP MLA Pam Barrett was aggressively "hugged" by a succession of male Conservative MLAs; a female Conservative cabinet minister was groped by a cabinet colleague, and another female minister was demeaned with the label "Miss Pretty Minister."[54] Manitoba's Sharon Carstairs received the tired, clichéd, sexist message directed at "uppity" women:

> Shortly after I was elected leader of the opposition, a card arrived at my office. [My assistant] assumed that it contained a congratulatory message, so she put it on my desk unopened. I took the card out of the envelope and read the outside message which said, "WHAT IS AN

EIGHT LETTER WORD FOR WHAT YOU NEED?" Inside it read, "AGOODLAY."[55]

In the Ontario legislature in the early 1990s, opposition members demeaned female members of the Rae government by mocking their voices and blowing kisses at them, prompting cabinet minister Marion Boyd to observe: "I work in a very hostile workplace." Another NDP MPP said she experienced the angry and antagonistic legislative culture, particularly the constant yelling, "almost as abuse or violence."[56] Marion Boyd was so concerned about negative working conditions for women in the Ontario legislature that she made a submission to the Standing Committee on the Legislative Assembly in 1992. In her report, Boyd highlighted the incidence of "language demeaning to women; efforts to humiliate and intimidate women; the use of sexist language; and a general mood of disrespect in the House."[57] This type of behaviour has not disappeared along with the twentieth century. In the BC legislature, when NDP leader Joy MacPhail "rises to challenge Campbell's government during Question Period, Liberal MLA's behind her whisper obscenities and other rude comments."[58]

MP Barbara Greene told the House of Commons in 1991 that "systemic sexual discrimination and harassment are rampant."[59] Greene and the late *Toronto Star* columnist Carol Goar had both been physically assaulted in a poorly-lit Commons parking lot, prompting women MPs and staff to approach the Speaker's office and demand better lighting in the parking area. These and other incidents involving lack of safety and chauvinism, including the misogynist comments, rudeness, and outright harassment such as that experienced by Sheila Copps and others, prompted female MPs to cross party lines and form the Association of Women Parliamentarians (AWP) in 1990. The AWP sprang into action in 1991 when a Conservative MP called Sheila Copps a "slut" during a Commons debate. The AWP condemned the remark, countering with a proposal to increase the power of the Speaker of the House to discipline MPs who make sexist, homophobic, or racist comments. While the association lasted only as long as the thirty-fourth Parliament, it brought together women from the three major parties to address matters of mutual concern, especially the obstacles to women's participation in political life. Cross-party cooperation among legislators is very rare indeed, especially in parliamentary systems.[60] The creation of the AWP is itself evidence of the severity of the problems it sought to address as all women legislators felt their negative experiences demonstrated the need for reforms.

BOX 5.4: A Hostile Profession

Women legislators confront:
- verbal insults, name-calling, and gender-specific criticisms;
- intimidation through aggressive speech or body-language;
- sexual harassment—comments about looks, weight, and sexuality, as well as inappropriate gestures and comments; and
- sexual assault—from sexual advances and propositions to attacks.

Women politicians often find support and encouragement inside their party caucuses from both male and female colleagues, but encounter hostility and harassment in their interactions with members of opposing parties. Women in the NDP caucus of Saskatchewan's Romanow government reported that, while the relatively large number of women in caucus provided a supportive atmosphere, interactions between parties remained unchanged.[61] For instance, male NDP MLAs called Liberal leader Lynda Haverstock the "princess of darkness." A legislative reporter described their highly personalized attacks on the opposition leader as vicious and disrespectful. Similarly, Manitoba MLAs related positive, collegial relationships within caucus, regardless of party, and said the increased numbers of women prompted new standards of behaviour in the House, including replacing the traditional desk-thumping with clapping. However, the women legislators also endured sexist comments and behaviours in the legislature. In the 1980s, a male MLA suggested "that a female member deserved a slap." As recently as the early 1990s, male MLAs made gun-shooting gestures and pelvic thrusts at women when they rose to speak. Manitoba NDP politician Judy Wasyliycia-Leis recalled that the harassment became more overt and opposition MLAs more hostile when members spoke in support of women's issues.[62]

Female politicians who adopt the label "feminist" or voice women's policy demands often come in for a particularly nasty brand of criticism. "In the 1970s, Flora MacDonald was regularly heckled in the House— sometimes by her own Tory colleagues—for raising women's concerns, such as the unfairness of laws that robbed women of pensions after their husband died."[63] Marie Laing, who served in the Alberta legislature from 1986 to 1993, persisted in raising women's experiences with discrimination and demanded policy changes to raise the status of women. She reported at times feeling personally attacked in the legislature because of her support for women. For instance, (then) Conservative back-bencher Stockwell Day accused Laing of "browbeating" members of the assembly with her "irresponsible" views on women's rights."[64] Years later, Laing recalled feeling emotionally battered when she left the chamber at the end of sessions.

Catch-22: How to Entice More Women without More Women?

The perils of the "testosterone tabernacle" create a dilemma. According to federal cabinet minister Anne McLellan, "More women aren't going to go into politics until they start to see a more constructive tone, less about theatre, less about scoring points and more about actually work-ing on the issues of the day in a constructive way that gets things done."[65] Alberta Liberal MLA Laurie Blakeman agrees, arguing that the compet-itive and nasty elements of political life may discourage some women from contemplating a political career: "Do they really want to put them-selves in a position where they are heckled about their weight, their looks, whether they are wearing makeup or not?"[66] The CBC-Angus

Reid survey of women politicians found widespread agreement that electing more women would help make legislatures more civilized and respectful places in which to work.

There is some evidence to suggest that electing more women can change the tone and style of legislative debate. For example, during the period from the mid-1960s to the mid-1980s in PEI, "the mood among the major parties and in the Assembly remained chilly, and at times hostile, toward participation by and representation of women." But the presence of more women in the PEI assembly in the early 1990s led one MLA to say that decorum had improved and that the language had become more gender-neutral.[67] NDP women in Ontario succeeded in achieving a more collegial atmosphere, at least for the duration of the Rae government. Pat Duncan reported that the Yukon legislature, while home to the highest percentage of women representatives, agreed to adopt non-sexist language. As well, while Premier, she pressed for consensus on the need to avoid violent terms and images in parliamentary debates.[68]

But these types of changes will not happen unless more women are represented. As already shown in Chapter 3, the numbers are not going up. Herein lies the classic catch-22. As former BC MLA Rosemary Brown puts it, because "both the hierarchical structure and the patriarchal history and nature of politics make it a hostile profession for women, it has for too long been the private and exclusive domain of men."[69] Journalist Susan Delacourt agrees the system needs to be fixed before many more women will be enticed to enter legislatures, but is unlikely to be renovated by men. And the "cost of *not* fixing it could be a political world that alienates everyone except the old boys who created it."[70]

Conclusion

Canada's newly elected women—the "Spice Girls" who claim "girl power" in the political arena—enter legislatures full of optimism, bursting with ideas and potential, and eager to make change. Flush with success in their personal and professional lives outside politics, empowered by their electoral victories, they may believe they can accomplish whatever they set their minds to do. And perhaps some of them can, despite the circles of constraint drawn by a legacy of institutionalized sexism and gender-based assumptions about a woman's proper place. The continued bad behaviour of the "Old Spice Boys"—men who resist women's entry into political life because it challenges their own power and privilege— enervates some women legislators. Sexist assumptions, verbal and sexual harassment, and anti-feminist rhetoric serve notice to women politicians that they have overstepped time-honoured gender boundaries. But often the biggest obstacle to women seeking a place in political life is resistance to change. Change, much needed though it is, has been slow and piece-meal. The lack of meaningful social change designed to make elected office more women-friendly continues to buttress a destructive form of circular reasoning: "Politics is a man's game; that's just the way things are." Knowing all this, why would women choose a career in politics? The answer is simple. Many do not.

As long as the behaviour inside legislatures is allowed to continue, as long as the media persist in questioning the competence of women politicians,[71] and as long as the public is encouraged by politicians and the media alike to evaluate women legislators according to a gendered double-standard, women will not take their rightful place in public life. Comments on women's looks, personalities, and sex lives litter women's experiences with electoral politics. Observations about Ellen Fairclough's hats in the 1950s, Judy LaMarsh's favourite recipes in the 1960s, the "**Flora Syndrome**" in the 1970s (where party members promised to support Tory MP Flora MacDonald's leadership bid but did not actually vote for her), Sheila Copps's assertive style in the 1980s, and Kim Campbell's love life in the 1990s—all illustrate a pattern of inappropriate scrutiny of female politicians' personal lives.[72] Until sexism is seen for what it is, challenged, and changed, this socially inappropriate behaviour will continue to prevent women from receiving balanced, equitable, and fair treatment in electoral politics in Canada.

CHAPTER 6

Counting for Something:
Women in Politics Can Make A Difference

Introduction

The purpose of the **electoral project** is to elect more women to legislatures, with an eventual target of about 50 per cent seats for women. Regardless of what phrase is used to describe this goal—the electoral project, equality in representation, **gender parity**—its aims are balance, equity, and fairness. To suggest otherwise is to imply that women, who comprise more than half the population, do not merit their fair share of political power. In addition, many of the advocates for increasing the political presence of women, like us, are not content with **symbolic representation**, though we recognize its importance. We also think women in politics ought to make a difference for women. However, there is strong disagreement about who can do this and how. According to former NDP leader Alexa McDonough, electing more women will not actually benefit women unless female legislators are willing actively and persistently to voice women's policy goals:

> I don't know if there is a magic number [of women]. You don't have to look any further than Prince Edward Island to see a good example of how it doesn't make much difference when the women support the same policies as the men who came before them. If they're not prepared to be feminists and activists, then I don't really think it makes any difference. Sometimes I think it can actually be counter-productive, because if women are going to carry on the old boys' traditions, then the system becomes hostile to progress that the majority of women really need.[1]

Is it true that women only make a genuine difference when they act as advocates for women, that is, when they accept the **mandate of difference** and focus on representing women's aspirations and needs? This controversial topic is the subject of the present chapter. What does making a difference for women mean in conceptual and practical terms? What are the political and structural factors shaping the ability of women elected to Canadian legislatures to have a demonstrable impact on political outcomes? Are some legislators more likely to achieve this goal than others? Is McDonough right when she says that female politicians who are not prepared to be feminist advocates will not count for much in the quest for gender equality?

We begin this chapter by exploring the strategies available to legislators who want to voice women's concerns and indicating the types of change that with a concerted effort can be made. The second part of the chapter argues that counting for something is certainly more than an issue of numbers, as the rules and practices of the parliamentary system shape what legislators can do and say while in office. We summarize three studies on the political impact of electing more female representatives to serve in Canada's legislatures. These studies confirm that an elected representative's ability to influence policy is determined in large part by the system of political representation itself and the rules that operate in it as well as by the structures of political power. Any evaluation of women's political contribution to legislative outcomes, therefore, must take these institutional constraints into consideration.

One of the key features of parliamentary government is executive dominance. Accordingly, policy-making power lies in cabinets. The third section of the chapter considers the numbers of women who sit at the cabinet table in contemporary Canadian governments. We argue that the trend illustrated in Chapter 2—that the percentage of women appointed to prestigious and powerful positions reflects the percentage of women elected—is borne out by the data on women in cabinets. In the future, women's access to powerful portfolios will become another measure of the advances women make in holding top jobs on an equal footing with men.

The final part of this chapter is the most controversial. We part ways with many feminist scholars on the issue of which women politicians actually count for something. Feminist political scientists, politicians, and women's movement activists tend to believe that female representatives make a difference for women when they actively promote the status of women. After all, if female representatives fail to voice women's concerns, what is the point of electing more of them? In contrast, we argue that it is necessary to elect more women, and more diverse women, from right-wing non-feminists like Reform and now Canadian Alliance MP Deborah Grey to left-leaning feminist advocates such as Alexa McDonough. In this section, we outline our reasons for maintaining that all women, regardless of their ideological position, stance on feminism, or for that matter, their ethnicity, sexual orientation, and able-bodied-ness, deserve a representative voice in public office.

How Can Women Politicians Count for Something?

If you question five different people about what they think is meant by "women making a difference in politics," you will likely come up with five different answers. What is the mandate of difference? Is there only one? As well, how do political representatives make a difference for women? Let us start with how many women it takes to make a difference: anywhere from 10 per cent to 20 per cent to 40 per cent or higher, depending on which answer one accepts. One in ten, one in five, two in five, or more women legislators may be needed depending on the type of electoral system and the ideology of the party in power for women legislators to begin to produce results that benefit women. For women to achieve equality for women more generally in society, the percentage needed in legislatures might be 60 per cent or even higher. We are not even close to that goal.

The electoral project is animated by the belief that change can be made by and for women through formal institutions of political power. In other words, electing more women creates the possibility that women's presence will alter behaviour in legislative settings and policy outcomes in legislation. Women have different experiences than their male counterparts because of physiological factors (reproduction, child-bearing, and so on) and the social construction of gender in Canadian society (socialization, roles, income, and dependency on the state based on sex). The sexual division of labour and gendered role expectations are reflected in women's unequal status in the job market, unequal pay, and continued responsibility for child care and domestic duties. As well, because women are no more a universal category than men, women's "difference" includes their diversity. "Class, age, ethnicity, race, physical ability, sexuality, parenting and life stage have a determining effect on women's lives, much the same as they do on men's lives."[2]

While some scholars and activists question the ability of a few women to make change from the inside,[3] many believe that some women politicians will engage in gender-based representation. According to political scientist Lisa Young, the mandate of difference includes the expectation that "women, once elected, will act in the interests of women."[4] But the interests of women appear to be as varied and diverse as the women who hold them. Women's needs and policy demands may, in fact, conflict.

Some may dismiss the mandate of difference argument on the grounds that women's interests are neither singular nor homogeneous and, thus, cannot become the basis for measuring the contribution of women legislators to modern governance. We do not expect men's interests to be easily summed up, so why would anyone expect women's interests to be uniform and consistent? It seems more reasonable to argue that the wide-ranging interests, ideas, and legislative goals held by women and men can only be fully represented by electing legislators with a diversity of backgrounds and ideologies.

Conceding that women's interests are indeed complex and diverse does not mean there is no such thing as representing women's interests. Women's policy needs are more likely to be expressed effectively when legislators are willing to represent both **women's issues** and **women's perspectives**. Women's issues are defined as those matters "where policy consequences are likely to have a more immediate and direct impact on significantly larger numbers of women than on men."[5] Women's issues, such as breast cancer research, pay equity, and domestic violence, mainly affect women, though they certainly have an impact on men. Approaches to women's issues may be feminist in orientation, focusing on women's rights or other feminist goals, such as measures to increase the number of women elected to Parliament or to ensure reproductive rights.

However, women's issues may also be framed in a more traditional manner, reflecting the sexual division of labour. This is evident when men are regarded as categorically "best" at performing functions related to the public sphere of government while women are seen to "thrive" in the private sphere of the domestic home and family.[6] For example, while the implementation of a homemaker's pension is controversial in the feminist community, it can certainly be classified as a women's issue. Clearly, there are multiple policy options concerning any given women's issue. For instance, on the issue of child care, parties operating from a neo-conservative orientation are likely to stress women's needs as mothers and advocate measures designed to strengthen the traditional family model. Left-leaning or social democratic parties, on the other hand, are more likely to focus on women's roles as workers and their need for flexible, affordable child care, thus arguing for an enhanced role for governments in child care provision and promotion of parental leave.

"Making a difference for women" goes beyond policy measures in areas designated as women's issues. Something important is left out of this analysis: policies may not affect larger numbers of women than men but may actually affect some women *differently* than many or all men. A differential effect may be experienced based on gender in matters as diverse as taxation, health, and international development. We can call this aspect of representation women's perspectives, since it involves introducing women's views on all policy concerns. For instance, changes to the Canadian Employment Insurance rules that require workers to put in a certain number of consecutive hours on the job before they can qualify for benefits have affected many women differently than most men. Women are more likely to be employed in part-time and casual positions and, thus, are less likely to meet the changed EI requirements. Representation of women's perspectives should reveal the gendered implications of such a policy move. How can elected legislators bring up women's issues and perspectives? Linda Trimble's work on women in the Alberta legislature reveals five different, but overlapping, strategies for expressing women's issues and women's perspectives in Canadian legislatures.[7]

The first strategy is to alter the masculine, aggressive style of legislative politics by changing (or at least challenging) the traditional, adversarial, and conflict-ridden style of legislative debate described in Chapter 5. Advocating a more cooperative style may encourage greater collegiality and even cross-party cooperation, thus allowing legislators to eschew the "game" and focus instead on issues and ideas. Changing the approach to political discourse and decision-making may also attract more women to political careers.

Secondly, women can exercise their legislative voice by articulating women's diverse experiences, ideas, needs, and policy goals. This strategy involves introducing concerns typically considered "private matters" into political debate, thus engaging the feminist strategy of making the personal political. As well, it includes recognition that women speak with many voices, and have different experiences based on class, ethnicity, sexual orientation, language, country of origin, and ability.

The third strategy is advocacy: interacting with women's groups and organizations that provide services to women in an effort to link the women's movement to the state. This link can go two ways; it can provide legislators with "ground up" information about women's lived realities, and it can allow legislators to interpret government policies for the women's movement.

Fourthly, female legislators can introduce gender-based policy analysis by engaging in gender-and-diversity sensitive analysis of policy proposals or legislation in all areas, from taxation to social services, and in all phases, from the initiation to the implementation stage of policy deliberation. Such analysis can identify policy gaps and improve outcomes.

The fifth and perhaps most important strategy is action. Elected women can demand results and outcomes that benefit women and introduce policies designed to meet women's needs or enhance the status of women.

According to the International Institute for Democracy and Electoral Assistance (IDEA), employing these strategies can lead to four types of change, each of which can produce measurable outcomes for women.[8] The first is institutional and procedural change or alterations to representative institutions themselves, designed to make legislatures more "woman-friendly." Such measures include the procedural changes discussed in Chapter 5 (regular hours, elimination of night sittings, on-site child care, firm legislative calendar), as well as increased gender awareness and sensitivity to diversity in legislative procedures and discussions.

The second type of change is representational, and it includes measures to secure and improve women's rates of electoral success, including changes to electoral laws and regulation of political parties designed to boost the number of women candidates. Also, rules requiring the appointment of women to important parliamentary and government positions can affect women's access to power.

Thirdly, women can influence legislative outputs by changing laws and policies in women's favour. "This includes both putting women's issues on the agenda and ensuring that all legislation is woman-friendly or gender-sensitive."[9]

Discourse change is the fourth avenue for reform; this involves changing the language and content of political discussions both inside and outside of legislatures so that women's perspectives are regarded as valid, important, and intrinsic to political discussions. Discourse change stretches the boundaries of the political agenda so that discussions of matters such as domestic violence, stalking, gay rights, and mobility needs of persons with disabilities are considered to be valid topics for political discussion and action.

BOX 6.1: Strategies for Change

How Can Legislators Make Change for Women?

- By *altering* the style and format of political debate.
- By *voicing* women's diverse experiences, ideas and policy needs.
- By *advocating* on behalf of, and providing information and advice to, women and women's groups.
- By *analyzing* policy issues with women's interests and perspectives in mind.
- By *acting* to promote women's policy demands and meet women's diverse needs.

What Types of Changes Can be Made to Improve the Status of Women?

- *Institutional change:* making representative institutions more accommodating to women.
- *Discourse change:* promoting recognition and validation of women's perspectives and issues, in all their diversity.
- *Impact/Output change:* changing laws in women's favour; policy changes promoting the status of women.
- *Representational Change:* improving women's representation in politics and legislatures.

Do women legislators employ these strategies and achieve these types of change? Studies conducted around the world conclude that sometimes they do, and sometimes they do not. It depends. Female legislators are not free radicals, able to act independently and autonomously to make change. They are constrained by rules, long-standing practices, and procedures. As we saw in Chapter 5, their ability to act is shaped by the "taken for granted" world of unspoken but powerful traditions. And the numbers game is important, too.

When Do Women Count for Something?

According to the International IDEA, the "actual impact women parliamentarians can make will depend on a number of variables, including the political context in which the assembly functions, the type and number of women who are in parliament, and the rules of the parliamentary game."[10] In Canada, all of these factors are important. As has been found in other countries, electing women in sufficient number is a crucial first step towards substantive representation of women's interests and perspectives.

The Critical Mass Hypothesis

Studies conducted when women were very poorly represented in political office in the United States and Western European nations found that the primary impact of female politicians was symbolic.[11] That is, while their presence shook up established gender boundaries and challenged the conception of politics as a man's game, these female legislators seemed reluctant to give voice to women's perspectives, discuss women's issues, or promote feminist policy measures. Sociological studies also indicated the difficulties experienced by women entering male-dominated professions in changing the professional ethos. These studies suggest that women can only make a substantial difference to political discourse and public policy when they are present in more than token numbers. In other words, a **critical mass** of women is a prerequisite for change.

Evidence from Norway suggests that "when female representation [in Parliament] reaches at least fifteen percent it begins to make a difference."[12] However, there is no consensus on the number of women required for a critical mass, as even small numbers can produce significant results in some cases, while in others larger numbers of women may not have a measurable impact. Some scholars suggest "the presence of even one woman will alter male behavior,"[13] but others argue that 30 per cent or more women legislators will be insufficient to challenge long-established patterns of discourse, decision-making, and institutional norms.[14] In general, though, studies of western democratic countries with larger numbers of women in legislatures, especially in Scandinavian countries, find that as the number of women legislators grows, it becomes easier to exercise the mandate of difference.

The presence of women in more than token numbers "normalizes" their existence as legislators and makes them feel more comfortable when articulating new ideas, challenging rules, or directing policy. For example, Liberal MP Mary Clancy served in the first Chrétien government, 1993–97, and remembers pressing the party brass to include women on the finance committee: "[they said] women have never been on the finance committee. I said, 'I don't care!'"[15] Do it because it is the right thing to do, she implied. As well, if sufficient numbers of female legislators discuss women's issues and introduce women's perspectives in legislative settings, their male counterparts seem inclined to follow suit.[16]

Rules of the Game: The Parliamentary System

There is a link between the number of women elected and the difference they can make to the policy discussions and outcomes of legislatures, but it is not a clear and uncomplicated connection. The rules of parliamentary systems shape their ability to voice women's concerns. Even if female legislators are motivated to introduce women's perspectives and discuss women's issues, they must abide by the procedures governing participation in legislative processes such as debates, committees, party caucuses, question period, and votes. With the exception of the Northwest Territories and Nunavut, where no political parties exist to structure debate, the Canadian parliamentary system features strong **party discipline**. As discussed in Chapter 5, party caucuses (all those elected to serve under the banner of a particular party) serve as cohesive, united teams, and members are expected to accept the party line, or behave as if they accept it, as well as to vote in support of the party's position.

Party discipline, which is the practice of legislators voting with their party, is particularly important to the party in government, because losing a vote on an important piece of legislation, or failing to defeat an opposition party's motion of non-confidence in the government, means the executive (first minister and cabinet) must resign. In short, if a governing party loses a vote, it loses power, and an election typically follows. While party discipline is less crucial to opposition parties, it is important that they appear to have a unified and coherent purpose, especially if they wish to be seen as a "government in the making." Parties that display political infighting, air fractious policy stances in public, or permit leadership disputes to come to light, are, as the examples of turmoil in the Canadian Alliance and federal Liberal Party clearly indicate, criticized by other parties as well as the mass media for their lack of direction and cohesion.

For women legislators who are motivated to represent women's issues and perspectives, party discipline may present either an opportunity or an obstacle. On the one hand, if their party addresses women's issues in its platform, is willing to engage in at least some of the four types of change discussed above, and encourages caucus members to employ various strategies to introduce women's perspectives and goals, then party discipline can empower representation by and for women. If, on the other hand, the party sees women's perspectives as particularistic "special interests," and is anti-feminist to the extent that it regards women's issues as contrary to the public good, party discipline will thwart legislators who seek to make change. Women legislators who wish to speak with a feminist voice on women's issues are not likely to be

drawn to the second type of party. But what about parties whose ideological stance situates them somewhere in the middle, or whose strategy
is pragmatic, or, for that matter, who simply have not developed a clear
consensus on gender issues? In these instances, the existence of a critical mass of women within the party caucus may be the determining
factor; if they can build coalitions with men in the caucus, they may be
able to build support for women's perspectives and develop stances on
women's issues. In sum, party ideology and party positions on policy
issues are a key determinant of all legislators' ability to speak and act for
women regardless of their gender.

In parliamentary systems, like Canada's, the connection between
numbers and power is mediated by the structure of power and the
nature of decision-making. As Trimble found, what "Canadian women
say and do in legislatures depends largely on where they sit."[17] Except for
Nunavut and NWT, Canadian legislatures are organized into the
government and opposition, and the government is further divided into
front and back benches. For the party in power, the front benches are
occupied by the prime minister or premier and the members of cabinet.
The so-called "backbench" consists of all the members of the governing
party caucus without cabinet responsibilities. Policy-making is largely
in the hands of first ministers and their cabinets, though sometimes
"ordinary" representatives, that is, opposition members and governing
party backbenchers, can wield a measure of authority. Any elected representative can shape political discourse by raising issues, challenging
government positions or lack of action, and introducing motions, peti-
tions, and private members' bills. Sometimes such actions lead governments to respond by changing policy or introducing new legislation.
However, the simple fact of the matter is that policy is made by the executive; thus, women who make it to the cabinet table will have significantly more policy-making power than their female counterparts on the
backbenches or in the opposition ranks.

The final aspect of parliamentary systems affecting women's substantive representation is the structure of debate and discussion. Members

cannot simply speak when they want, on the subjects of their choice. And different types of debates offer varying levels of freedom when it comes to speaking one's mind. Parliamentary procedures include debates on motions, daily question period, private members bills, private members' notices of motion, and private members' statements to the House. Smaller venues for discussion include caucus and committee meetings. Voting is another avenue of expression, though it tends to be tightly organized along party lines, as noted above. Free votes, instances where legislators are freed from party allegiances to "vote their conscience," are very rare in Canada. Even so, they provide another window of opportunity for coalition-building and innovation. These processes can be assessed for the opportunities and constraints each poses for legislators wishing to speak and act for women's interests.

It is often assumed that legislators have their say during debates, which allow them to speak for an allotted period of time on a motion, usually a motion to introduce legislation for second or third reading of a proposed bill, though motions can be about matters other than legislation. MPs and MLAs generally toe the party line in debates unless they are to be followed by a free vote.[18] In other words, the party position usually determines whether or not a legislator can introduce a gendered analysis. Also, the main players in debates are cabinet ministers, as they are the ones who table legislation and speak in support of it. Party leaders also may play key roles, though private members can choose to play supporting roles.

What about the most visible aspect of parliamentary politics, the daily question period? As discussed in Chapter 5, the purpose of the question-and-answer exercise is for opposition party "teams" to attack the government, score public opinion points, and win the attention of the media. Question period is highly scripted and controlled, with opposition party leaders having first and privileged positions in the speaking order, and cabinet ministers replying according to the topic of the question. Accordingly, first ministers, cabinet ministers, and party leaders get the most "air time" in question period. Other opposition members are allowed to ask questions in their areas of policy expertise (sometimes called critic areas) when they fit within the overall party strategy for critiquing the government. Government party backbenchers can also ask questions of ministers, though these tend to offer sycophantic and self-serving queries, designed to curry favour with the party brass. The largest window of opportunity here is for opposition party members who see the government as vulnerable on women's issues. However, if gender equality is not on the public agenda, a women's perspectives strategy for critiquing the government will likely fall flat. There will be no uptake on the government side to demonstrate that it takes the issue seriously and will act.

Normally bills are introduced by the political executive (cabinet ministers), but rules occasionally allow legislation to be introduced by private members (opposition members and government party back-benchers). Though they rarely come to a vote, thus rarely make it into law, private members' bills provide an opportunity to introduce new policy ideas, thus pointing out gaps in the government's policy agenda. In the early 1980s Alberta opposition and government MLAs persisted in introducing legislation to create an Advisory Council on the Status of Women, thus drawing attention to the government's refusal to do so.[19] Again, if the legislator does not wish to run afoul of his or her party, such bills should be consistent with, or at least not contrary to, party policy.

Because they are appointed, senators may have more leeway in this area than their elected counterparts. For instance, in February 2002, Liberal Senator Vivienne Poy introduced a private member's bill to make the words of the Canadian Anthem, *O Canada*, gender-inclusive. Poy's bill was supported by at least one Conservative senator, Gerald Beaudoin, but opposed by a female senator from Poy's party, Anne Cools.[20] It is difficult to imagine such a bill being introduced by a Liberal MP in the House of Commons.

Private members' notices of motions and statements allow private members another avenue for voicing their own opinions (or those of their constituents) in legislatures. Motions are proposals that must be brought to a vote; members' statements can be made on any topic. These processes allow some flexibility, granting legislators "a sphere of autonomy to pursue and promote ... issues they consider to be important."[21]

Caucus meetings arguably provide legislators with the best opportunity to have their say without censure. These are private, usually confidential discussions of party business, designed to shape or consolidate policy stances and strategies for debates, question period, and other House business. Weekly caucus meetings are supposed to give legislators a safe place to disagree openly with their party, on the understanding that once agreement on a party line has been reached in caucus, the member will toe that line. Since party discipline is more important for governing parties, it is likely that governing party caucus meetings provide less freedom to challenge official party stances on women's issues. As we saw in Chapter 2, Liberal MP Carolyn Bennett's public criticism of the newly reconstituted cabinet led the prime minister to upbraid her in a caucus meeting. However, because the incident was quickly reported to the media, and because many Liberal backbenchers rushed to Bennett's defense, the prime minister then back-pedaled, publicly praising Bennett's work on behalf of women as Chair of the Women's Caucus.

Committee meetings can provide another opportunity for influence if the circumstances are right. The job of committees is to oversee policy development, so members of committees scrutinize legislation, question ministers and officials, and hold hearings. Committees can recommend legislation or offer suggestions for changes to proposed bills. Party discipline tends to determine the behaviour of Canadian parliamentary committees, but committees occasionally allow legislators to cooperate across party lines. A notable example of this is provided by the subcommittee on the status of women, formed in 1989 by the House of Commons Standing Committee on Health and Welfare, Social Affairs, Seniors, and the Status of Women. The sub-committee featured cross-party cooperation among women from three political parties on issues of violence against women and health care. The subcommittee's report, titled *The War Against Women*, "offered a holistic feminist analysis of the problem of violence against women" and made a variety of recommendations for policy change, some of which were acted on by the federal government.[22] Firearms regulations, sexual assault legislation, and breast cancer screening policies were influenced by the work of this sub-committee.

Finally, after all the caucus and committee meetings and debates are over, legislators vote on bills or motions. Unless the vote is a free vote, which releases legislators from the constraints of party discipline, those who do not vote with their party may be punished in a variety of forms such as being denied perks, ostracized, and even expelled from the caucus.

Two key conclusions can be drawn from this discussion of parliamentary rules and procedures in the Canadian context. First, there is not much leeway within the confines of party discipline and parliamentary procedures. Secondly, while parties heavily influence opportunities for influence, knowledge of rules and procedures is essential to any strategy for change. Legislators who want to make change for women need to learn the rules about law-making processes, hierarchical structures, traditions, and procedures, and they need to learn how to use them effectively. This type of knowledge can be gained from legislative experience, training, or effective mentoring. As such, it is likely that the ability to raise women's issues and perspectives increases with experience on the job.

The Evidence: Does Electing Women Matter?

Given these constraints, has the election of women to approximately 15 to 20 per cent of the seats in Canadian legislatures had a significant impact on parliamentary procedures, policy discussions, or outcomes? Three quantitative studies analyze the impact of women legislators in Canada. Sandra Burt and Elizabeth Lorenzin examined legislators' discussion of women's concerns during member's statements, question period, and debates in the first and third sessions of the NDP government in Ontario (1990–95). Manon Tremblay compared attention by male and female MPs to women's issues during the thirty-fifth Parliament (1993–97). Trimble tested the critical mass hypothesis at the provincial level by examining the impact of increasing numbers of female legislators in Alberta on the style, content, and direction of political debates between 1972 and 1995. All three studies showed that gender is not a significant concern of parliamentarians, as Canadian political representatives spend precious little time thinking about women's diverse experiences, discussing women's issues, or formulating policy with women's perspectives in mind. To a large extent, gender equality issues are not on the political agenda. Are women more likely than their male counterparts to put them there?

The answer, according to these three studies, is yes. In addition, Burt and Lorenzin emphasize the role played by partisanship, primarily the NDP, concluding that some parties are more open than others to women's perspectives. Tremblay demonstrates that some parliamentary activities are more susceptible to influence from women's perspectives than others. And Trimble shows how party ideology can mitigate the potential of a critical mass to benefit women.

Burt and Lorenzin's study of Bob Rae's NDP government in Ontario from 1990 to 1995 provides some evidence to support the proposition that women are more likely than men to talk about women's concerns.[23] Burt and Lorenzin expected the success of the NDP, a party that had a long history of support for feminist policy initiatives, coupled with a "critical mass of women" in the Ontario legislature (22 per cent) to produce measurable outcomes for women. As well, several of the women in the government caucus and in cabinet had been active in women's organizations prior to their election. This finding led the investigators to anticipate considerable attention to gender-related policy issues. They quantified the amount of attention given to women's issues as expressed in member's statements and during question period during the first and third legislative sessions and found, as expected, that the NDP were more likely to refer to women's interests than members of other parties. Seven per cent of the NDP speaking times mentioned women's concerns, compared to 3 per cent by Liberals and 4 per cent by Conservatives in the first session. The attention to gender-related issues increased in the third session in which 8 per cent of NDP speeches discussed women, compared with 5 per cent for the Liberals and 6 per cent for the Conservatives.

With the exception of the Liberal party, most of the limited attention to women's issues was voiced by male MPPs, but female legislators were proportionately more likely to mention women.[24] For example, in the first session, Liberal women, who comprised 13 per cent of the Liberal caucus, were responsible for 65 per cent of Liberal references to gender. Women in the governing NDP comprised 24 per cent of the caucus but were responsible for only 5 per cent of the party's statements on women in the first session. However, in the third session, NDP women registered 44 per cent of the party's statements on women's issues. Women in the NDP cabinet explained the first session results by saying they refused to take sole responsibility for women's concerns, urging all ministers to deal with women's issues from their own ministries.[25] For instance, questions about child care were directed to the minister responsible, instead of being handled by the (female) minister responsible for women's issues.

Burt and Lorenzin also considered the willingness of legislators to introduce women's perspectives during discussion of legislation by examining debates during second reading of all bills presented during the first session of the legislature. They found that NDP members "were more sensitive to women's concerns in the debates on legislation."[26] In particular, in debates on child support, male and female New Democrats alike discussed the experiences of friends and family, thereby engaging in the feminist strategy of making the personal political.

Manon Tremblay's study of the impact of women in the thirty-fifth Parliament (1993–97) also found some support for the proposition that female legislators are more likely than their male counterparts to speak about women's issues. Recognizing that certain parliamentary processes offer more freedom to speak outside the party's platform or introduce issues not on the government's legislative agenda, Tremblay distinguished between private members' bills, notices of motion, and statements, on the one hand, and legislative debates on the other. The former offer MPs more leeway in their individual interpretation of topics, while the latter are more directly influenced by party discipline. In the case of private members' bills, notices of motion, and statements, few MPs used these mechanisms to represent women's interests. Women's issues were raised infrequently and more often by female rather than male MPs, leading Tremblay to conclude that, despite the fact that women put women's issues onto the legislative agenda more often than men, "the results of their efforts may still be extremely limited."[27]

Legislative debates, while more restrictive, offer significantly greater opportunities for voicing women's issues and perspectives than do private member's bills, notices, and statements because debates comprise a much larger share of the House's business. During the course of the thirty-fifth Parliament, debates on a number of women's issues and issues of concern to women took place, including discussion of support payments, violence against women, gun control, and International Women's Day. Tremblay found that women MPs were more likely to seize these opportunities to address women's issues, as 93 per cent of them spoke on women's issues during debates, compared to 75 per cent of male MPs. On average, female parliamentarians spoke twice as often as men about women's issues in the House (14 and six times respectively). More women than men took advantage of the daily question period to intervene on women's issues, leading Tremblay to conclude that without the presence of a critical mass of women in the House of Commons, women's perspectives would have received significantly less attention in debates on issues concerning women. Still, women's issues are not of great concern to parliamentarians of either sex: "while women's issues represent a relatively minor field of interest for both women and men in Canada's House of Commons, they occupy a clearer place in the political universe of a larger proportion of female MPs."[28]

In the third study Trimble used content analysis to compare the role and impact of women politicians in Alberta from the early 1970s, when few women were elected, to the mid-1990s when female MLA's comprised a critical mass of over 20 per cent of the legislators.[29] She identified three time periods based on women's numeric representation in the legislature.

BOX 6.2: Women's Representation in the Alberta Legislature

- *1972–1985*

  Women held fewer than 8 per cent of the seats, and there were no female opposition members.

- *1986–1993*

  Women legislators increased first to 12 per cent, and then 16 per cent. The size of the opposition grew, and women members of the opposition parties participated in criticizing the government.

- *1993–1995*

  The Klein government came to power. Women made up almost 20 per cent of the members of the legislature. The NDP were no longer represented in the legislature.

Through the three periods, Trimble tabulated the participation of male and female legislators in all types of legislative debates, including motions, debates on bills, question period, and member's statements. By distinguishing between opposition and government members, as well as between cabinet and backbench MLAs, she was able to show how party affiliation and parliamentary role intersect with gender to shape the ability (and willingness) of legislators to voice women's interests and concerns. She found that numbers alone do not make the difference for women. **Opportunity structures** ("forces, structures and ideas that characterize official political systems and enhance or deter women's political participation"[30]) also exist and must be put to use.

As did the other studies, Trimble's research found scant attention had been paid to women's issues and perspectives overall, particularly during the first phase, 1972–85, when only a handful of women sat in the legislature. These few women all represented the governing Conservatives, who were at best indifferent, and at worst hostile, to feminist analysis and the claims of the women's movement. As Trimble comments, "the topic of irrigation ditches received more attention than did women."[31]

Still, she found that the context of legislative debate shaped opportunities for voicing a variety of women's interests. The Conservative women MLAs, none of whom identified themselves as feminists, nonetheless did use a "safe" space to discuss women's perspectives on a variety of issues. This space was created by debate on a motion advancing the creation of an advisory council on the status of women. It had no chance of coming to a vote and so posed no threat to official government policy. Several of the governing party backbenchers used their relative freedom during this debate to discuss a variety of issues facing women, including pay equity, farm women, pensions, and domestic violence.[32]

Trimble found that the amount of discussion about women's interests increased as more women joined the opposition side of the House after the 1986 and 1989 elections. The second phase, 1986–91, increased the number of women in the legislature, with the 1989 election providing a critical mass (15 per cent) of female MLAs. Perhaps more importantly, these elections greatly increased the size of the Liberal and NDP caucuses, thereby creating a critical mass of opposition MLAs and opening up possibilities for challenging the governing Conservatives. Confront them they did, with gender equality issues sometimes taking centre stage in the debates, and opposition women clearly taking the lead in advancing critiques of the government's record on the status of women.[33] Moreover, the presence of these opposition women, despite their relatively small numbers, had a significant impact on both the content and style of legislative debate, leading Trimble to argue that "a few good women" can effect considerable change. Larger numbers of women legislators matter less when the opportunity structures are receptive.

From 1986 to 1989, four opposition women were able to give voice to some women's experiences, offer a gender-sensitive analysis of policy initiatives, and demand policies to promote the status of women. Why? Because their parties either championed or did not oppose a woman-centred approach to policy analysis. In addition, both opposition parties benefited from such an approach. The Conservative government was vulnerable on women's issues, and opposition parties quickly seized on this weakness. As a result, women in the opposition (Liberals and NDP) were able to use the full range of parliamentary procedures (debates, question period, and private members' bills and motions) to advance women's issues and perspectives. The opportunity structures amplified the difference the women made.

Trimble found that women sometimes subvert traditional parliamentary processes in the interest of supporting each other and adopting a different style of legislative debate. During this period, women from all three parties avoided adversarial and bombastic rhetoric, often choosing instead to compliment each other in public and across party lines for good work on motions, statements, or legislation. For instance, a female cabinet minister praised the work of a female opposition member, calling her a "wonderful advocate for women." Behind the scenes, women from all three parties supported each other's efforts to represent women by passing notes of encouragement.[34]

However, despite increased discussion of women's issues generally, only certain groups of women had their interests and experiences represented during this period. Only one female MLA consistently spoke to women's different needs as shaped by ethnicity, culture, sexual orientation, mental or physical disability, and official citizenship status. Generally, women's diversity was ignored or glossed over, leading Trimble to conclude that while "the white, able-bodied heterosexual woman, in the guise of 'generic woman,' has at times been represented in the Alberta legislature, most of her real-life sisters have not."[35]

The election of the Klein Conservatives in June 1993 brought more women into the legislature, temporarily cast out the NDP from the House, and brought neo-liberal and neo-conservative policy ideas to the fore, many of which were in direct opposition to women's equality claims. In this altered opportunity structure, larger numbers of women legislators did not translate into beneficial legislative outcomes for women.

Trimble's research on the very first years of the Klein governments, from 1993 to 1995, shows that party ideology can easily overwhelm a critical mass of women legislators. The Liberals and Conservatives alike campaigned on a deficit-reduction platform, and the Liberal's fiscally conservative election rhetoric limited their post-election criticisms of the government. Attention to women's issues declined, and female MLAs no longer took the lead when advancing women's perspectives. Most of the gender-related discussion focused on the Klein government's dramatic deficit reduction measures, including spending cuts, privatization and de-regulation. What little attention was given to the differential impact of the program on different groups of women produced no substantial changes.[36] Women in general were victimized by the cuts, but solidarity among women legislators failed at a time when their concerted efforts were most needed.

Cooperation among women across party lines disappeared as a strategy, and legislative debates became increasingly testy and argumentative. While women in the Liberal opposition did critique the Klein government's policies on the grounds that they were harmful to women, their contributions to the legislative debate had no impact on public policy outcomes. The Conservative cabinet included several women, all of whom embraced the government's neo-liberal agenda. Where women at the cabinet table might have been expected to dampen the negative impacts of policy on women, in this case partisan commitment outweighed gender.

Attention to critical mass on its own only tells the tale when the opportunity structure remains receptive and stable over time. When the opportunity structures change—a partisan realignment, ideological retrenchment, or changes in the environment such as an economic downturn or perceived crises—what it takes to benefit women may also change. Numbers in and of themselves are not enough. However, without the numbers there are fewer possibilities of positive change for women.

BOX 6.3: Factors Affecting Women Legislators' Ability to Count for Something

---

- Their position in the legislature—governing versus opposition party, backbench or cabinet position.
- Willingness to speak up in support of women's perspectives.
- Party—some parties are more supportive than others.
- Party ideology can dampen or amplify the effects of having a critical mass of women legislators.

In summary, these three studies show that electing more women can make a difference for women, to the extent that women's interests become a topic of conversation for legislators from time to time. The evidence suggests that female representatives may be more likely than their male counterparts to put women's issues on the political agenda and to analyze legislation with women's perspectives in mind. Still, the link between the sex of the legislator and the ability to speak about women depends largely on the individual legislator's willingness to do so. Other factors also come into play such as party affiliation, legislative role, the character of party competition in the legislature, and the processes of parliamentary debate. Given all of these potentially countervailing factors, it is not at all surprising to find that even when hurdles to effective representation for women are overcome, and women's issues are discussed, the concerns being articulated by no means represent the experiences and policy needs of all women.

Women at the Cabinet Table

Trimble's analysis of legislative debates in Alberta shows that legislators representing opposition parties are somewhat less confined by party discipline than those sitting with governing parties, not the least of all because it is the job of the opposition to criticize the government. With their party's support and a firm grasp of legislative procedure, women on the opposition side of the House can enjoy more freedom to voice and act on women's issues. But they have little power to shape public policy, as this is the purview of the governing party. Women in cabinets have the greatest access to the levers of decision-making. At the same time, they are most tightly limited by party discipline because of the principle and practice of cabinet solidarity. Once policy decisions are reached in cabinet, all ministers must support the policy in public as well as in the legislature. As a result, cabinet solidarity can provide opportunities for women's activism, but it can also act as a barrier to the promotion of women's interests.

While women in opposition and governing party backbenches can raise issues of concern to women and press governments for gender-sensitive policy measures, women in cabinet in some circumstances can make policy decisions of benefit to women and other relatively economically disadvantaged groups. Of course, there is no guarantee that the presence of women legislators in decision-making positions will translate into concrete policy decisions designed to improve the status of women. In fact, women in cabinet may make no further advances for women at all. Our point is simply that gender-sensitive policy is more likely to be made with women at the cabinet table.

Rosemary Brown, a NDP MLA elected to serve in British Columbia in 1972, campaigned unabashedly as a feminist, defying her leader by calling for the creation of a women's ministry. Premier Barrett did not appoint Brown to his cabinet. In her memoirs Brown reflected on the implications of her exclusion from the inner circle:

> There is power, prestige, influence and money attached to a cabinet appointment. In cabinet I could have done more for women, visible minorities and other disadvantaged groups who made up my constituency. The Black community would have been proud and it would have been a clear and positive message to feminists about the NDP's support for women's rights.[37]

High quality representation increasingly requires genuine diversity in the representatives selected to serve in top jobs. Rosemary Brown's analysis points the direction in which future discussions of representation will go as voter turnouts at elections continue to sink.

TABLE 6.1: Women in Federal, Provincial, and Territorial Cabinets (July 2002)[1]

Jurisdiction	Government Party	Women Cabinet Ministers/ Total Cabinet Ministers	% Women in Cabinet	Women in Government Party Caucus	
				%	#/total
Canada (federal)	Liberal	10/39	26%	24%	40/170
British Columbia	Liberal	8/28	29%	21%	16/77
Alberta	Conservative	5/24	21%	20%	15/74
Saskatchewan	New Democrat	2/15	13%	24%	7/29
Manitoba	New Democrat	5/16	31%	28%	9/32
Ontario	Conservative	6/25	24%	16%	9/57
Quebec	Parti Québécois	6/30	20%	26%	18/69
New Brunswick	Conservative	3/15	20%	17%	8/47
Nova Scotia	Conservative	1/12	8%	10%	3/31
Newfoundland	Liberal	5/18	28%	26%	7/27
Prince Edward Island	Conservative	2/10	20%	23%	6/26
Yukon[2]	Liberal	4/8	50%	50%	4/8
Northwest Territories	N/A	0/8	0%	N/A	N/A
Nunavut	N/A	1/8	13%	N/A	N/A
Totals		**58/256**	**23%**	**22%**	**142/647**

[1] Junior ministers were not included in the tabulations.

[2] As this book was going to press, the Yukon Party won the November 4, 2002 Yukon election, defeating the Liberals. Only one of the 12 Yukon Party caucus members is female (8.3%); therefore, women will not be well represented in the new cabinet. Premier elect Dennis Fentie had not announced his cabinet by our publisher's deadline, so check the Still Counting website for an update of this table (http://stillcounting.athabascau.ca).

Sources: Federal, provincial, and territorial government websites (downloaded July 2002).

Since first ministers choose cabinet members from among their party caucuses, the number of women elected by the governing party delimits the female **pool of eligibles** for these prestigious, and powerful, positions. Table 6.1 shows that the impact of the numbers game is very clear.

In 2002 the percentage of women in cabinet was roughly proportionate to the percentage of women in the governing party caucus in all provinces and territories. Women held on average 22 per cent of the seats in governing party caucuses across the country and occupied about the same percentage of cabinet positions (23 per cent). In short, the number of women elected for the governing party determines the number of women in cabinet. The exception is Saskatchewan, where, as of 2002, women comprise 24 per cent of the NDP caucus but hold only two of 15 cabinet positions (13 per cent). This underrepresentation of women in cabinet may reflect the minority government status of the NDP, which holds power thanks to an alliance with a group of former Liberals who now sit as independents; two of them hold posts in the Calvert cabinet.

In the Canadian political system the presence of women at the cabinet table, where they have the opportunity to shape public policy in ways that reflect women's diverse needs and interests, is crucial to representative outcomes. Cabinet ministers oversee policy initiation, design, and implementation; consequently, they possess sufficient power to make decisions that have profound implications for the everyday lives of Canadian men, women, and children. As the cartoon at the beginning of this chapter illustrates, when she was Justice Minister Anne McLellan forwarded the gun control agenda that had been championed by many women's groups and victim's rights organizations. She implemented a firearms registry despite vocal opposition from the gun lobby, especially in her own Edmonton riding. We conclude, then, that the number of women at the cabinet table is arguably as important, and at times perhaps more important, than the overall number of women elected.

The Deb Effect

Deborah Grey (or "Deb," as she likes to be called) entered the federal legislative scene in 1989 when she won a by-election in Beaver River, Alberta, becoming the first member of the Reform Party of Canada to hold a seat in Parliament. Hers was the first voice on Parliament Hill to combine western alienation and "new right populism" and to put issues of concern to many Western Canadians on the public agenda. Active in Reform's transformation into the Canadian Alliance, Grey has remained true to her original political commitments over time, even to the point of being expelled from the Alliance for allegedly fuelling internal discontent and rancor over the issue of who can best lead the party. In July 2001 Grey joined the Democratic Representative Caucus, which cooperated for a time with the Progressive Conservatives in the House of Commons. After the March 2002 leadership contest, from which Stephen Harper emerged victorious over the increasingly unpopular Stockwell Day, overtures were made to the disaffected MPs. Deb Grey and her colleagues, minus one dissident, returned to the Alliance Party, their quarrel about the leadership resolved.

Grey happily claims her status as Mrs. Lewis Larson, declaring that she is neither a feminist nor a "Suzy, Miss stay at home in the kitchen."[38] Despite serving as interim leader of the Alliance party from March to September, 2001, and thereby as the first woman leader of the official opposition, Grey has been quick to deny any long-term leadership aspirations within her own party. While a Reform MP, she repeatedly told the media that she was pleased to follow a leader like Preston Manning. In turn, Manning described her as "the Prairie Margaret Thatcher."[39] Indeed, she expresses views that are non-feminist, even to the point, at times, of being anti-feminist. For instance, Grey is quoted as saying "women are just trying to lift themselves up to the detriment and expense of men."[40] On the other hand, she supported Sheila Copps in condemning John Crosbie's personal and sexist remarks in the House. Some women admire Grey's self-assertiveness; others decry her unwillingness to become a standard-bearer for women's issues. The "debutante" for a fiscally conservative right-wing agenda, Grey represents the "coming out" of the self-confident, right-wing woman, which is significant in and of itself. In the federal election held in 2000, for example, more women voted for the Alliance than for the NDP.[41] Small "c" conservative women are worthy of representation by one of their own as are feminists. Or are they? There is no consensus on the answer to this question.

Is it better to elect women, any women, or only the right sort of women? Some argue that "only one kind of elected woman has a chance to do any good—a firm feminist who makes it her business to enact legislation that eradicates inequality."[42] Others take this point even further. Is it not better for women, so the argument goes, to have as one's elected representative a progressive male such as Svend Robinson rather than a conservative woman like Deb Grey? The answer coming from the Left and the women's movement has generally been, "Better no woman than a non-feminist woman. A male supporter of feminism is preferable to Deb Grey." We disagree; in our capacity as feminists, women, citizens, and political scientists we support the election of diverse individuals regardless of their party stripe. If successful, the **Deb Effect** will produce beneficial outcomes for all women as well as for some groups of men that have received relatively poor representation.

By the Deb Effect we mean the deliberate choice to make considerably more public space available to more, and increasingly more diverse, sorts of women. The opening up of the representational function implied by a public commitment to diversity will be crucial to the future of Canada as a nation. In addition to the effect that principles of equity and fairness can bring to women's substantive representation, equality and democratic governance confer legitimacy to the entire political system, improving national unity, social cohesion, and the vitality of civil society. We may have to wait a considerable length of time for the merit of fair and equitable political representation as described here to become strongly enough rooted to support the social change required for women to become genuine co-participants in public life, on an equal footing and in roughly equal numbers with men. In the meantime, many more debutantes like Grey are needed. The public discussion of equality for women would be better served than is the situation at present by having many more women of every political stripe advance women's multiplicity of views.

Four reasons support our confidence in the Deb Effect as a motivator of change for women. First of all, the assertion that women will invariably receive "better" representation from a feminist man like

Robinson than a non-feminist woman like Grey implies that electing more women is a risky, perhaps even dangerous, proposition for women, while electing more men offers a "safer" representational outcome. How can the continued overrepresentation of men be "better" for women?

Secondly, the idea that women may be better represented by a feminist man than a non-feminist woman introduces a double standard. On the one hand, elected women all too often have been required to be superior to men in order to gain positions already held by disproportionate numbers of men without similar demands being made on them. On the other hand, male candidates are not required to be supporters of feminism in order to be considered electable. At the same time, non-feminist men are implied to be preferable to a non-feminist woman candidate. Women legislators ought to be able to be as mediocre, non-feminist, and in some instances as crude and offensive as many of the men who get elected and to hold poorly reasoned positions just as much as some of the men do. In the absence of balance, equity, and fairness, women politicians' skills and abilities are expected to exceed the general standards and to achieve a higher quality of representation. Women legislators should not be held to a higher standard than either men or most women. Once women are elected in proportions equal or superior to men, there will then be ample time to reconsider which women ought best to hold the range of seats available.

The third reason for championing the election of more women, including non-feminist women, is to ensure that women's interests and needs, in all their diversity, are represented in political debates and policy-making processes. The "Deb Grey versus Svend Robinson" choice wrongly suggests women's interests are somehow more homogenous than men's, requiring a certain type of representation. However, women's lived experiences and policy demands involve **representational diversity** (ideological, geographic, ethnic, linguistic, and so on). For both genders, representational diversity produces high quality representation.

The phenomenon we call "the Deb Effect" reminds us that the desire for diversity among our legislators is ideological as well as sociological.

Non-feminist women contribute as valuably to Canadian women's access to public life as feminist women legislators. Not only feminist women are in short supply. Any and all women, regardless of their ideological or partisan affiliation, ethnicity, ability, sexual orientation, and country of origin, are needed and valuable. We contend that the more women there are, the easier it becomes for them to differentiate themselves according to the political ideas they hold. Instead of being wrongly portrayed any longer as unwitting champions of a singularly coherent women's view, women legislators will then begin to be seen for what they have always been—diverse, relatively ordinary, and more unequivocally human than when their every utterance became "the women's view."

Deborah Grey provides a fine example. She has perhaps been the most eloquent and effective speaker in Parliament on the destructiveness of drunk driving. Outspoken women legislators like her, whether feminist or not, have the useful effect of dislodging complacency by introducing new ideas. Love her views or hate them, they engage citizens and the media in the public process. In the absence of continuity among the Reform/Alliance, Grey's voice continues to be heard in question period, in media scrums, and on news clips. Had she been with any party other than Reform, she probably would have had a good shot at a top job, perhaps even the top job. She is clearly not a creature of the political party culture that demands loyalty and discipline as a qualification for promotion. Grey still supports the advancement of women by broadening the public platform from which women address public issues. Even so, some feminists dislike her politics, going so far as to demean her contribution to women's presence in politics. Doing so, in our view, diminishes the cause of women's equality.

A fourth reason to support non-feminist and anti-feminist women's capacity to make a difference is its contribution to normalizing women's presence, without expecting them to be either "one or the boys," or "one of the girls." The presence of women legislators who are other than feminist both expands the pool of eligibles and promotes internal diversity among women legislators. The comfort level for all women legislators increases as they are further encouraged to be who they are as individuals rather than as mere standard bearers.

This brings us back to the numbers and our fifth and final reason for seeing positive outcomes from electing women with diverse ideological positions. For women, electoral representation is not a choice between being "better" represented by Deborah Grey or Svend Robinson; it is a matter of equality and democratic governance. The issue is equity and fairness, not men's inflated sense of entitlement or women's alleged "special interests." It may well be that women legislators perform at times better, as well, and, as poorly, as male legislators. Having women govern in the name of the electorate brings to bear principles of balance, equity, and fairness. Electoral politics in Canada remains largely a cipher for men's political ambition, power hoarding, and the reproduction of their own excessive sense of entitlement. The situation is changing but ever so slowly.

BOX 6.6: Rationale for Supporting the Deb Effect

- Progressive representation by men is no substitute for balanced, equitable, and fair representation by women.
- It challenges the double standard which embodies different, more stringent, expectations of female legislators.
- Diversity in representatives improves the quality of representation for everybody.
- Diversity normalizes the individual representative's capacity to feel comfortable being themselves.
- The issue is balance, equity, and fairness, not men's entitlements or women's alleged "special interests."

The results of gender-based representation that is balanced, equitable, and fair can be measured over time. In consequence, numbers continue to matter as one important indicator of social change. Electing more women, even many more right-wing women, will assist all women to advance further in Canadian society than holding out the hope that only feminist women or women whose partisanship is left of centre can make gender count for something in our legislatures and in public life. This is so because, as we have demonstrated in earlier chapters, women's influence in politics remains very much a numbers game. It is true that small numbers of dedicated and openly feminist women can and have influenced political outcomes. However, occasional successes are no substitute for the goal of approximating gender parity in our legislatures. As established in Chapter 2, as the numbers go, so go the chances of women being selected for top positions related to public life. The numbers of women legislators remain as they have always been the principal indicator of what women can expect as members of Canadian society.

Conclusion

Women do make a difference in politics. There is considerable evidence to suggest that when more women enter Canada's Parliament and legislatures, they alter the style, tone, content, and outcomes of political debate. Since women can only make a gender-sensitive difference in political life if they are present to do the work, effective representation of women's interests by women is only possible when women occupy half of the seats in legislatures and in cabinets. In short, women will exercise their fair share of formal decision-making power, including control of public policy directions and parity at the cabinet table only once the glass ceiling is shattered.

We think all female politicians make a difference for women regardless of their support for feminism, their varying desire to advocate on behalf of the women's movement, or their party affiliation and ideology. The election of a critical mass of women is insufficient effectively to represent women's many ideologies, experiences, and interests. Success at the glass ceiling level of 20 to 25 per cent may boost the attention given to women's issues, but these issues are typically discussed from a very limited range of perspectives. As we saw with the case of Alberta, aboriginal, ethno-racial minority, immigrant, poor, and disabled women and lesbians do not see their experiences and identities represented in the legislature. Electing more, and more diverse, women is essential to the full realization of the "Deb Effect," whereby a multiplicity of interests can be voiced, acknowledged, debated, and possibly even reconciled.

CHAPTER 7

Conclusion:
Halfway to Equal?

Anyone concerned about women's equality must still count numbers, although numbers certainly are not all that count. Attention needs also to be given to policy issues, as well as to broadening the range of people selected and the diversity of political perspectives aired. Until the numbers of women elected approach gender parity, however, the quality of representation will remain constrained by sex and race bias and the discrimination and artificial narrowing of viewpoints that implies. Equality between the genders remains an important political goal because it remains a key indicator of social change. Much work remains to be done if equality is to be realized.

Now, a few years after the turn of the century, fundamental political equality has yet to be achieved in Canada, a country championed as one of the world's leading examples of democratic governance. At present, women occupy about 20 per cent of the seats in this country's legislatures.

We have demonstrated that inequality in political representation continues to disadvantage women by denying them half of the seats, posts, appointments, and honours that would be theirs in a society in which gender was neutral. We conclude, then, that there continues to be a problem: without equality in political representation, women as a group are denied equal chances to plan and live their lives without having to endure the effects of disadvantages that result from gender bias. The level of women's electoral representation provides a quick, easy, and objective measure of Canada's social progress toward equality. Advances there have been, for some women. However, despite all of the public education and effort so far, the results across the country produced by the electoral system in election after election remind all Canadians that women are only halfway to equality. It is a good start, but it is not good enough.

In the chapters of this book we have shown that renewed attention to women's overall capacity to win elected office in record numbers is needed for the following reasons.

BOX 7.1: Reasons For Requiring Women's Success in Electoral Politics

- Women's presence in elected life has social meaning more generally for women's place in public life and Canadian society. Women's access to top jobs in public life is an important indicator of how a society values the status of women.
- Very real limits constrain prospects for further advancement in terms of women's electoral success for at least the next ten to 15 years.
- A leadership vacuum continues to underrepresent women. High ranking political positions remain a male preserve.
- Political life continues to exude masculinist and racialized assumptions, norms, and behaviours, which have the effect of excluding women, thereby denying them full opportunities for the exercise of political power.
- Despite all the constraints and obstacles, feminist and

> non-feminist women alike do make a difference in politics and will continue to do so.
> - The addition of many more, and more diverse, women in public life will enrich the social and political fabric of our country.

Taken together, the effect of the first four factors lead us to conclude that in the next 15 years the Canadian public is unlikely to see the changes needed to bring parity to Canadian political life.

> ### BOX 7.2: Electoral Changes Required to Bring Parity
>
> - Women elected to 50 per cent of the seats in Canada's legislatures.
> - Female legislators who reflect the full sociodemographic range of diversity among Canadian women.
> - At least one, and ideally several, woman elected to be first minister from among the current female legislators.
> - Women as leaders of political parties at roughly the same rate that women are legislators.
> - Women in 50 per cent of the positions of top jobs that give a human face to Canada at home and abroad.

With the exception of Sheila Copps, who will likely take a second run at the leadership of the federal Liberals, there are presently no strong female contenders for the leadership of any of the major political parties nor in other powerful political positions. This is very worrisome for what it suggests about future improvements in women's status in Canadian society in the short term. Women have their foot in the door and can sit among the country's leading political decision-makers, but they are not positioned to assume leadership of political parties, regardless of their personal qualities.

The political environment remains masculinist, much to the peril of any woman who dares presume to be able to do what other women politicians have failed to do. Women remain unlikely to attain leadership positions that actually entitle the winner to govern. Based on years of study of women who had a shot at such a role, we predict that in the next ten to 15 years, women's aspirations for political leadership will not be achieved, although a full century has passed since many women became eligible to vote and stand for election.

While political life has had a handful of women leaders, the structural sexism that prevents many more women from making a career in electoral politics is due, we maintain, to three factors.

BOX 7.3: Factors Leading to the Lack of Women in Political Life

---

- The length of time it took to move from eligibility for some to electability for a few: 50 years.
- The short 20–year span in which the underrepresentation of women in politics received attention as an identifiable problem on the public agenda worthy of policy solutions, that is, from roughly the mid to late 1960s to the mid to late 1980s.
- Current complacency with the status quo.

In short, the existing gendered leadership gap indicates gross underrepresentation by women, and this pattern will continue unless there is a concerted effort to address the problem. This gap is important for two reasons. First, it affects women's overall access to power; secondly, it shapes their ability to use political power to achieve social and political change. The absence of women in powerful decision-making positions has been explained time and time again in terms of collective success in getting elected to the House of Commons.

The rough rule is that women are selected to represent and speak for governments once they prove their electoral mettle. Successful election has been a very important indicator of what women could expect, and how visible they would be in public life. Such a presence also sets an example for women's participation in government and public-sector employment, as well as, in general, for the role of women as valued members of the body politic. Moreover, increased representation for women, in all their diversity, has the potential to change political discussions, decision-making processes, and policy outcomes. The persistence of a leadership gap means that women cannot count on the arena of formal politics for adequate representation or for much-needed changes to the way politics works.

Increases in the numbers of women elected in the last 15 years tend to overshadow the fact that now, more than 80 years after some women were eligible to stand for election to legislatures, Canadian women as a group are only halfway to equal. When we look at specific categories of women, it is plain that even less progress has been made. Aboriginal, poor, disabled, lesbian, and racial minority women are not even halfway toward the goal of fair and equitable representation. The truth of the matter is that going the distance to achieve equality with men in elected public office remains a formidable challenge. Energy for the struggle is flagging, although recent gains sustain continued hope that the rest will look after itself in due course. We will be happy if that turns out to be the case. However, our studies of the first leg of the race to equality leads us to conclude that the finish line is nowhere in sight.

Not Even Halfway to Equal

Canada exhibits a level of representation that is not even halfway to equal as measured by two key indicators: percentage of women leaders across Canada and percentage of women legislators. Chronic underrepresentation provides an objective measure of our nation's failure to value women by electing and appointing them to top jobs. This book has documented the fact that women are markedly, severely, and grossly underrepresented in key positions such as prime minister or premier as well as in cabinets and legislatures. These social facts present a public policy problem because they provide consistent and damning evidence of a gendered democratic deficit that reproduces systemic bias, thereby lending additional support to the opinion that women are entitled to less than men by virtue of their gender.

Redressing the gender skew in legislatures will go a long way toward ensuring that women take their rightful place in all areas of human endeavour. Reducing the gender imbalance and inequity will increase fairness by addressing a gendered democratic deficit. Women's place is in the legislatures, the courts, the government, and every walk of life. Ensuring that all citizens can make their life plans and realize them without being hindered by gender discrimination would go a long way toward eliminating other bases of discrimination as well.

BOX 7.4: Underrepresentation of Canadian Women

- Gross Underrepresentation: Less than 15 per cent
  - ° Women's presence in leadership of political parties, 1916 to the present
- Severe Underrepresentation: 15–30 per cent
  - ° Women's presence in most legislatures, including most Cabinets, barely achieved and only in most recent years
- Marked Underrepresentation: 30–45 per cent
  - ° Not achieved at any level of public life by women, including the Senate

---

Women legislators encounter glass ceilings, sticky floors, and revolving doors at the entry to leadership positions; uncertain opportunities for alliance building within and across parties; and attitudes and conventions of behaviour that constrain their capacity to act effectively. Their feminist, non-feminist, or anti-feminist identification is used to pit feminist women against humanists when any woman legislator can be one or both or none. At present, feminism divides women legislators along ideological lines, despite the fact that most female legislators believe that Canadian women, and men, have been well served by the presence of women in Canada's legislatures. Even if we disagree with any or all long-serving women legislators about their views, how they vote, or, even if they think women are important in public life, they deserve our thanks and high praise for persevering in a difficult, often ruthless, and highly competitive work environment.

In addition to valuing the courage and perseverance of women legislators, we need to step up the research agenda that documents opportunities to leverage increased prominence in public life for women. For example, which constituencies have never elected a woman representative, and which ones have elected many? Are women more likely to be elected in urban or rural ridings? Are some regions and parties more welcoming to women aspirants than others? Do women have better chances of being elected to vacant seats or of unseating incumbents? The lack of comprehensive, cross-jurisdictional answers to these sorts of questions itself deters women from entering political life. Moreover, who is responsible for making the appointments that deny women fair shares of top political appointments? What role does the Prime Minister's Office play in perpetuating the status quo? Can status of women's caucuses within parties get better results for women? Do we need an annual list of women leadership prospects who could be called up from the farm teams? One thing is certain. Complacency is the strongest factor to be considered. If women legislators, party executives, and the media do not demand more and better for Canadian women, nothing much will change.

For young women to choose politics as a career, a great deal more information and analysis is required. Without basic information on women's chances of electoral success, the pattern of severe underrepresentation by women will continue for at least the next three elections. Public education, media interest, and many more "uppity" women are needed to break the current impasse.

Canadian women demand equality that is real and meaningful. Legislatures with substantially less than half women further reproduce and intensify the disadvantages already experienced by girls and women by virtue of being female. Equality will be achieved once 40 to 60 per cent of seats in legislatures are held by women. Reaching that goal is a matter of fairness and equity for all Canadians. In the absence of the achievement of basic fairness for women we are ... still counting.

Appendix I:
Women Legislators and Senators, 1916–1969

Rank	Name	Elected/ Appointed	End Date yy.mm.dd	Years	Jurisdiction	Party
1	Louise McKinney	1917.06.07	1921.07.18	4	AB-MLA	Ind.
2	Roberta MacAdams Price	1917.06.07	1921.07.18	4	AB-MLA	n/a
3	Mary Ellen Smith	1918.01.24 1920.07.18 1924.06.20	1920.07.18 1924.06.20 1928.07.18	10 ½	BC-MLA	Ind.
4	Sarah Ramsland	1919.07.27 1921.06.09	1921.06.09 1925.06.02	6	SK-MLA	Liberal
5	Edith McTavish Rogers	1920.06.29 1922.07.18 1927.06.29	1922.07.18 1927.06.29 1932.06.16	12	MB-MLA	Liberal
6	Nellie McClung	1921.07.18	1926.06.28	5	AB-MLA	Liberal
7	Irene Parlby	1921.07.18 1926.06.28 1930.06.19	1926.06.28 1930.06.19 1935.07.22	14	AB-MLA	United Farmers
8	Agnes Macphail	1921.12.06 1925.10.29 1926.09.14 1930.07.28 1935.10.14 1943.08.04 1948.01.01	1925.10.29 1926.09.14 1930.07.28 1935.10.14 1940.03.06 1945.06.04 1951.11.22	18 ¼ 5 ¾	ON-MP ON-MLA	Progressive United Farmers
9	Helena Squires[1]	1930.05.17	1932.06.11	2	NF-MLA	
10	Helen Douglas Smith	1933.11.02 1937.06.01	1937.06.01 1941.10.21	8	BC-MLA	Liberal

[1] Newfoundland was not a province of Canada at this date.

Rank	Name	Elected/ Appointed	End Date yy.mm.dd	Years	Jurisdiction	Party
11	Cairine Wilson	1930.02.15	1962.03.03	32	PM-Senate	Lib Appt
12	Dorothy G. Steeves	1934.07.14 1937.06.01 1941.10.21	1937.06.01 1941.10.21 1945.10.25	11¼	BC-MLA	CCF/NDP
13	Iva Fallis	1935.07.20	1942.12.10	7½	ON-Senate	Cons Appt
14	Edith Gostick	1935.08.22	1940.03.21	4½	AB-MLA	Social Credit
15	Edith Rogers	1935.08.22	1940.03.21	4½	AB-MLA	Social Credit
16	Martha Louise Black	1935.10.14	1940.03.21	4½	YK-MP	Ind Cons
17	Salome Halldorson	1936.07.27	1941.04.22	4¾	MB-MLA	Ind.
18	Shannon Foster	1936.07.27 1941.04.22	1941.04.22 1945.10.15	9¼	MB-MLA	Liberal
19	Laura Jamieson	1939.05.01 1941.10.21 1949.06.15 1945.10.25 1952.06.12	1941.10.21 1945.10.25 1952.06.12 1949.06.15 1953.06.09	14	BC-MLA	Liberal
20	Cornelia Wood	1940.03.21 1944.08.08 1948.08.17 1952.08.05 1959.06.18 1963.06.17	1944.08.08 1948.08.17 1952.08.05 1955.06.29 1963.06.17 1967.05.23	23¼	AB-MLA	Social Credit
21	Dorise Winnifred Nielson	1940.03.26	1944.06.15	4¼	SK-MP	Unity
22	Cora Casselman	1941.06.02	1945.06.11	4	AB-MP	Liberal
23	Grace MacInnis	1941.10.21 1965.11.08 1968.06.25 1972.10.30	1945.10.25 1968.06.25 1972.10.30 1974.07.08	4 8¾	BC-MLA BC-MP	CCF/NDP
24	Nancy Hodges	1941.10.21 1945.10.25 1949.06.15 1952.06.12 1953.11.05	1945.10.25 1949.06.15 1952.06.12 1953.06.09 1965.06.12	11½ 11½	BC-MLA BC-Senate	Liberal Lib Appt
25	Tilly Jean Rolston	1941.10.21 1945.10.25 1949.06.15 1952.06.12	1945.10.25 1949.06.15 1952.06.12 1953.06.09	11¾	BC-MLA	PC

Rank	Name	Elected/ Appointed	End Date yy.mm.dd	Years	Jurisdiction	Party
26	Margarette Lucock	1943.08.04	1945.06.04	2	ON-MLA	CCF/NDP
27	Beatrice Trew	1944.06.15	1948.06.24	4	SK-MLA	CCF/NDP
28	Marjorie Cooper	1952.06.11 1956.06.20 1960.06.08 1964.04.22	1956.06.20 1960.06.08 1964.04.22 1967.09.25	15 ¼	SK-MLA	CCF/NDP
29	Edith Thurston	1944.08.08	1948.08.17	4	AB-MLA	Soc. Credit
30	Rose Wilkinson	1944.08.08 1948.08.17 1955.06.29 1952.08.05 1959.06.18	1948.08.17 1952.08.05 1959.06.18 1955.06.29 1963.06.17	19	AB-MLA	Soc. Credit
31	Gladys Strum	1945.06.11 1960.06.08	1949.06.27 1964.04.22	4 4	SK-MP SK-MLA	CCF/NDP
32	Ellen Fairclough	1950.05.15 1953.08.10 1957.06.10 1958.03.31 1962.06.18	1953.08.10 1957.06.10 1958.03.31 1962.06.18 1963.04.08	13	ON-MP	Progressive Conservative
33	Elizabeth Robinson	1953.12.21 1955.06.29 1959.06.18	1955.06.29 1959.06.18 1963.06.17	9 ½	AB-MLA	Soc. Credit
34	Mariana Jodoin	1953.05.19	1966.06.01	13	QU-Senate	Lib Appt
35	Muriel McQueen Fergusson	1953.05.19	1975.05.23	22	NB-Senate	Lib Appt
36	Lydia Augusta Arsens	1953.06.09	1956.09.19	3 ¼	BC-MLA	Soc. Credit
37	Sybil Bennett	1953.09.10	1957.06.10	3 ¾	ON-MP	Progressive Conservative
38	Marie Ann Shipley	1953.08.10	1957.06.10	3 ¾	ON-MP	Liberal
39	Margaret Aitken	1953.08.10 1957.06.10 1958.03.31	1957.06.10 1958.03.31 1962.06.18	8 ¾	ON-MP	Progressive Conservative
40	Florence Elsie Inman	1955.07.28	1986.05.31	30 ¾	PEI-Senate	Lib Appt
41	Mary Batten	1956.06.20 1960.06.08	1960.06.08 1964.03.18	7 ¾	BC-MLA	Liberal
42	Buda Hosmer Brown	1956.09.19 1960.06.08	1960.06.08 1962 died	6	BC-MLA	Soc. Credit

Rank	Name	Elected/ Appointed	End Date yy.mm.dd	Years	Jurisdiction	Party
43	Lois Mabel Haggen	1956.09.19 1960.09.12 1963.09.30	1960.09.12 1963.09.30 1966.09.12	10	BC-MLA	CCF/NDP
44	Jean Casselman Wadds	1958.09.29 1962.06.18 1963.04.08 1965.11.08	1962.06.18 1963.04.08 1965.11.08 1968.06.25	9¾	ON-MP	Progressive Conservative
45	Thelma Forbes	1959.11.26 1962.12.14 1966.06.23	1962.12.14 1966.06.23 1969.06.25	9½	MB-MLA	Progressive Conservative
46	Ethel Wilson	1958.11.26 1963.06.17 1967.05.23	1963.06.17 1967.05.23 1971.08.30	12¾	AB-MLA	Soc. Credit
47	Olive Lillian Irvine	1960.01.14	1969.11.01	9¾	MB-Senate	PC Appt
48	Gladys Porter	1960.09.11 1963.10.08	1963.10.08 1967.05.30	6¾	NS-MLA	PC
49	Julia (Judy) LaMarsh	1960.10.31 1962.06.18 1963.04.08 1965.11.09	1962.06.18 1963.04.08 1965.11.08 1968.06.25	7¾	ON-MP	Liberal
50	Josie Quart	1960.11.16	1980.04.17	19½	AB-Senate	PC Appt
51	Carolyne Morrison	1960.11.25 1962.12.14 1966.06.23	1962.12.14 1966.06.23 1969.06.25	8½	MB-MLA	PC
52	Camille Mildred Mather	1960.09.12	1963.09.30	3	BC-MLA	CCF/NDP
53	Margaret Mary MacDonald	1961.05.29 1962.06.18	1962.06.18 1963.04.08	2	PEI-MP	Progressive Conservative
54	Marie-Claire Kirkland Casgrain	1961.12.14 1962.11.14 1966.06.05 1970.04.29	1962.11.14 1966.06.05 1970.04.29 1973.10.29	12	QU-MLA	Liberal
55	Margaret Frances Hobbs	1962.09.04	1963.09.30	1	BC-MLA	Liberal
56	Isabel J. Tibbie Hardie	1962.06.18	1963.04.08	¾	NWT-MP	Liberal
57	Margaret Konantz	1963.04.08	1965.11.08	2½	MB-MP	Liberal
58	Pauline Jewett	1963.04.08 1979.05.22 1980.02.18 1984.09.04	1965.11.08 1980.02.18 1984.09.04 1988.11.21	2½ 9½	ON-MP ON-MLA	Liberal NDP

Rank	Name	Elected/ Appointed	End Date yy.mm.dd	Years	Jurisdiction	Party
59	Ada Pritchard	1963.09.25 1967.10.17 1971.10.21	1967.10.17 1971.10.21 1975.09.18	12	ON-MLA	PC
60	Eloise Jones	1964.06.22 1965.11.08	1965.11.08 1968.06.25	4	SK-MP	PC
61	Margaret Isabel Rideout	1964.11.09 1965.11.08	1965.11.08 1968.06.25	3½	NB-MP	Liberal
62	Eileen Elizabeth Dailly	1966.09.12 1969.08.27 1972.08.30 1975.12.11 1979.05.10	1969.08.27 1972.08.30 1975.12.11 1979.05.10 1983.05.05	16½	BC-MLA	CCF/NDP
63	Isabel Pearl Dawson	1966.09.12 1969.08.27	1969.08.27 1972.08.03	6	BC-MLA	Soc. Credit
64	Sally Merchant	1964.04.22	1967.10.11	3½	SK-MLA	Liberal
65	Grace Mary McCarthy	1966.09.12 1969.08.27 1975.12.11 1979.05.10 1983.05.05 1986.10.22	1969.08.27 1972.08.30 1979.05.10 1983.05.05 1986.10.22 1991.10.17	22	BC-MLA	Soc. Credit
66	G. Jean Gordon	1967.09.11	1970.09.08	3	YK-MLA	None
67	Mary Kinnear	1967.04.06	1973.04.03	6	ON-Senate	Lib Appt
68	Margaret Renwick	1967.10.17	1971.10.21	4	ON-MLA	CCF/NDP
69	Brenda Robertson	1967.10.23 1970.10.26 1974.11.18 1978.10.23 1982.04.06 1984.12.21	1970.10.26 1974.11.18 1978.10.23 1982.04.06 1984.12.21 2000+	17¼ 15	NB-MLA NB-Senate	PC
70	Agnes Kripps	1969.08.27	1972.08.30	3	BC-MLA	Soc. Credit

Elected and Appointed Women Legislators, 1916–1969

Jurisdiction	Date	Number	Years	Average
Members of Parliament	1917–1969	18	102	6
Senators	1930–1969	9	120	13
Members of Provincial and Territorial Legislative Assemblies[2]	1916–1969	47	~331	~7
ALL	1917–1969	70	553	~8

[2] No women elected in Yukon or Northwest Territories

Appendix II:

Women Legislators and Senators, 1970–1985

Rank	Name	Elected/ Appointed	End Date yy.mm.dd	Years	Jurisdiction	Party
72	Hilda P. Watson	1970.09.08 1974.11.18	1974.11.18 1978.11.20	8	YK-MLA	Progressive Conservative
73	Anne Bell	1970.10.07	1989.11.29	19	BC-Senate	Lib Appt
74	Thérèse Casgrain	1970.10.07	1971.07.10	¾	QU-Senate	Lib Appt
75	Jean Canfield	1970.05.11 1974.04.29	1974.04.29 1979.04.23	9	PEI-MLA	Liberal
76	Lena Pederson	1970.12.21	1975.03.10	4 ¼	NWT-MLA	Ind.
77	Catherine Chichak	1971.08.30 1975.03.26 1979.03.04 1982.11.02	1975.03.26 1979.03.04 1982.11.02 1986.05.08	14 ¾	AB-MLA	Progressive Conservative
78	Helen Hunley	1971.08.30 1975.03.26 1985.01.22	1975.03.26 1979.03.14 1991.03.11	7 ½ 6	AB-MLA AB-LG	Progressive Conservative PC Appt
79	Margaret Scrivener	1971.10.21 1975.09.18 1977.06.09 1981.03.19 1985.05.02	1975.09.18 1977.06.09 1981.03.19 1985.05.02 1987.09.10	16	ON-MLA	Progressive Conservative
80	Margaret Birch	1971.10.21 1975.09.18 1977.06.09 1981.03.19	1975.09.18 1977.06.09 1981.03.19 1985.05.02	13 ½	ON-MLA	Progressive Conservative
81	Louise Marguerite Lapointe	1971.11.10	1987.01.03	15	QU-Senate	Lib Appt

Rank	Name	Elected/ Appointed	End Date yy.mm.dd	Years	Jurisdiction	Party
82	Margaret Campbell	1972.04.27 1975.09.18 1977.06.09	1975.09.18 1977.06.09 1981.03.19	9	ON-MLA	Liberal
83	Margaret Norrie	1972.04.27	1980.10.16	8½	NS-Senate	Lib Appt
84	Rosemary Brown	1972.08.30 1975.12.11 1979.05.10	1975.12.11 1979.05.10 1983.05.05	10¾	BC-MLA	CCF/NDP
85	Karen Elizabeth Sandford	1972.08.30 1975.12.11 1979.05.10 1983.05.05	1975.12.11 1979.05.10 1983.05.05 1986.10.12	14	BC-MLA	CCF/NDP
86	Daisy Webster	1972.08.30	1975.12.11	3¼	BC-MLA	CCF/NDP
87	Phyllis Florence Wheeler	1972.08.30	1975.12.11	3¼	BC-MLA	CCF/NDP
88	Joan Neiman	1972.09.01	1995.09.09	23	ON-Senate	Lib Appt
89	Monique Bégin	1972.10.30 1974.07.08 1979.05.22 1980.02.18	1974.07.08 1979.05.22 1980.02.18 1984.09.04	12	QU-MP	Liberal
90	Flora MacDonald	1972.10.30 1974.07.08 1979.05.22 1980.02.18 1984.09.04	1974.07.08 1979.05.22 1980.02.18 1984.09.04 1988.11.21	16	ON-MP	PC
91	Albanie Morin	1972.10.30 1974.07.08	1974.07.08 1976.09.30	4	QU-MP	Liberal
92	Aideen Nicholson	1974.07.08 1979.05.22 1980.02.18 1984.09.04	1979.05.22 1980.02.18 1984.09.04 1988.11.21	14¼	ON-MP	Liberal
93	Jeanne Sauvé	1972.10.30 1974.07.08 1979.05.22 1980.02.18 1984.05.14	1974.07.08 1979.05.22 1980.02.18 1984.02.18 1990.01.29	11¼ 5¾	QU-MP CA-GG	Liberal
94	Lise Bacon	1973.10.29 1981.04.13 1985.12.02 1989.09.25	1976.11.15 1985.12.02 1989.09.25 1994.09.12	16½	QU-MLA	Liberal

Rank	Name	Elected/ Appointed	End Date yy.mm.dd	Years	Jurisdiction	Party
95	Coline M. Campbell	1974.04.02 1980.02.18 1988.11.21	1979.05.22 1984.09.04 1993.10.25	14 ½	NS-MP	Liberal
96	Melinda Jane MacLean	1974.04.02	1978.09.19	4 ½	NS-MLA	Liberal
97	Simma Holt	1974.07.08	1979.05.22	5	BC-MP	Liberal
98	Shirley Dysart	1974.11.18 1978.10.23 1982.10.12 1987.10.13 1991.09.23	1978.10.23 1982.10.12 1987.10.13 1991.09.23 1995.09.11	20 ¾	NB-MLA	Liberal
99	Iona Campagnola	1974.07.08 2001.09.25	1979.05.22 n/a	5 —	NB-MLA BC-LG	Liberal
100	Ursula Appolloni	1974.07.08 1979.05.22 1980.02.18	1979.05.22 1980.02.18 1984.09.04	10	ON-MP	Liberal
101	Eleanor Millard	1974.11.18	1978.11.20	4	YK-MLA	None
102	Florence Whyard	1974.11.18	1978.11.20	4	YK-MLA	None
103	Barbara B. Wallace	1975.12.11 1979.05.10	1979.05.10 1983.05.05	7 ½	BC-MLA	Liberal
104	Linda Clifford	1975.06.11	1978.10.18	3 ¼	SK-MLA	Liberal
105	Evelyn Edwards	1975.06.11	1978.10.18	3 ¼	SK-MLA	Liberal
106	Marion Bryden	1975.06.11 1977.06.09 1981.03.19 1985.05.02 1987.09.10	1977.06.09 1981.03.19 1985.05.02 1987.09.10 1990.08.06	15	ON-MLA	Liberal
107	Bette Stephenson	1975.06.11 1977.06.09 1981.03.19 1985.05.02	1977.06.09 1981.03.19 1985.05.02 1987.09.10	12 ¼	ON-MLA	PC
108	Hazel MacIsaac	1975.06.11	1979.06.18	4	NF-MLA	PC
109	Evelyn Gigantes	1975.09.18 1984.12.13 1985.05.02	1977.06.09 1985.05.02 1987.09.10	4 ½	ON-MLA	Liberal
110	Louise Cuerrier	1976.04.29	1981.04.13	5	QU-MLA	PQ
111	Thérèse Lavoie-Roux	1976.04.29 1981.04.13 1985.12.02	1981.04.13 1985.12.02 1989.09.25	13 ½	QU-MLA	Liberal

Rank	Name	Elected/ Appointed	End Date yy.mm.dd	Years	Jurisdiction	Party
112	Denise Leblanc-Bantey	1976.04.29	1981.04.13	5	QU-MLA	PQ
113	Jocelyne Ouellette	1976.04.29	1981.04.13	5	QU-MLA	PQ
114	Lise Payette	1976.04.29	1981.04.13	5	QU-MLA	PQ
115	Jean Pigott	1976.10.18	1979.05.22	2½	ON-MP	PC
116	Norma Price	1977.10.11	1981.11.17	4	MB-MLA	PC
117	Florence Bird	1978.03.23	1983.01.15	4¾	ON-Senate	Lib Appt
118	Doris Anderson	1978.03.23	1990.08.07	12¼	ON-Senate	Lib Appt
119	Joan Duncan	1978.10.18 1982.04.26 1986.10.20	1982.04.26 1986.10.20 1991.10.21	13	SK-MLA	PC
120	Nancy Clark	1978.10.23 1982.10.12	1982.10.12 1987.10.13	9	NB-MLA	PC
121	Mabel DeWare	1978.10.23 1982.10.12	1982.10.12 1987.10.13	9	NB-MLA	PC
122	Meg S. McCall	1978.11.20	1982.06.07	3½	YK-MLA	PC
123	Alice P. McGuire	1978.11.20	1982.06.07	3½	YK-MLA	Liberal
124	Nellie Cournyea	1979.10.01 1983.11.21 1987.10.05 1991.10.15	1983.11.21 1987.10.05 1991.10.15 1995.10.16	16	NWT-MLA	None
125	Sheila Embury	1979.03.14 1982.11.05	1982.11.05 1986.05.08	7	AB-MLA	PC
126	Shirley Cripps	1979.03.14 1982.11.05 1986.05.08	1982.11.05 1986.05.08 1989.03.20	10	AB-MLA	PC
127	Mary Le Messurier	1979.03.14 1982.11.05	1982.11.05 1986.05.08	7	AB-MLA	PC
128	Myrna Fyfe	1979.03.14	1982.11.05	3½	AB-MLA	PC
129	Constance Osterman	1979.03.14 1982.11.05 1986.05.08 1989.03.20	1982.11.05 1986.05.08 1989.03.20 1992.05.05	13	AB-MLA	PC
130	Leone Bagnall	1979.03.23 1982.09.27 1986.04.21 1989.05.29	1982.09.27 1986.04.21 1989.05.29 1993.03.29	14	PEI-MLA	PC

Rank	Name	Elected/ Appointed	End Date yy.mm.dd	Years	Jurisdiction	Party
131	Marion Reid	1979.03.23 1982.09.27 1986.04.21	1982.09.27 1986.04.21 1989.05.29	10	PEI-MLA	PC
132	Dalia Wood	1979.03.26	1999.01.31	19¾	QU-Senate	Lib Appt
133	Yvette Rousseau	1979.03.27	1988.03.17	9	QU-Senate	Lib Appt
134	Judith Erola	1979.05.22 1980.02.18	1980.02.18 1984.09.04	5¼	ON-MP	Liberal
135	Céline Hervieux-Payette	1979.05.22 1980.02.18 1995.03.21	1980.02.18 1984.09.04 2000.+	5¼ 4¾+	QU-MP QU-Senate	Liberal
136	Marie Thérèse Killens	1979.05.22 1980.02.18 1984.09.04	1980.02.18 1984.09.04 1988.11.21	9½	QU-MP	Liberal
137	Margaret Mitchell	1979.05.22 1980.02.18 1984.09.04	1980.02.18 1984.09.04 1988.11.21	9½	BC-MP	NDP
138	Diane Rose Stratas	1979.05.22	1980.02.18	¾	ON-MP	PC
139	Hazel Newhook	1979.06.18 1982.04.06	1982.04.06 1985.04.02	5¾	NF-MLA	PC
140	Lynn Verge	1979.06.18 1982.04.06 1985.04.02 1989.04.20 1993.05.03	1982.04.06 1985.04.02 1989.04.20 1993.05.03 1996.02.22	16¾	NF-MLA	PC
141	June Westbury	1979.10.16	1981.11.17	2	MB-MLA	Liberal
142	Solange Chaput Rolland	1979.11.14	1981.04.13	1½	QU-MLA	Liberal
143	Martha Bielish	1979.09.27	1990.09.26	11	AB-Senate	PC Appt
144	Lynda Sorenson	1979.10.01	1983.11.21	4	NWT-MLA	None
145	Suzanne Beauchamp-Niquet	1980.02.18	1984.09.04	4½	QU-MP	Liberal
146	Pat Carney	1980.02.18 1984.09.04	1984.09.04 1988.10.01	8½	BC-MP	Liberal
147	Eva Coté	1980.02.18	1984.09.04	4½	QU-MP	Liberal
148	Mary Elizabeth Dolin	1981.04.13	1985.04.10[1]	4	MB-MLA	NDP

[1] Died April 10; succeeded by her husband Matthew who was then re-elected in 1986.

Rank	Name	Elected/ Appointed	End Date yy.mm.dd	Years	Jurisdiction	Party
149	Maureen Hemphill	1980.02.18 1981.11.17 1986.03.18 1988.04.26	1981.11.17 1986.03.18 1988.04.26 1990.09.11	10½	MB-MLA	NDP
150	Charlotte L. Oleson	1981.04.13 1981.11.17 1986.03.18 1988.04.26	1981.11.17 1986.03.18 1988.04.26 1990.09.11	9½	MB-MLA	NDP
151	Myrna A. Phillips	1981.11.17 1986.03.18	1986.03.18 1988.04.26	6½	MB-MLA	NDP
152	Muriel Ann Smith	1981.11.17 1986.03.18	1986.03.18 1988.04.26	6½	MB-MLA	NDP
153	Sheila Copps	1981.03.19 1984.09.04 1988.11.21 1993.10.15 1997.06.02	1984.07.10 1988.11.21 1993.10.15 1997.06.02 2000+	3¼ 15¼	ON-MLA ON-MP	Liberal Liberal
154	Susan Fish	1981.03.19 1985.05.01	1985.05.01 1987.09.10	6½	ON-MLA	PC
155	Joan Dougherty	1981.04.13 1985.12.02	1985.12.02 1989.09.25	8½	QU-MLA	Liberal
156	Louise Harel	1981.04.13 1985.12.02 1989.09.25 1994.09.12 1998.11.30	1985.12.02 1989.09.25 1994.09.12 1998.11.30 2000+	18¾	QU-MLA	PQ
157	Carmen Juneau	1981.04.13 1985.12.02	1985.12.02 1989.09.25	8½	QU-MLA	PQ
158	Huguette Lachapelle	1981.04.13	1985.12.02	4¾	QU-MLA	PQ
159	Pauline Marois	1981.04.13 1989.09.25 1994.09.12 1998.11.30	1985.12.02 1994.09.12 1998.11.30 2000+	14½	QU-MLA	PQ
160	Alexa McDonough	1981.10.06 1984.11.06 1988.09.06 1993.05.25 1997.06.02	1984.11.06 1988.09.06 1993.05.25 1996.06.04 2000+	14½ 2½	NS-MLA NS-MP	NDP
161	Ida Reid	1982.04.06	1985.04.02	3	NF-MLA	PC

Rank	Name	Elected/ Appointed	End Date yy.mm.dd	Years	Jurisdiction	Party
162	Margaret Joe	1982.06.07 1989.02.20 1992.10.19	1989.02.20 1992.10.19 1996.09.30	14¼	YK-MLA	NDP
163	Beatrice Firth	1982.06.07 1985.05.13 1989.02.20 1992.10.19	1985.05.13 1989.02.20 1992.10.19 1996.09.30	14¼	YK-MLA	PC
164	Katherine Emma Nukon	1982.06.07	1985.05.13	3	YK-MLA	PC
165	Shirley Janet Koper	1982.11.02 1986.05.08	1986.05.08 1988(died)	5	AB-MLA	PC
166	Jennifer Cossitt	1982.10.12 1984.09.04	1984.09.04 1988.11.21	6	ON-MP	PC
167	Lynn McDonald	1982.10.12 1984.09.04	1984.09.04 1988.11.21	6	ON-MP	NDP
168	Gay Caswell	1982.04.26	1986.10.20	4½	SK-MLA	NDP
169	Evelyn Bacon	1982.10.12	1986.10.20	4½	SK-MLA	NDP
170	Jo-Ann Zazelenchuk	1982.10.12	1986.10.20	4½	SK-MLA	PC
171	Eliza Lawrence	1983.05.05	1987.10.05	4½	NWT-MLA	None
172	Rita Johnston	1983.05.05 1986.10.22	1986.10.22 1991.10.17	13¼	BC-MLA	Soc. Credit
173	Madeleine Bélanger	1983.12.05 1985.12.02 1989.09.25 1994.09.12 1998.11.30	1985.12.02 1989.09.25 1994.09.12 1998.11.30 2000+	16	QU-MLA	Liberal
174	Aline Saint-Amand	1983.12.05	1985.03.25	1¼	QU-MLA	Liberal
175	Anne Cools	1984.01.13	2000+	16	ON-Senate	Lib Appt
176	Lorna Marsden	1984.01.24	1992.08.31	8½	ON-Senate	Lib Appt
177	Ann Sloat	1984.12.13	1985.05.02	¼	ON-MLA	PC
178	Joyce Fairbairn	1984.06.29	2000+	5½	AB-Senate	Lib Appt
179	Gabrielle Bertrand	1984.09.04 1988.11.21	1988.11.21 1993.10.25	9	QU-MP	PC
180	Suzanne Blais-Grenier	1984.09.04 1988.09.21	1988.09.21 1988.11.21	4	QU-MP	PC Independent
181	Anne Blouin	1984.09.04	1988.11.21	4	QU-MP	PC
182	Lise Bourgault	1984.09.04 1988.11.21	1988.11.21 1993.10.25	9	QU-MP	PC

Rank	Name	Elected/ Appointed	End Date yy.mm.dd	Years	Jurisdiction	Party
183	Pauline Browes	1984.09.04 1988.11.21	1988.11.21 1993.10.25	9	QU-MP	PC
184	Andrée Champagne	1984.09.04 1988.11.21	1988.11.21 1993.10.25	9	QU-MP	PC
185	Mary Collins	1984.09.04 1988.11.21	1988.11.21 1993.10.25	9	BC-MP	PC
186	Suzanne Duplessis	1984.09.04 1988.11.21	1988.11.21 1993.10.25	9	QU-MP	PC
187	Sheila Finestone	1984.09.04 1988.11.21 1993.10.25 1997.06.02 1999.08.11	1988.11.21 1993.10.25 1997.06.02 1999.08.10 2000+	15 ¼	QU-MP QU-Senate	Liberal Lib Appt
188	Carole Jacques	1984.09.04 1988.11.21	1988.11.21 1993.10.25	9	QU-MP	PC Independent
189	Monique Landry	1984.09.04 1988.11.21	1988.11.21 1993.10.25	9	QU-MP	PC
190	Claudy Mailly	1984.09.04	1988.11.21	4	QU-MP	PC
191	Shirley Martin	1984.09.04 1988.11.21	1988.11.21 1993.10.25	9	ON-MP	PC
192	Barbara Jean McDougall	1984.09.04 1988.11.21	1988.11.21 1993.10.25	9	QU-MP	PC
193	Lucie Pépin	1984.09.04 1997.04.08	1988.11.21 2000+	4 2¼	QU-MP Senate	Liberal Lib Appt
194	Barbara Jane (Bobbie) Sparrow	1984.09.04 1988.11.21	1988.11.21 1993.10.25	9	AB-MP	PC
195	Monique Tardif	1984.09.04 1988.11.21	1988.11.21 1993.10.25	9	QU-MP	PC
196	Monique Vézina	1984.09.04 1988.11.21	1988.11.21 1993.10.25	9	QU-MP	PC
197	Maxine Cochran	1984.11.06	1988.09.06	4	NS-MLA	PC
198	Cora Etter	1984.11.06	1988.09.06	4	NS-MLA	PC
199	Elizabeth Smith	1985.05.02 1987.09.10 1990.09.06	1987.09.10 1990.09.06 1995.06.08	10	ON-MLA	NDP
200	Lily Munro	1985.05.02 1987.09.10 1990.09.06	1987.09.10 1990.09.06 1995.06.08	10	ON-MLA	Liberal

Rank	Name	Elected/ Appointed	End Date yy.mm.dd	Years	Jurisdiction	Party
201	Ruth Grier	1985.05.02 1987.09.10 1990.09.06	1987.09.10 1990.09.06 1995.06.08	10	ON-MLA	NDP
202	Margaret Marland	1985.05.02 1987.09.10 1995.06.08 1999.06.03	1987.09.10 1990.07.30 1999.06.03 2000+	14½	ON-MLA	PC
203	Elinor Caplan	1985.05.02 1987.09.10 1990.09.06 1995.06.08	1987.09.10 1990.09.06 1995.06.08 1997.09.05[2]	12¼	ON-MLA	NDP
204	Jeanne L. Blackburn	1985.12.02 1989.09.25 1994.09.12	1989.09.25 1994.09.12 1998.11.30	13	QU-MLA	PQ
205	Madeleine Bleau	1985.12.02 1989.09.25	1989.09.25 1994.09.12	8¾	QU-MLA	Liberal
206	Pierrette Cardinal	1985.12.02 1989.09.25 1994.09.12	1989.09.25 1994.09.12 1995.11.30	10	QU-MLA	Liberal
207	France Dionne	1985.12.02 1989.09.25 1994.09.12	1989.09.25 1994.09.12 1998.11.30	13	QU-MLA	Liberal
208	Monique Gagnon-Tremblay	1985.12.02 1989.09.25 1994.09.12 1998.11.30	1989.09.25 1994.09.12 1998.11.30 2000+	14	QU-MLA	Liberal
209	Claire-Hélène Hovington	1985.12.02 1989.09.25	1989.09.25 1994.09.12	8¾	QU-MLA	Liberal
210	Yolande Legault	1985.12.02	1989.09.25	3¾	QU-MLA	Liberal
211	Christiane Pelchat	1985.12.02 1989.09.25	1989.09.25 1994.09.12	8¾	QU-MLA	Liberal
212	Louise Robic	1985.12.02 1989.09.25	1989.09.25 1994.09.12	8¾	QU-MLA	Liberal
213	Violette Trepanier	1985.12.02 1989.09.25	1989.09.25 1994.09.12	8¾	QU-MLA	Liberal

[2] Succeeded by her eldest child, David.

Rank	Name	Elected/ Appointed	End Date yy.mm.dd	Years	Jurisdiction	Party
214	Cécile Vermette	1985.12.02	1989.09.25	14	QU-MLA	PQ
		1989.09.25	1994.09.12			
		1994.09.12	1998.11.30			
		1998.11.30	2000+			

Elected and Appointed Women Legislators, 1970–85

Jurisdiction	Number	Years	Average
Members of Parliament	39	152	~ 4
Senators	18	126	~7
Members of Provincial and Territorial Legislative Assemblies	102	496	~5
ALL	159[3]	774	~7

[3] 1 MP, 4 Senators, and 10 MLAs had served before 1970.

Glossary

balanced, equitable, and fair representation: "Fairness in a free and democratic society presupposes a foundation of justice, in which the equality of citizens to participate in governance requires a fair opportunity to influence political institutions and public policy."[1] For electoral representation to be seen to be fair it must provide equitable access to candidacy and assign seats to legislative jurisdictions with due regard for communities of interest that exist. The integrity of the electoral process affects Canadians' confidence in their capacity to access, exercise and enjoy their democratic rights.

complacency: Self-satisfaction of the sort that tends to support the status quo. Not predisposed to produce self-reflection or reform, complacency actually contributes to the continued failure to see, study, or change gender gaps in order to achieve equality for women.

contagion effect: A phenomenon observed in Canadian electoral politics whereby one party's promotion of a higher number of female candidates results in increasing numbers of female candidates advanced by other political parties.

critical mass: The idea that, in order to make a difference to political debate and public policy, women must be present in sufficient numbers; for example 15 to 30 per cent of elected officials must be women.[2]

Deb effect: The public policy choice to make considerably more public space available to more, and increasingly more diverse, women as a matter of balanced, equitable, and fair representation.

democratic deficits: Gaps or flaws in the democratic political system that diminish its effectiveness and legitimacy. The continued underrepresentation of women in political life, especially in leadership positions, constitutes a democratic deficit.

electoral project: Organized efforts, typically led by women's groups, to increase the number of women elected to municipal and legislative office.

Flora syndrome: Refers to the promise of party members to support Tory MP Flora MacDonald's bid for the leadership of the party; support that failed to materialize.

gender bias: Gender-based discrimination benefits men while producing disadvantages and inequitable outcomes for women.

gender parity: Numerically equal representation for women; gender parity will be achieved in Canadian legislatures when women, who comprise slightly more than 50 per cent of the population, win at least 50 per cent of the seats.

gendered leadership gap: Gaps in knowledge and public policy occur when topics have not been accorded the attention that they subsequently are seen to merit. For example, in the past it was not a matter of general concern, let alone a public policy question, that leadership roles in politics are taken up predominantly, and at times almost exclusively, by men. The gendered leadership gap draws attention to the under-representation of women in positions of political leadership and has been identified as a problem that needs to be solved.

glass ceiling: The invisible barriers that keep women from rising beyond a certain level in hierarchical organizations.[3] The electoral variant of the glass ceiling for women sits at or below 25 per cent of the available seats.

identity politics: "Political movements organized around aspects of individuals' identities such as their sex (women's movements) … sexual orientation (gay/lesbian movements) … or disability (movements of people with disabilities). The emphasis is on the right to self-describe or name their identity in culture and as the basis for political choices and alliances."[4]

incumbency: The person who presently holds a legislative seat is called the incumbent. When the number of incumbents seeking re-election is high, voter preference for sitting members over challengers produces low-rates of legislative turnover.

local riding association autonomy: The power of riding (also known as constituency) associations (comprised of party members in the riding) to choose candidates at nomination meetings. Each party member in good standing in the riding can cast a ballot for the nominee of their choice. The ability of local ridings to control candidate selection makes it difficult for party elites to introduce equity programs or impose gender quotas.

mandate of difference: The idea that female legislators will see their gender difference as politically salient and interpret their legislative mandate to include making a difference for women, for instance, by voicing women's policy needs and supporting policies designed to raise the status of women.

neo-conservative principles: Neo-conservatism, often called moral or social conservatism, typically supports use of the state's coercive powers to impose law and order and shore up social hierarchies like the patriarchal family.

neo-liberal restructuring: Neo-liberalism favours the economic market and in so doing tends to pursue policies that shrink the size and fiscal obligations of the state. As such, neoliberal restructuring includes cost and program cutting, privatization, decentralization, and deregulation.

opportunity structures: "Forces, structures and ideas that characterize official political systems and that enhance or deter women's political participation."[5]

opposition party syndrome: Coined to describe the Conservative Party's travails during its years in opposition. Opposition parties in their frustration over failing to win elections tend to lapse into self-defeating internal conflicts. Party leaders are challenged, personality disputes are allowed to get out of hand, and the party's "dirty laundry" is aired in public. The leadership crisis in the Alliance party after the 2000 federal election, which culminated in a caucus revolt and the leader's eventual resignation, provides a recent example of this syndrome in operation.[6]

partisan CPR: The selection of a leader whose main task is to keep the party functioning rather than having any real hope of forming the next government.

party discipline: The practice of legislators voting in support of their party's position. Party discipline is very strong in Canada, and legislators are offered "carrots" for toeing the party line (better office space, travel, and other perks) and threatened with "sticks" for noncompliance (removal from critic or committee positions, demotion, even ejection from the party).

party elites: Elites are small groups of people who wield disproportionate amounts of power within their organizations. In political parties, the preferences and activities of elites may comprise the leader, top officials, and influential party members and backers.

political equality and freedom: Political equality and freedom are key to electoral democracy, as these principles require that each adult citizen has the same freedom and opportunity as every other adult citizen to participate in electoral and decision-making processes, with reasonable exceptions. In Canada, these principles have prompted the extension of the franchise to women, racial minority groups, Aboriginal peoples, persons with disabilities, and the homeless, and have prompted Elections Canada to ensure that every eligible voter has access to the electoral process.

pool of eligibles: The group of people with the qualifications and characteristics essential to success in the job. The "pool of eligibles" for public office generally includes those individuals whose professional status and personalities are similar to those who previously have been successful at winning election.

popular consultation: In representative democracies, citizens delegate their decision-making power to elected representatives. This democratic principle holds that citizens have a right to be consulted by their representatives and elected representatives in their turn are held accountable to their constituents through the electoral process.

popular sovereignty: Popular sovereignty means that decision-making power is vested in all the people and not in one of them or a small group of them. In representative democracies, citizens can delegate their decision-making power to elected representatives.

proportional representation (PR) or mixed-member plurality (MMP) electoral systems: In strict **PR** systems, the country (or province/territory) is divided into multi-member constituencies or comprises one multi-member constituency. Parties devise lists of candidates. Voters cast their ballots for a party, and the number of votes per party determines its proportion of the available seats. Roughly speaking, if a party receives 25 per cent of the vote, it will be allocated 25 per cent of the seats, and the candidates comprising the top quarter of the list are elected. **MMP** systems combine the PR and single-member plurality (SMP, see below) systems by electing half of the representatives with SMP, then, in an effort to address the vote/seat distortions resulting from this system, electing the other half with PR. Each voter casts two ballots, one for a candidate in an SMP constituency and one for a party list.[7]

public policy legacy: Public policy is classically defined as a course of action or inaction chosen by governments to address issues or problems. Like institutions that convey a society's norms and values across several generations, public policy has similar long-term effects, often shaping and even restraining choices of future governments.

representational diversity: The actualization of the Deb Effect.

revolving door (for female party leaders): The pattern of women's party leadership, which is typically short-lived, as Canadian women party leaders serve, on average, only 2 years in the post.

sacrificial lambs: The habit of political parties fielding a female candidate in a riding they do not expect to win. By doing so, they can "cut their losses" by claiming a "moral victory" in improving their participation rate.[8]

sex-based discrimination: Differential treatment based on gender, usually directed against women. Related to systemic sex bias and systemic sexism, defined below.

single-member plurality system (SMP): Electoral systems which divide the country or province/territory into single-member constituencies. The voter casts a ballot for one candidate, and one person is elected in each constituency. The candidate with the plurality of votes (more votes than any other candidate) wins the seat. Often called the "first past the post" system.

symbolic representation: Token representation with little or no lasting effect; symbolic representation remains important for demonstrating unrealized potential. Having "a foot in the door" is no replacement for unimpeded access, although it may be all that is possible in the early phases of a struggle to achieve equality.

systemic sex bias: Attitudes and behaviour that "form part of a system of structural discrimination" preventing some people from "realizing opportunities or receiving equal protection or benefit of the law."9

systemic sexism: Sexism refers to the different treatment of women because of their sex. Sexism is systemic when it is evident in social, economic, and political systems and is manifested in both the public sphere of business and government and in the domestic sphere of home and family.

top jobs: Positions that are prized for the status they confer, and the evidence of ability and leadership as well as many years of relevant work experience they require. Being selected to lead political parties and appointments representing the Crown or the federal or provincial government at the highest levels are examples of employment of this kind.

uncompetitive political parties: Political parties with little or no representation in the legislature. As a result, such parties are unlikely to become the governing party or official opposition in the near future.

underrepresentation: The extent to which the proportion of women in Parliament or legislatures is less than their proportion of the population. Women constitute 52 per cent of Canada's population but hold only slightly more than 20 per cent of the seats in the House of Commons. Aboriginal people, racial minorities, and people with disabilities are also currently underrepresented. The degree of underrepresentation varies: *gross* underrepresentation (less than 15 per cent) is evident in the leadership of political parties across Canada by women; *severe* is the case of women legislators (15 to 30 per cent); and *marked* (35 to 45 per cent) would occur if the recent trend to appoint increasing proportions of women to the Senate surpasses percentages achieved in recent years by another 10 per cent.

welfare state: An approach to governance that took root in Canada between the 1940s and 1960s and which was developed further throughout the 1970s and 1980s. Based on the idea that the state has obligations to provide for the social well-being of its citizens, this policy framework inspired the introduction of public education, universal health care services, income security, and wage replacement programs.

windows of opportunity: A combination of circumstances which together create opportunities for women to contest, and win, election. For example, low rates of incumbency combined with electoral volatility may propel unlikely candidates to electoral victory as occurred for some candidates in the first Mulroney government.

winnable ridings: Ridings where the party (and thus the candidate) has a reasonable chance of winning the election because an incumbent is in place, or because the party has won election in that riding in several previous elections. Safe seats are those a particular party is virtually guaranteed to win.

women's issues: Those matters "where policy consequences are likely to have a more immediate and direct impact on significantly larger numbers of women than on men."[10]

women's perspectives: Women's range of views as well as their approaches to all policy issues, not just those with an immediate and direct impact on women. A women's perspectives approach leads legislators to consider gender differences when making policy decisions in all areas, from taxation to agricultural subsidies.

Endnotes

PREFACE   Why Are We Still Counting?

1   Gwen Brodsky and Shelagh Day, *Canadian Charter Equality Rights for Women: One Step Forward or Two Steps Back?* (Ottawa: Canadian Advisory Council on the Status of Women, 1989).

CHAPTER 1   Introduction: Still Counting

1   Sheila Copps, *Nobody's Baby* (Toronto: Deneau, 1986) 169.

2   Azza Karam, ed., *Women in Parliament: Beyond Numbers* (Stockholm, Sweden: International Institute for Democracy and Electoral Assistance [IDEA], 1998), or the IDEA website, "Gender and Political Participation," http://www.idea.int/gender/index.htm including international and regional electronic links, http://www.idea.int/gender/links.htm. The Inter-Parliamentary Union tracks gender representation worldwide. See http://www.ipu.org/wmn-e/world.htm. At present Canada does slightly better than the world average. In general, worldwide, as in Canada, there are four men for every woman in our national legislatures.

3   Hugh Winsor, "The Power Game. Under Chrétien, Political Clout Goes to the Men," *Globe and Mail* 8 February 2002: A6.

4   Tom Flanagan, "Women and Other Party Animals: MacBeth is the Latest in a Short Line of Losing Female Pols," *National Post* 15 March 2001, http://www.nationalpost.com (downloaded 22 March 2001).

5   Cerise D. Morris. "No More than Simple Justice: The Royal Commission on the Status of Women and Social Change in Canada," diss., McGill University, 1982.

6   Candace Savage, *Foremothers: Personalities and Issues From the History of Women in Saskatchewan* (Saskatoon, SK: C. Savage, 1975) 41–42.

7   Judith McKenzie, *Pauline Jewett: A Passion for Canada* (Montreal and Kingston: McGill-Queen's University Press, 1999) 172.

8   Larry Johnsrude, "Lots of Sparring, But No Knockout Punches," *Edmonton Journal* 28 February 1997: A1.

9   Inter-Parliamentary Union, http://www.ipu.org/wmn-e/world.htm

CHAPTER 2 Counting Matters: The Number's Game and Women's Political Power

1 Canadian Bar Association, Taskforce on Gender Equality in the Legal Profession, *Touchstones for Change: Equality, Diversity and Accountability* : Report of the Canadian Bar Association Task Force on Gender Equality in the Legal Profession (Ottawa: Canadian Bar Association, 1993); Task Force on Barriers to Women in the Public Service, *Beneath the Veneer*, 4 vols. (Ottawa: Ministry of Supply and Services, 1990); Kathleen Archibald, *Sex and the Public Service* (Ottawa: Queen's Printer, 1970).

2 Jane Arscott, "'More Women': The RCSW and Political Representation, 1970," *Women and Political Representation in Canada*, ed. Manon Tremblay and Caroline Andrew (Ottawa: University of Ottawa Press, 1998) 145–68, especially 150.

3 Interview with Monique Bégin, 15 July 1996. Bégin had been the secretary to the RCSW. She later had a successful career in federal politics.

4 Canada, Royal Commission on the Status of Women (RCSW), *Report* (Ottawa: Queen's Printer, 1970) 339. There had been 134 federal and provincial elections between 1917 and June 1970, and 6,845 people have been elected. Of these, 67 were women.

5 RCSW, Report 339.

6 The second half of the chapter discusses women's involvement in political parties, thus addressing the question commissioners knew was of greatest interest to the government. National Archives, RCSW, Vol. 23, File 1, 4.

7 The RCSW recognized the contribution of the voluntary sector to the vibrancy of public life, and women were acknowledged as leaders in religious, charitable, and community-based organizations. See Anne Carver, *The Participation of Women in Political Activities in Canada* (Ottawa: Information Canada, 1970). This study was funded by the RCSW.

8 Arscott, "'More Women'" 147.

9 For the RCSW the problem of women's participation in electoral politics was clearly separate from women's leadership in their own organizations. See Carver, cited in the note 8.

10 National Archives RCSW, Margaret MacGill Papers, Toronto, 18 April 1967 (MG31 K7), Vol. 7, File 7.

11 Canada, Royal Commission on Electoral Reform and Party Financing, "Fairness as the Pre-Eminent Value in the Electoral Process," *Reforming Electoral Democracy*, Vol. 1 (Ottawa: Minister of Supply and Services Canada, 1991) 322.

12 Charlotte Whitton, "The Right Honorable Margaret," *Chatelaine* August 1929: 42.

13 Agnes Macphail, "If I Were Prime Minister," *Chatelaine* January 1933: 13, 46.

14 No comparison can be made to the provincial and territorial elections because this data has never been compiled so far as we know.

15 No counts are readily available to provide the same information province by province. The tally is made more difficult because of the numbers of candidates who used only their initials or whose first names can indicate both males and females. Electoral offices in each jurisdiction could easily make this information available by reviewing their records and presenting the material on their websites to match the categories already available on the federal site, dividing the material clearly between that which is of current and historical interest.

16 See the website of the Famous Five Foundation, www.famous5.org.

17 "Women WANT Women in Public Life?," *Chatelaine* January 1948: 12, 13, 55.

18 Barbara Frum, "Why There Are so Few Women in Ottawa," *Chatelaine* October 1971: 33, 110; Doris Anderson, "Let's Desegregate the Commons," *Chatelaine* October 1972: 45.

19 For specific dates, see the information boxes in Arscott and Trimble, *In the Presence of Women*, 1997.

20 Doris Anderson, "The MPs Who Care and the MPs Who Don't," editorial, *Chatelaine* May 1972: 1.

21 For a discussion of this approach to "ethnicity" in Canadian political science, see Yasmeen Abu-Laban, "Challenging the Gendered Vertical Mosaic," *Citizen Politics: Research and Theory in Canadian Political Behaviour*, ed. Joanna Everitt and Brenda O'Neill (Toronto: Oxford University Press, 2002) 268–82.

22 See Canada, *A History of the Vote in Canada* (Ottawa: Public Works and Government Services, 1997) 70–100.

23 Fraser Valentine and Jill Vickers, "'Released from the Yoke of Paternalism and Charity': Citizenship and the Rights of Canadians with Disabilities," *International Journal of Canadian Studies* 14 (1996): 155, 173.

24 Alain Pelletier, "Politics and Ethnicity: Representation of Ethnic and Visible-Minority Groups in the House of Commons," *Ethnocultural Groups and Visible Minorities in Canadian Politics: The Question of Access*, ed. Kathy Megyery (Toronto: Dundurn Press, 1991) 101–59.

25 Jerome Black, "Differences that Matter: Minority Women MPs, 1993–2000," *Women and Electoral Politics in Canada*, ed. Manon Tremblay and Linda Trimble (Toronto: Oxford University Press, forthcoming 2003).

26 Ibid.

27 Abu-Laban 270.

28 The percentage of women in the Senate in 2000 was 35 per cent due to a number of vacancies subsequently filled by more men than women.

29 Janine Brodie, *Women and Politics in Canada* (Toronto: McGraw-Hill Ryerson, 1985); Sylvia Bashevkin, *Toeing the Lines: Women in Party Politics in English Canada* (Toronto: Oxford University Press, 1985).

30 Susan Riley, "PM Lashes Out, and Loses," *Edmonton Journal*, 30 January 2002: 12.

31 Heather Sokoloff and Tim Naumetz, "MPs Rally Around Scolded Colleague," *National Post*, 29 January 2002; www.nationalpost.com (downloaded 7 February 2002).

CHAPTER 3 The Electoral Glass Ceiling

1 The authors gratefully acknowledge the research assistance of Mark Blythe, PhD candidate in political science at the University of Alberta, who collected some of the data on women candidates in recent elections.

2 Susan Delacourt, *Shaughnessy* (Toronto: Macfarlane, Walter and Ross, 2000) 145. Delacourt writes that for some time the new women's lavatory was referred to as the Shaughnessy Cohen Memorial Washroom.

3 Regarding the "toilet thing" in the House of Commons, see Sydney Sharpe, *The Gilded Ghetto* (Toronto: HarperCollins, 1994) 37; on Manitoba, see Kathy Brock, "Women and the Manitoba Legislature," *In the Presence of Women: Representation in Canadian Governments*, ed. Jane Arscott and Linda Trimble (Toronto: Harcourt, 1997) 182.

4 Erin Anderssen, "No Memoirs for McDonough Yet," *Globe and Mail* 6 June 2002: A4.

5 Rosemary Brown, *Being Brown: A Very Public Life* (Toronto: Random House, 1989) 142. Linda Trimble sympathizes with Brown's story. Her office is in a building on the University of Alberta campus clearly designed to accommodate more men than women, as there are men's washrooms on every floor but women's facilities only every other floor (but not her floor!). Women in the department staged a protest several years ago, and the twelfth-floor facilities were converted using the "box covering the urinal" approach.

6 Canada, Royal Commission on Electoral Reform and Party Financing, *Report*, Volume 1 (Ottawa: Supply and Services Canada 1991) 268–73; Alexandra Dobrowolski and Jane Jenson, "Reforming the Parties: Prescriptions for Democracy," *How Ottawa Spends: A More Democratic Canada?*, ed. Susan D. Phillips (Ottawa: Carleton University Press, 1993) 53–54.

7   Lisa Young and Elaine Campbell, "Women and Political Representation," *Party Politics in Canada*, 8th ed., ed. Hugh Thorburn and Alan Whitehorn (Toronto: Prentice Hall, 2001) 65.

8   See the website of the InterParliamentary Union, http://www.ipu.org/wmn-e/world.htm. (downloaded 6 August 2001).

9   Jane Arscott and Linda Trimble, "Introduction" Arscott and Trimble, *In the Presence of Women* 4.

10 Linda Trimble, "Who's Represented? Gender and Diversity in the Alberta Legislature," Tremblay and Andrew 257–89.

11 A fairly extensive body of literature on glass ceilings in bureaucracy and public administration has recently emerged. See Elisabeth Gidengil and Richard Vengroff, "Representative Bureaucracy, Tokenism and the Glass Ceiling: the Case of Women in Quebec Municipal Administration," *Canadian Public Administration* 40 (1997): 457–58. On the topic of glass ceilings, see also Katherine Naff and Sue Thomas, "The Glass Ceiling Revisited: Determinants of Federal Job Advancement," *Policy Studies Review* 13:3 (1994): 251; Katherine Naff, "Through the Glass Ceiling: Prospects of Advancement of Women in the Federal Civil Service," *Public Administration Review* 54:6 (1994): 507; Angela S. Bullard and Deil S. Wright, "Circumventing the Glass Ceiling: Women Executives in American State Governments," *Public Administration Review* 53:3 (1993): 189.

12 Journalist Susan Riley points to the underrepresentation of women in politics as evidence of a glass ceiling; "PM Lashes Out and Loses," *Edmonton Journal* 30 January 2002: A12.

13 Brodie, *Women and Politics in Canada* 85.

14 Chantal Maillé, *Primed for Power* (Canada: Canadian Advisory Council on the Status of Women, 1990) 6–7.

15 Young and Campbell 66–67.

16 On this point, see Lynda Erickson, "Parties, Ideology and Feminist Action: Women and Political Representation in British Columbia Politics," Arscott and Trimble, *In the Presence of Women* 114–16; Louise Carbert, "Governing on 'the Correct, the Compassionate, the Saskatchewan Side of the Border,'" Arscott and Trimble, *In the Presence of Women* 173; Brock 186–87; Sandra Burt and Elizabeth Lorenzin, "Taking the Women's Movement to Queen's Park: Women's Interests and the New Democratic Government of Ontario," Arscott and Trimble, *In the Presence of Women* 207; Manon Tremblay, "Quebec Women in Politics: An Examination of the Research," Arscott and Trimble, *In the Presence of Women* 232.

17 Lynda Erickson discusses the importance of electoral volatility to women's recent electoral successes; see Erickson, "Parties, Ideology and Feminist Action" 110.

18 Donley Studlar and Richard Matland, "The Dynamics of Women's Representation, in the Canadian Provinces, 1975–1994," *Canadian Journal of Political Science* 29:2 (1996): 280.

19 Chantal Maillé, *Les Québécoises et la conquête du pouvoir politique* (Montreal: Saint-Martin, 1990) 109–14.

20 Studlar and Matland 273; and Lynda Erickson, "Women and Political Representation in British Columbia," *Politics, Policy and Government in British Columbia*, ed. R.K. Carty (Vancouver: UBC Press, 1996) 122.

21 Lynda Erickson, "Entry to the Commons: Parties, Recruitment, and the Election of Women in 1993," Tremblay and Andrew 232.

22 Réjean Pelletier and Manon Tremblay, "Les femmes sont-elles candidates dans les circonscriptions perdues d'avance?" *Canadian Journal of Political Science* 25:2 (June 1992): 266; Studlar and Matland 287.

23 Jane Arscott and Linda Trimble, "Women's Electoral Space: Glass Ceilings, Flying Wedges and Revolving Doors," paper presented to the Department of Political Science, University of Waterloo, October 1997.

24 Maillé, *Primed for Power* 10.

[25] Elisabeth Gidengil, "Gender and Attitudes Towards Quotas for Women Candidates in Canada," *Women & Politics* 16:1 (1996): 38–39.

[26] Ken MacQueen, "PM's Policy to Pick Women Candidates Draws Criticism," *Edmonton Journal* 12 March 1997: A3.

[27] Leonard Preyra, "If Chrétien Really Wants to Get More Women Into Parliament ..." *Globe and Mail* 14 March 1997: A21.

[28] Anne McIlroy, "PM Picks Four Women to Run," *Globe and Mail* 12 March 1997: A4.

[29] See, for instance, Brock 188–89.

[30] Erickson, "Entry to the Commons" 235–36.

[31] Young and Campbell 67.

[32] Brodie, *Women and Politics in Canada* 1.

[33] Arscott and Trimble, *In the Presence of Women* 4.

[34] Trimble, "Who's Represented?"

[35] Arscott and Trimble, *In the Presence of Women* 4.

[36] Lise Gotell and Janine Brodie, "Women and Parties in the 1990s: Less Than Ever an Issue of Numbers," *Party Politics in Canada*, 7th ed., ed. Hugh Thorburn (Scarborough: Prentice Hall, 1996) 54–71; Trimble, "Feminist Politics in the Alberta Legislature"; and Gurston Dacks, Joyce Green, and Linda Trimble, "Road Kill: Women in Alberta's Drive Toward Deficit Elimination," *The Trojan Horse: Alberta and the Future of Canada*, ed. Trevor Harrison and Gordon Laxer (Montreal: Black Rose, 1995) 271–80.

[37] Arscott and Trimble, *In the Presence of Women* 5.

[38] Janine Brodie, "Women and the Electoral Process in Canada," *Women in Canadian Politics: Toward Equity in Representation*, ed. Kathy Megyery (Toronto: Dundurn Press, 1991) 40.

[39] Manon Tremblay, "Women and Political Participation in Canada," *Electoral Insight* 3:1 (January 2001): 6.

[40] Linda Trimble, "'Good Enough Citizens': Canadian Women and Representation in Constitutional Deliberations," *International Journal of Canadian Studies* 17 (Spring 1998): 145.

[41] For a clear overview of how these systems work, see Heather McIvor, "Proportional and Semi-proportional Electoral System: Their Potential Effects on Canadian Politics" *Electoral Insight* 1:1 (June 1999): 12–16.

[42] An organization called "Fair Vote Canada" is presently leading the chorus of voices demanding some form of proportional electoral system. See www.fairvotecanada.org

[43] See Appendix B, "Two-Member Constituencies and Gender Equality: A 'Made in Nunavut' Solution," Arscott and Trimble, *In the Presence of Women* 374–80; also, see Jens Dahl, Jack Hicks, and Peter Jull, eds., *Nunavut: Inuit Regain Control of Their Lands and Their Lives* (Copenhagen: International Work Group for Indigenous Affairs, 2000) 70–74.

CHAPTER 4   It's a Drag: Where Have All the Party Leaders Gone?

[1] Dennis Bueckert, "Drag Queen Antes Up $24,000 to Join Alliance Leadership Race," *Edmonton Journal*, 7 December 2001: A3. In fact, Anderson was unable to produce the required deposit and signatures and was forced to step out of the race. For more about Enza, see her website: www.enza.ca.

[2] Linda Trimble, "Can Women Break the 25 Per Cent Electoral Barrier?" *Folio* 12 May 2000: 5. (Available on-line at www.expressnews.ualberta.ca/expressnews/archives.cfm)

[3] Casgrain was appointed to the Senate by Pierre Trudeau in 1970. See Susan Mann Trofimenkoff, "Thérèse Casgrain and the CCF in Quebec," *Beyond the Vote: Canadian Women and Politics*, ed. Linda Kealey and Joan Sangster (Toronto: University of Toronto Press, 1989) 139–68.

4 Joyce Hayden, *Yukon's Women of Power: Political Pioneers in a Northern Canadian Colony* (Whitehorse: Windwalker Press, 1999) 112–15.

5 Ken MacQueen, "Why Don't Female Leaders Last in Canadian Politics?," *Ottawa Citizen* 29 November 1996: A1.

6 http://www.enza.ca/enzasays.htm.

7 Flanagan.

8 Kelly Torrance, "Back To Where The Votes Are?" *Alberta Report* 29 September 1997: 13.

9 This schema is based on the women leaders' experiences and a measure of party competitiveness reflecting electoral wins and losses. The categories, and the assignment of various women to them, are interpretive devices not evaluative pronouncements.

10 David Roberts, "Bitter Leader Quits Job With Rancorous Liberals," *Globe and Mail* 13 November 1995: A4.

11 Sharon Carstairs, *Not One of the Boys* (Toronto: Macmillan Canada, 1993) 48.

12 See Carstairs 128–51, for a discussion of her party's role in the Meech Lake debate.

13 John Crossley, "Picture This: Women Politicians Hold Key Posts in Prince Edward Island," Arscott and Trimble, *In the Presence of Women* 291.

14 Canadian Press, "Manitoba Liberals Red-Faced Over Wrong Results," *Edmonton Journal* 7 December 1997: A10. In October 1998, former federal cabinet minister Jon Gerrard defeated Jerry Fontaine, chief of the Sagkeeng First Nation, and assumed the leadership of the Manitoba Liberal party. See David Roberts, "Former Federal Minister to Lead Manitoba Liberals," *Globe and Mail* 19 October 1998: A4.

15 Don Desserud, "Women in New Brunswick Politics: Waiting for the Third Wave," Arscott and Trimble, *In the Presence of Women* 273.

16 Kim Lunman, "It's no Joy Being a Party of Two," *Globe and Mail* 6 August 2001: A4.

17 Cartoon, *Vancouver Province*, 29 September 1993: A28; Editorial, "A Faith Healer for Still-Sick Socreds," *Victoria Times-Colonist*, 9 November 1993: A4.

18 *Vancouver Sun* 19 February 1994: A23.

19 "Some Top Socreds 'Tired' of Grace," *Vancouver Sun* 22 April 1994: A4; Keith Baldrey, "Leadership Crisis Grips Socred party; McCarthy's Resignation Urged by Two Directors," *Vancouver Sun* 22 April 1994: A3.

20 New Democratic Party of Alberta press release, 12 January 1999 http://www.newdemocrats.ab.ca/newsreleases/Jan1299.html (downloaded 30 December 2001).

21 Allison Jeffs, "Barrett Resigns … Again. 'Near-death Experience' at Dentist Prompts ND Leader to Quit," *Edmonton Journal* 3 February 2000: A1.

22 MacQueen A1.

23 Kim Campbell, *Time and Chance: The Political Memoirs of Canada's First Woman Prime Minister* (Toronto: Doubleday Canada, 1996) 263.

24 "Liberals Continue to Draw Votes," *Canadian News Facts* 27:1 (1 January 1993–15 January 1993): 4865.

25 Sharpe 22, 13–33, 22; see also Campbell.

26 After MacBeth was selected, a member of the Liberal caucus, Gene Zwozdesky, crossed the floor to join the Conservatives, leaving 17 Liberal MLAs.

27 Mark Lisac, "MacBeth Might Challenge Klein to Try For a Last Hurrah," *Edmonton Journal* 19 April 1998: A3; Tom Arnold, "Liberals' New Leader Braces for Next Fight," *Edmonton Journal* 20 April 1998: A1; Jac MacDonald, "Tories Foolish Not to Take MacBeth Seriously," *Edmonton Journal* 20 April 1998: A6.

28 Ian McDougall, "MacBeth Resigns: Liberal Leader Ends Her Political Career," *Edmonton Sun* 16 March 2001: A1. Indeed, the reporter wrote that MacBeth "threw herself on her own sword."

[29] Amy Smith and David Jackson, "Helen at Helm: Party Picks NDP Veteran as New Leader in 3rd Round," *Halifax Chronicle Herald* 16 July 2000: A1–A2.

[30] Parker Barss Donham, "Exit Helen MacDonald," *Halifax Daily News* 24 April 2001.

[31] Audrey McLaughlin, with Rich Archbold, *A Woman's Place: My Life & Politics* (Toronto: MacFarlane, Walter & Ross, 1992) 61.

[32] McLaughlin 87.

[33] Hugh Winsor, "Matters of Sex, Substance," *Globe and Mail* 2 December 1992: A4.

[34] See Justine Hunter, "McDonough Sets Stage for Departure," *National Post* 26 February 2001, http://www.nationalpost.com (downloaded 25 February 2001).

[35] Juliet O'Neill, "NDP Keeps McDonough, Rejects Hard Swing to Left: Vote Ends Hours of Stormy Debate at Weekend Convention," *National Post* 26 November 2001, www.nationalpost.com (downloaded 29 January 2001).

[36] Erin Anderssen, "No Memoirs for McDonough Yet," *Globe and Mail* 6 June 2002: A4.

[37] Susan Riley, "McDonough's Common Sense Political Lesson," *Edmonton Journal* 10 June 2002: A 10.

[38] Susan Riley, "PM Lashes Out, and Loses. Jean Chrétien Shows Women He's Really a Grumpy Old Patriarch," *Edmonton Journal* 30 January 2002: A12.

[39] Richard Mackie, "A Leader Who Doesn't Fit the Traditional Image of One," *Globe and Mail* 9 February 1993: A9.

[40] MacQueen A1.

[41] Nadine Pedersen, "Liberals Win Yukon Majority," *Canoe news* 17 April 2000; http://www.canoe. ca/CNEWSPolitics0004/18_yukon.html (downloaded 30 December 2001).

[42] Gillis, Charlie. "New Yukon leader promises more open style of government," *National Post* 6 November 2002, www.nationalpost.com (downloaded 6 November 2002).

[43] This analysis of the Yukon situation was provided by Floyd McCormick, Deputy Clerk of the Yukon Legislature, via e-mail correspondence, 12 September 2002.

[44] Robert Sheppard, "Premier Callbeck's Departure," *Globe and Mail* 14 August 1996: A19.

[45] Sheppard; MacQueen A1.

[46] "Men and Farmers in PEI Government," *Canadian Press Newswire Service* 6 October 1993.

[47] MacQueen A1.

[48] Shannon Sampert and Linda Trimble, "'Wham, Bam, No Thank You Ma'am': Gender and the Game Frame in National Newspaper Coverage of Election 2000," Tremblay and Trimble.

[49] Elizabeth Gidengil and Joanna Everitt, "Tough Talk: How Television News Covers Male and Female Leaders of Canadian Political Parties," Tremblay and Trimble.

[50] Sampert and Trimble.

[51] Gertrude Robinson and Armande Saint-Jean, "Women Politicians and Their Media Coverage: A Generational Analysis," Megyery 127–69.

[52] Lunman A4.

[53] Ian McDougall, "Poll Position OK by ND," *Edmonton Sun* 3 March 1997: 5.

[54] Sharpe, 23, 26–27; Lysianne Gagnon, "Why Isn't Campbell Judged by the Same Yardstick As Male Politicians?" *Globe and Mail* 5 June 1993: D3.

[55] Jane Taber, "Kim Campbell's New Man is 'No Bimbo,'" *National Post* 23 January 1999: B10; Alexandra Gill, "Dating Young: How Kim Campbell Got her Groove Back," *Globe and Mail* 22 July 2000: R1, R6.

[56] Shawn McCarthy, "PM Pushes for Early Election," *Globe and Mail* 16 September 2000: A1, A4.

[57] Mike Sadava, "Leaders Take Their Corners," *Edmonton Journal* 27 February 1997: A6; Johnsrude, "Lots of Sparring."

58 Campaign Notebook, "Dressed to Kill," *Edmonton Journal* 27 February 1997: A6.

59 Maurine Beasley, "How Can Media Coverage of Women be Improved?," *Women, Media and Politics*, ed. Pippa Norris (New York: Oxford University Press, 1997) 244.

60 Rhéal Séguin, "Marois Opts Out of PQ Race," *Globe and Mail* 27 January 2001: A2.

61 See Edward Greenspon, "Can She Get to First Position?" *Globe and Mail* 25 May 2001: A17.

62 Joan Bryden, "Masochists or Optimists?" *Edmonton Journal* 19 April 1999: A10.

63 Susan Delacourt, "Put Off by Parliament," *Elm Street* February/March 2001: 53–62.

64 Scott Feschuk, "Poll Favours Klein, But He Says No," *Globe and Mail* 28 March 1998: A1, A6; also see Scott Feschuk, "Tories Search for Segal Alternatives," *Globe and Mail* 9 April 1998: A5.

65 Norma Greenaway, "Tories Foolish to Stick with Clark, Says Activist," *Edmonton Journal* 6 July 2002.

66 Brian Laghi, "Ablonczy Gauging her Support," *Globe and Mail* 1 September 2001: A4.

67 Larry Johnsrude, "In Politics, Being a Woman is a Drag," *Edmonton Journal* 11 March 2002: A1, A2.

68 Steven Chase and Jeff Sallot, "New Democrats Face a Crucial Choice," *Globe and Mail* 6 June 2002: A1, A4.

69 Riley, "McDonough's Common Sense Political Lesson."

Chapter 5   Spice Girls and Old Spice Boys: Getting There is Only Half the Battle

1 Jerry Ward, "Spicing Up the House," *Edmonton Sun* 28 April 1998: 5.

2 Steve Chase, "MacBeth's Return Greeted with Jeers," *Calgary Herald* 21 April 1998: A1, A2.

3 Copps 50.

4 This term was coined by Sydney Sharpe. In *The Gilded Ghetto* she devotes a chapter to the travails of women politicians in male-dominated legislatures (see 34–52).

5 Crossley 282.

6 Sheila Copps, Audrey McLaughlin, Sharon Carstairs, and many others make this point in their autobiographies.

7 Catherine Cleverdon, *The Woman Suffrage Movement in Canada*, 2nd ed. (Toronto: University of Toronto Press, 1974) 5–7.

8 Alison Prentice, et al., *Canadian Women: A History*, 2nd ed. (Toronto: Harcourt Brace, 1996) 195–96.

9 For a brief discussion of women's citizenship, see Linda Trimble, "The Politics of Gender," *Critical Concepts: An Introduction to Politics*, 1st ed., ed. Janine Brodie (Scarborough: Prentice-Hall, 1999) 307–10.

10 Mark Kingwell, *The World We Want: Virtue, Vice, and the Good Citizen* (Toronto: Penguin, 2000) 10–11.

11 Prentice 143, 146.

12 Sharpe 36.

13 Judy LaMarsh, *Memoirs of a Bird in a Gilded Cage* (Toronto: McClelland and Stewart, 1968) 283.

14 Erickson, "Parties, Ideology and Feminist Action" 111.

15 Desserud 261–62.

16 Sharpe 45.

17 See Jerome H. Black, "Representation in the Parliament of Canada: The Case of Ethnoracial Minorities," Everitt and O'Neill 355–72.

18 Brown 94, 119.

19 Copps 25, 28.

20 Anderssen A4.

21 Robinson and Saint-Jean 136.

22 Brodie, *Women and Politics in Canada* 79.

23 Copps 85.

24 Quoted in Sharpe 152.

25 Robert Matas, "Women Politicians Called Backlash Victims," *Globe and Mail* 10 June 1993: A3.

26 Brodie, *Women and Politics in Canada* 81.

27 Copps 85.

28 Johnsrude, "In Politics, Being a Woman is a Drag" A1, A2.

29 See Sharpe 144–63, for accounts of role strain experienced by women politicians.

30 Brown 126.

31 Sharpe 47. Indeed, when 29–year old Sheila Copps ran for the leadership of the Ontario Liberal party opponents circulated anonymous notes accusing her of "lesbian tendencies." See Copps 45.

32 McKenzie 59.

33 Erickson, "Parties, Ideology and Feminist Action" 121.

34 At a June 2002 Edmonton YWCA "One Woman One Vote" brainstorming session attended by Linda Trimble, women politicians discussed the dilemma posed by breakfast meetings for women responsible for seeing their young children off to day care or school. One municipal politician said that, when her children were small, she insisted on scheduling meetings at "child-friendly" hours.

35 Pat Carney, *Trade Secrets: A Memoir* (Toronto: Key Porter, 2000) 191–93.

36 Campbell 122.

37 Downloaded from Angus Reid, www.angusreid.com/wip/sld002.htm, 10 May 1997.

38 "Gentleman" was removed from the title when, for the first time, a woman (Mary McLaren) assumed the post, in 1997. Now the position is referred to as "Usher of the Black Rod" or just "Black Rod."

39 Sharpe 37.

40 The monument was unveiled on 18 October, 2000, over 70 years after the Judicial Committee of the Privy Council declared that women could be considered persons under the law. See the Famous Five Foundation website www.famous5.org/html/famous5.html for a photograph of the monument, a history of the Persons Case, and biographies of the Famous Five.

41 Sharpe 35. Calling another member a "liar" is against parliamentary rules, but the same rule book is silent about many of the epithets thrown at women legislators.

42 Copps 93.

43 Hayden 634.

44 Delacourt, "Put Off by Parliament" 53–62.

45 Delacourt, "Put Off by Parliament" 54.

46 McLaughlin 27–28.

47 Erickson, "Parties, Ideology and Feminist Action" 121.

48 Desserud 270.

49 When Linda Trimble was trying to come up with a title for a paper on women in the Alberta Legislature, her colleague Fred Judson offered, not very seriously, "Babes in Boyland." She decided on "A Few Good Women," but Fred's suggestion was not forgotten. This phrase seems an apt description of the legislative climate for women.

50 Sharpe 44.

51 Copps 24–27; 74.

52 Anderssen A4.

53 Copps 29.

54 Sharpe 216. These events led Sharpe to label the Alberta legislature the most sexist in the country.

55 Carstairs 217.

56 Sharpe 185, 187.

57 Burt and Lorenzin 211.

58 Sam Schecter, "Political Stonecutters: Joy MacPhail and Jenny Kwan," *Forward Magazine*, 27 August 2001, http://www.forwardmagazine.org/articles/PoliticalStonecutters.html (downloaded 12 December 2001).

59 Sharpe 48.

60 Lisa Young, "Fulfilling the Mandate of Difference: Women in the Canadian House of Commons," Arscott and Trimble, *In the Presence of Women* 92–93.

61 Carbert 163–64.

62 Brock 190–193, 194, 195.

63 Sharpe 38.

64 Linda Trimble, "Feminist Politics in the Alberta Legislature, 1972–1994," Arscott and Trimble, *In the Presence of Women* 143.

65 Delacourt, "Put Off by Parliament" 62.

66 Johnsrude, "In Politics, Being a Woman is a Drag," A2.

67 Crossley 284, 304.

68 Hayden 638.

69 Brown 141.

70 Delacourt, "Put Off by Parliament" 62.

71 Susan Carroll and Ronnee Schreiber, "Media Coverage of Women in the 103rd Congress," Norris 132; Kim Fridkin Kahn, "The Distorted Mirror: Press Coverage of Women Candidates for Statewide Office," *Journal of Politics* 56:1 (1994): 170–71.

72 The Flora Syndrome refers to Conservative MP Flora MacDonald's bid for the Tory leadership in the 1970s; numerous activists and party members promised to support MacDonald but failed to deliver their votes; according to some observers, many delegates could not bring themselves to support a woman. Regarding Kim Campbell and the double standard, see Lysiane Gagnon, "Why Isn't Campbell Judged by the Same Yardstick as Male Politicians?" *Globe and Mail* 5 June 1993: D3.

CHAPTER 6   Counting for Something: Women in Politics Can Make A Difference

1 Quoted in Sharpe 215.

2 Joni Lovenduski and Azza Karam, "Women in Parliament: Making a Difference," Karam 129.

3 See Jill Vickers, "Toward a Feminist Understanding of Representation," and Chantal Maillé, "Challenges to Representation: Theory and the Women's Movement in Quebec," Arscott and Trimble, *In the Presence of Women* 20–46 and 47–63, respectively.

4 Young 89–90.

5 Susan J. Carroll, *Women as Candidates in American Politics*, 2nd ed. (Bloomington, IN: Indiana University Press, 1994) 15.

6 See Manon Tremblay, "Do Female MPs Substantively Represent Women? A Study of Legislative Behaviour in Canada's 35th Parliament," *Canadian Journal of Political Science* 31:3 (September 1998): 439–40.

7 Linda Trimble, "Feminist Politics in the Alberta Legislature, 1972–1994," Arscott and Trimble, *In the Presence of Women* 130–31.

8 Lovenduski and Karam 129–30.

9 Lovenduski and Karam 130.

10 Lovenduski and Karam 126.

11 Linda Trimble, "A Few Good Women: Female Legislators in Alberta, 1972–1991," *Standing on New Ground: Women in Alberta*, ed. Catherine Cavanaugh and Randi Warne (Edmonton, AB: University of Alberta Press, 1993) 88–89.

12 Jill Bystydzienski, "Influence of Women's Culture on Public Politics in Norway," *Women Transforming Politics*, ed. J. Bystydzienski (Bloomington and Indianapolis, IN: Indiana University Press, 1992) 15.

13 Lovenduski and Karam 128.

14 See Hege Skjeie, "The Rhetoric of Difference: On Women's Inclusion into Political Elites," *Politics and Society* 19:2 (1991): 235.

15 Meredith Ralston, *Why Women Run* (Toronto: National Film Board, 1999).

16 Trimble, "Feminist Politics in the Alberta Legislature" 147–48.

17 Trimble, "Feminist Politics in the Alberta Legislature" 131.

18 See, for instance, Manon Tremblay and Guylaine Boivin, "La question de l'avortement au Parlement canadien: de l'importance du genre dans l'orientation des débats," *Revue juridique la femme et le droit* 4 (1991): 459–76. Tremblay and Boivin found that, in a debate on abortion followed by a free vote, there was a consensus of women from all parties on a pro-choice position.

19 After 14 years of pressure, the Alberta government finally created an Advisory Council on the Status of Women in 1986. However, it was disbanded just ten years later in 1996, as part of the Klein government's deficit reduction program.

20 Jack Aubry, "Le May Doan Forced to Sing Sexist Anthem, Senator Says," *National Post* 22 February 2002, www.nationalpost.com (downloaded 22 February 2002).

21 Tremblay, "Do Female MPs Substantively Represent Women?" 444.

22 Young 93–98.

23 Burt and Lorenzin 202–27.

24 This assertion involves a re-interpretation of Burt and Lorenzin's Table 9.2 (212), based on a comparison of the percentage of statements on women's issues made by male and female legislators of each party with the proportion of male and female legislators in each party. For instance, women comprised 24 per cent of the NDP caucus and, in the third session, were responsible for 44 per cent of the instances when women's issues were raised in members' statements and question period. Only 13 per cent of the Liberal caucus was female, but they were responsible for 64 per cent of the statements on women in the third session.

25 Burt and Lorenzin 212.

26 Burt and Lorenzin 215.

27 Tremblay, "Do Female MPs Substantively Represent Women?" 457.

28 Tremblay, "Do Female MPs Substantively Represent Women?" 459, 463.

29 See Trimble, "A Few Good Women" and "Feminist Politics in the Alberta Legislature"; also, Trimble, "Who's Represented?" 257–89.

30 Jill Vickers, *Reinventing Political Science: A Feminist Approach* (Halifax: Fernwood, 1997) 200.

31 Trimble, "Who's Represented?" 263.

32 Trimble, "Feminist Politics in the Alberta Legislature" 137.

33 Trimble, "Feminist Politics in the Alberta Legislature" 139–41.

34 Trimble, "Feminist Politics in the Alberta Legislature" 145–46.

35 Trimble, "Who's Represented?" 258.

36 Trimble, "Who's Represented?" 281.

37 Brown 133.

38 Deborah Grey, Speech to Linda Trimble's Political Science 220 Class, Edmonton, 15 March 2002.

39 Christopher Gudgeon and Mark Leiren-Young, eds., *The Little Book of Reform* (Vancouver: Arsenal Pulp Press, 1994) 64.

40 Gudgeon and Leiren-Young 22.

41 Jeffrey Simpson, "Moderates Among the Ideological Heathen," *Globe and Mail* 8 March 2002: A 13.

42 Sharpe 214.

Glossary

1 Canada, Royal Commission on Electoral Reform and Party Financing, "Fairness as the Pre-Eminent Value in the Electoral Process," *Reforming Electoral Democracy*, Vol. 1 (Ottawa: Minister of Supply and Services Canada, 1991) 13; also 7, 9, 16.

2 Arscott and Trimble, *In The Presence of Women* 361.

3 Arscott and Trimble, *In the Presence of Women* 363.

4 Vickers, *Reinventing Political Science* 197.

5 Vickers, *Reinventing Political Science* 200.

6 See George Perlin, *The Tory Syndrome: Leadership Politics in the Progressive Conservative Party* (Montreal and Kingston: McGill-Queen's University Press, 1980).

7 For a more detailed account of these electoral systems and their implications for women, see Heather McIvor, "Women and the Canadian Electoral System," Tremblay and Trimble, forthcoming 2003.

8 Arscott and Trimble, *In The Presence of Women* 361.

9 Vickers, *Reinventing Political Science* 366.

10 Carroll 15.

Website Information and Web Links

Still Counting
http://www.stillcounting.athabascau.ca
This site will continually update data in this book.

International

IDEA [International Institute for Democracy and Electoral Assistance]
http://www.int-idea.se
See also for international and regional electronic links,
http://www.idea.int/gender/links.htm

InterParliamentary Union
See http://www.ipu.org/wmn-e/world.htm

Canadian

Famous Five Foundation
www.famous5.org/html/famous5.html
See this site for a photograph of the monument, a history of the Persons Case, and biographies of the Famous Five.

General Election Results (Canada)
http://www.elections.ca
See this site also for quick links to election sites in all other provinces and territories.

National Library

First Women in Provincial and Territorial Legislatures
http://www.nlc-bnc.ca/2/12/h12-278-e.html
This includes a list of key references on the "Canadian Women in Politics" topic.

Parliament of Canada

http://www.parl.gc.ca/common/index.asp?Language=E&Parl=37&Ses=1

See under "Senators and Members" for historical and current biographies.

Prince Edward Island

http://www.gov.pei.ca/election/provincial/historical/women/index.php3

This site summaries the achievements of elected women in its jurisdiction.

Research Centre on Women and Politics

http://www.crfp-rcwp.uottawa.ca

Offers data on women and politics in Canada, analysis of recent electoral trends, links to academic researchers and to feminist groups promoting women's political equality.

Works Cited

Books, Articles, Unpublished Documents

Abu-Laban, Yasmeen. "Challenging the Gendered Vertical Mosaic." Everitt and O'Neill 268–82.

Anderssen, Erin. "No Memoirs for McDonough Yet." *Globe and Mail* 6 June 2002, A4.

Archibald, Kathleen. *Sex and the Public Service.* Ottawa: Queen's Printer, 1970.

Arscott, Jane. "'More Women': The RCSW and Political Representation, 1970." Tremblay and Andrew 145–68.

Arscott, Jane, and Linda Trimble. "Women's Electoral Space: Glass Ceilings, Flying Wedges and Revolving Doors." Paper presented to the Department of Political Science, University of Waterloo, October 1997.

———, eds. *In the Presence of Women: Representation in Canadian Governments.* Toronto: Harcourt, 1997.

Bashevkin, Sylvia. *Toeing the Lines: Women in Party Politics in English Canada.* Toronto: Oxford University Press, 1985.

Beasley, Maurine. "How Can Media Coverage of Women be Improved?" Norris 235–44.

Black, Jerome. "Differences that Matter: Minority Women MPs, 1993–2000." Tremblay and Trimble.

———. "Representation in the Parliament of Canada: The Case of Ethnoracial Minorities." Everitt and O'Neill 355–72.

Brock, Kathy. "Women and the Manitoba Legislature." Arscott and Trimble, *In the Presence of Women* 180–200.

Brodie, Janine. "Women and the Electoral Process in Canada." *Women in Canadian Politics: Toward Equity in Representation.* Ed. Kathy Megyery. Toronto: Dundurn Press, 1991. 3–59.

Brodie, Janine. *Women and Politics in Canada.* Toronto: McGraw-Hill Ryerson, 1985.

Brodsky, Gwen, and Shelagh Day. *Canadian Charter Equality Rights for Women: One Step Forward or Two Steps Back?* Ottawa: Canadian Advisory Council on the Status of Women, 1989.

Brown, Rosemary. *Being Brown: A Very Public Life.* Toronto: Random House, 1989.

Bullard, Angela S., and Deil S. Wright. "Circumventing the Glass Ceiling: Women Executives in American State Governments." *Public Administration Review* 53:3 (1993): 189–202.

Burt, Sandra, and Elizabeth Lorenzin. "Taking the Women's Movement to Queen's Park: Women's Interests and the New Democratic Government of Ontario." Arscott and Trimble, *In the Presence of Women* 202–27.

Bystydzienski, Jill. "Influence of Women's Culture on Public Politics in Norway." *Women Transforming Politics.* Ed. J. Bystydzienski. Bloomington and Indianapolis, IN: Indiana University Press, 1992. 11–23.

Campbell, Kim. *Time and Chance: The Political Memoirs of Canada's First Woman Prime Minister.* Toronto: Doubleday Canada, 1996.

Canada. *A History of the Vote in Canada.* Ottawa: Public Works and Government Services, 1997.

Canada. Royal Commission on Electoral Reform and Party Financing. "Fairness as the Pre-Eminent Value in the Electoral Process." *Reforming Electoral Democracy.* Vol. 1. Ottawa: Supply and Services Canada, 1991.

Canada. Royal Commission on Electoral Reform and Party Financing. *Report.* Vol. 1. Ottawa: Supply and Services Canada, 1991.

Canada. Royal Commission on the Status of Women (RCSW). *Report.* Ottawa: Queen's Printer, 1970.

Canadian Bar Association, Taskforce on Gender Equality in the Legal Profession. *Touchstones for Change: Equality, Diversity and Accountability: Report of the Canadian Bar Association Task Force on Gender Equality in the Legal Profession.* Ottawa: Canadian Bar Association, 1993.

Carbert, Louise. "Governing on the Correct, the Compassionate, the Saskatchewan Side of the Border." Arscott and Trimble, *In the Presence of Women* 154–79.

Carroll, Susan J. *Women as Candidates in American Politics.* 2nd ed. Bloomington, IN: Indiana University Press, 1994.

Carroll, Susan, J. and Ronnee Schreiber. "Media Coverage of Women in the 103rd Congress." Norris 131–48.

Carstairs, Sharon. *Not One of the Boys*. Toronto: Macmillan Canada, 1993.

Carver, Anne. *The Participation of Women in Political Activities in Canada*. Ottawa: Information Canada, 1970.

Cleverdon, Catherine. *The Woman Suffrage Movement in Canada*. 2nd ed. Toronto: University of Toronto Press, 1974.

Copps, Sheila. *Nobody's Baby*. Toronto: Deneau, 1986.

Crossley, John. "Picture This: Women Politicians Hold Key Posts in Prince Edward Island." Arscott and Trimble, *In the Presence of Women* 278–307.

Dacks, Gurston, Joyce Green, and Linda Trimble. "Road Kill: Women in Alberta's Drive Toward Deficit Elimination." *The Trojan Horse: Alberta and the Future of Canada*. Ed. Trevor Harrison and Gordon Laxer. Montreal: Black Rose, 1995. 270–85.

Dahl, Jens, Jack Hicks, and Peter Jull, eds. *Nunavut: Inuit Regain Control of Their Lands and Their Lives*. Copenhagen: International Work Group for Indigenous Affairs, 2000.

Delacourt, Susan. "Put Off by Parliament." *Elm Street* February/March 2001: 53–62.

———. *Shaughnessy*. Toronto: Macfarlane, Walter and Ross, 2000.

Desserud, Don. "Women in New Brunswick Politics: Waiting for the Third Wave." Arscott and Trimble, *In the Presence of Women* 254–77.

Dobrowolski, Alexandra, and Jane Jenson. "Reforming the Parties: Prescriptions for Democracy." *How Ottawa Spends: A More Democratic Canada?* Ed. Susan D. Phillips. Ottawa: Carleton University Press, 1993. 43–81.

Erickson, Lynda. "Entry to the Commons: Parties, Recruitment, and the Election of Women in 1993." Tremblay and Andrew 219–55.

———. "Parties, Ideology and Feminist Action: Women and Political Representation in British Columbia Politics." Arscott and Trimble, *In the Presence of Women* 106–27.

———. "Women and Political Representation in British Columbia." *Politics, Policy and Government in British Columbia*. Ed. R.K. Carty. Vancouver: UBC Press, 1996. 103–22.

Everitt, Joanna, and Brenda O'Neill, eds. *Citizen Politics: Research and Theory in Canadian Political Behaviour*. Toronto: Oxford University Press, 2002.

Flanagan, Tom. "Women and Other Party Animals: MacBeth is the Latest in a Short Line of Losing Female Pols." *National Post* 15 March 2001. http://www.nationalpost.com (downloaded 22 March 2001).

Gidengil, Elisabeth. "Gender and Attitudes Towards Quotas for Women Candidates in Canada." *Women & Politics* 16:1 (1996): 21–44.

Gidengil, Elizabeth, and Joanna Everitt. "Tough Talk: How Television News Covers Male and Female Leaders of Canadian Political Parties." Tremblay and Trimble.

Gidengil, Elisabeth, and Richard Vengroff. "Representative Bureaucracy, Tokenism and the Glass Ceiling: the Case of Women in Quebec Municipal Administration." *Canadian Public Administration* 40 (1997): 457–58.

Gotell, Lise, and Janine Brodie. "Women and Parties in the 1990s: Less Than Ever an Issue of Numbers." *Party Politics in Canada*. 7th ed. Ed. Hugh Thorburn. Scarborough: Prentice Hall, 1996. 53–67.

Gotlieb, Sondra. *Wife Of: An Irreverent Account of Life in Powertown*. Washington, DC: Acropolis Books Ltd., 1985.

Gudgeon, Christopher, and Mark Leiren-Young, eds. *The Little Book of Reform*. Vancouver: Arsenal Pulp Press, 1994.

Hayden, Joyce. *Yukon's Women of Power: Political Pioneers in a Northern Canadian Colony*. Whitehorse: Windwalker Press, 1999.

Johnsrude, Larry. "In Politics, Being a Woman is a Drag." *Edmonton Journal* 11 March 2002, A1.

———. "Lots of Sparring, But No Knockout Punches." *Edmonton Journal* 28 February 1997, A1.

Kahn, Kim Fridkin. "The Distorted Mirror: Press Coverage of Women." *Journal of Politics* 56:1 (1994): 154–73.

Karam, Azza, ed. *Women in Parliament: Beyond Numbers*. Stockholm, Sweden: International Institute for Democracy and Electoral Assistance [IDEA], 1998.

Kingwell, Mark. *The World We Want: Virtue, Vice, and the Good Citizen*. Toronto: Penguin, 2000.

LaMarsh, Judy. *Memoirs of a Bird in a Gilded Cage*. Toronto: McClelland and Stewart, 1968.

Lovenduski, Joni, and Azza Karam. "Women in Parliament: Making a Difference." Karam 125–57.

Maillé, Chantal. "Challenges to Representation: Theory and the Women's Movement in Quebec." Arscott and Trimble, *In the Presence of Women* 47–63.

———. *Les Québécoises et la conquête du pouvoir politique*. Montreal: Saint-Martin, 1990.

———. *Primed for Power*. Canada: Canadian Advisory Council on the Status of Women, 1990.

McIvor, Heather. "Proportional and Semi-proportional Electoral Systems: Their Potential Effects on Canadian Politics." *Electoral Insight* 1:1 (June 1999): 12–16.

McKenzie, Judith. *Pauline Jewett: A Passion for Canada.* Montreal and Kingston: McGill-Queen's University Press, 1999.

McLaughlin, Audrey, with Rich Archbold. *A Woman's Place: My Life & Politics.* Toronto: MacFarlane, Walter & Ross, 1992.

Morris, Cerise D. "No More than Simple Justice: The Royal Commission on the Status of Women and Social Change in Canada." Diss., McGill University, 1982.

Naff, Katherine. "Through the Glass Ceiling: Prospects of Advancement of Women in the Federal Civil Service." *Public Administration Review* 54:6 (1994): 507–14.

Naff, Katherine, and Sue Thomas. "The Glass Ceiling Revisited: Determinants of Federal Job Advancement." *Policy Studies Review* 13:3 (1994): 249–72.

Norris, Pippa, ed. *Women, Media and Politics.* New York: Oxford University Press, 1997.

Pelletier, Alain. "Politics and Ethnicity: Representation of Ethnic and Visible-Minority Groups in the House of Commons." *Ethnocultural Groups and Visible Minorities in Canadian Politics: The Question of Access.* Ed. Kathy Megyery. Toronto: Dundurn Press, 1991. 101–59.

Pelletier, Réjean, and Manon Tremblay. "Les femmes sont-elles candidates dans les circonscriptions perdues d'avance?" *Canadian Journal of Political Science* 25:2 (June 1992): 249–67.

Perlin, George. *The Tory Syndrome: Leadership Politics in the Progressive Conservative Party.* Montreal and Kingston: McGill-Queen's University Press, 1980.

Prentice, Alison, et al. *Canadian Women: A History.* 2nd ed. Toronto: Harcourt Brace, 1996.

Ralston, Meredith. *Why Women Run.* Toronto: National Film Board, 1999.

Robinson, Gertrude, and Armande Saint-Jean. "Women Politicians and Their Media Coverage: A Generational Analysis." Megyery 127–69.

Sampert, Shannon, and Linda Trimble. "'Wham, Bam, No Thank You Ma'am': Gender and the Game Frame in National Newspaper Coverage of Election 2000." Tremblay and Trimble.

Savage, Candace. *Foremothers: Personalities and Issues From the History of Women in Saskatchewan.* Saskatoon: C. Savage, 1975.

Sharpe, Sydney. *The Gilded Ghetto.* Toronto: HarperCollins, 1994.

Skjeie, Hege. "The Rhetoric of Difference: On Women's Inclusion into Political Elites." *Politics and Society* 19:2 (1991): 232–63.

Studlar, Donley, and Richard Matland. "The Dynamics of Women's Representation in the Canadian Provinces, 1975–1994." *Canadian Journal of Political Science* 29:2 (1996): 269–93.

Task Force on Barriers to Women in the Public Service. *Beneath the Veneer.* 4 vols. Ottawa: Ministry of Supply and Services, 1990.

Tremblay, Manon. "Do Female MPs Substantively Represent Women? A Study of Legislative Behaviour in Canada's 35th Parliament." *Canadian Journal of Political Science* 31:3 (September 1998): 439–40.

———. "Quebec Women in Politics: An Examination of the Research." Arscott and Trimble, *In the Presence of Women* 228–51.

———. "Women and Political Participation in Canada." *Electoral Insight* 3:1 (January 2001): 4–7.

Tremblay, Manon, and Caroline Andrew, eds. *Women and Political Representation in Canada.* Ottawa: University of Ottawa Press, 1998.

Tremblay, Manon, and Guylaine Boivin. "La question de l'avortement au Parlement canadien: de l'importance du genre dans l'orientation des débats." *Revue juridique la femme et le droit* 4 (1991): 459–76.

Tremblay, Manon, and Linda Trimble, eds. *Women and Electoral Politics in Canada.* Toronto: Oxford University Press, forthcoming 2003.

Trimble, Linda. "A Few Good Women: Female Legislators in Alberta, 1972–1991. *Standing on New Ground: Women in Alberta.* Ed. Catherine Cavanaugh and Randi Warne. Edmonton, AB: University of Alberta Press, 1993. 87–114.

———. "Feminist Politics in the Alberta Legislature, 1972–1994." Arscott and Trimble, *In the Presence of Women* 128–53.

———. "'Good Enough Citizens': Canadian Women and Representation in Constitutional Deliberations." *International Journal of Canadian Studies* 17 (Spring 1998): 131–56.

———. "The Politics of Gender." *Critical Concepts: An Introduction to Politics.* 1st ed. Ed. Janine Brodie. Scarborough: Prentice-Hall, 1999. 307–10.

———. "Who's Represented? Gender and Diversity in the Alberta Legislature." Tremblay and Andrew 257–89.

Trofimenkoff, Susan Mann. "Thérèse Casgrain and the CCF in Quebec." *Beyond the Vote: Canadian Women and Politics.* Ed. Linda Kealey and Joan Sangster. Toronto: University of Toronto Press, 1989. 139–68.

Valentine, Fraser, and Jill Vickers. "'Released from the Yoke of Paternalism and Charity': Citizenship and the Rights of Canadians with Disabilities." *International Journal of Canadian Studies* 14 (1996): 155–77.

Vickers, Jill. *Reinventing Political Science: A Feminist Approach.* Halifax: Fernwood, 1997.

———. "Toward a Feminist Understanding of Representation." Arscott and Trimble, *In the Presence of Women* 20–46.

Young, Lisa. "Fulfilling the Mandate of Difference: Women in the Canadian House of Commons," Arscott and Trimble, *In the Presence of Women* 82–103.

Young, Lisa, and Elaine Campbell. "Women and Political Representation." *Party Politics in Canada.* 8th ed. Ed. Hugh Thorburn and Alan Whitehorn. Toronto: Prentice Hall, 2001. 61–74.

Newspapers and Magazines

Alberta Report

Calgary Herald

Canadian News Facts

Canadian Press Newswire Service

Canoe news

Chatelaine

Globe and Mail

Edmonton Journal

Edmonton Sun

Forward Magazine

Halifax Chronicle Herald

Halifax Daily News

National Post

Ottawa Citizen

Vancouver Province

Vancouver Sun

Victoria Times-Colonist

Index